FLUTTER ECHO

Flutter Echo: Living Within Sound
by David Toop

Introduction by Thurston Moore

INTRODUCTION: STORY TIME

There is the sense that free improvisation is conducted by an innate relationship between memory and the immediate now. Composing in real time with music (or on the tongue with improvised poetics, a phrase attributed to the late American poet iconoclast Allen Ginsberg) is to be engaged in the moment of creative impulse.

But regardless of any meditation-practice suggestion to Be Here Now there seems to be always a ghost of the artist's experiential past at play informing, for better or worse, his or her's performance, public or private.

Through all of David Toop's essaying - from various pieces in the communitarian published *MUSICS* (1975-79), *Collusion* magazine (1981-83), filing reports for The Face, a passionate fascination with ground zero hip hop in his 1984 study *Rap Attack* and onward to a host of acclaimed books examining the aspects and ramifications of sound, both intellectual and emotional, as sentient reflection - there is a quiet haunting, keeping the writer glancingly attentive to a chi-state David Toop seemingly regards with intrigue and humour.

*Flutter Echo*, as memoir, is adult voice sublime with child energy. And as the pages deal with ego and self-analysis, with an ever slight and knowing self-effacement and humility, the reader may glean the significance the Past and Present, the Now and Then, has for David as a writer and musician considering the sound-worlds he has historically been entranced with.

Investigations into animal sonics, indigenous musics of every marginal, arcane and non-Western culture on the planet, and a delight in the beyond-pretense bizarro discography of exotica and novelty all present the commonality that there is continually a story being told and shared, either underlying or blatant, primordial or anew.

A devoted listener to song can glean intrigue either in solace or amongst company. From reading David's writings, at least since *Ocean of Sound* in 1995 (published eleven years on from *Rap Attack*), I sense a listener more attuned to the qualities of living sonics while in a state of lone contemplation. Which could lead one to believe that whatever dynamics David has experienced with relationships, be they intimate or platonic, would be inconsequential to his meditations on music(s).

As it is, we find from *Flutter Echo* an engaged regard to the intrusions, collaborations, delights, romances, fall outs, encouragements, disappointments et al every person shares in their domestic and professional worlds. The writing suggests a thoughtfulness of friends and lovers having a very true effect on every aspect of daily existence all figuring directly with an artist's appreciations and practices.

David can strike the figure of a private person beyond his writing, performing and teaching. I can only imagine the resistance to be revealing in any way to personal relationships in and outside one's quarters.

But the story of this particular gentleman's music life is knowingly tied in with his community and David, with his unique perspective, allows the reader the merits of his history. With a slight smile towards the knowledge of the absurdities all Earth's children experience, he welcomes us in to his pages. Ghosts coming and going.

Thurston Moore, London MMXIX

David Toop performance with sounds of plastic

LISTEN WITH CAUTION

When it came to human foibles, Jane Austen's percipience was acute. "Those who tell their own story, you know," a character says in her unfinished novel, *Sanditon*, "must be listened to with caution." Mindful of this common failure of autobiographical truthfulness, it never occurred to me to write a memoir. I consider all of my writing to be personal, unashamedly grounded in my own experience if only because I present my ideas as emanations of my own practice, thinking, research and encounters, rather than somehow coming from a neutral or distanced source. Besides, who would want to know about me in any detail?

Then in May 2014 I was approached by a Tokyo based small-press publisher and editor, Takaaki Kurahashi, asking if I would be interested in writing a book for Japanese publication. His request was that I write about my "musical career, some inside stories of the record production, memories of your musical partners, etc." Later that year, dizzy with exhaustion at the end of a tour of Asia, I met with him in Tokyo and was disconcerted to discover that he possessed more detailed knowledge of my musical life than I did myself. I must confess that my agreement to write a memoir was influenced by the thought that it would be published in Japanese. In that sense it would remain a semi-secret. Any shameful lapses in taste, honesty, loyalty, accuracy of memory or self-awareness would be judged by only one language group. The book was written in 2015, almost immediately after I finished *Into the Maelstrom*, then translated by Mr. Kurahashi and Tomoko Okuto, and published in a very attractive edition by Du Books, Tokyo, in 2017.

A few friends asked me if it would be published in English. I thought not, wary of feeling so exposed in my own backyard. Then in July 2017, backstage after a trio gig by Thurston Moore, Steve Beresford and myself, the conversation came around to my so-called autobiography. Eva Prinz asked if she could read it so I sent her the manuscript, then put the whole thing out of my mind for the rest of the summer. In early autumn, she and Thurston expressed a strong wish to publish it. Grateful for their enthusiasm and encouragement I decided that shame was no big deal at my age and set to work in a sort of inactive way, considering how I might expand the text from its original remit. This final version retains some evidence of its origin as a memoir directed to those Japanese readers who have an interest in my work but it also goes more deeply into detail and the personal. The personal is tricky. Life and art are inextricably entangled. Each colours the other but in the end this is the story of a life immersed in sound and listening. Hopefully that shifting boundary has been negotiated without falling too far on one side or the other. On the other hand, some experiences are too powerful to treat lightly, either at the time or in

retrospect. There is current research to suggest that we are constantly improvising the story of ourselves and our 'tradition'; this aligns with my philosophy and I have tried to stay true to the cyclical, repercussive and imbricated nature of events, hopefully without creating any more confusion than is strictly necessary. In general I have tried to keep faith with Jane Austen's warning but inevitably there will be lapses. A high proportion of my activities are collaborative. In advance, I thank and apologise to anybody who has been dragged into these pages unwittingly, simply because of a past association with me.

A word about my title. **A flutter echo**, as I explain early in this book, is the term used by acousticians to describe a percussive sound reflecting rapidly back and forth between two hard parallel surfaces – the walls of a narrow alley, perhaps or a low ceiling and floor – to make a hard-sounding echo. The sound has emotional meaning for me, occupying a significant place in my childhood memories, so in that sense it causes a 'fluttering' of the heart. At the same time it echoes back from the deep time of life, a memory echoed by other experiences of similar flutter echoes.

## I. DEEP TIME

If every listening experience of our lives could be recollected the world would be transformed into an infinite space of sounds so layered in time, so thickly textured as to be a second nature. Our minds would be continually defending themselves from a waterfall of auditory impressions. Sound slips away from the memory in the same way that water dries on a rock, its stain gradually disappearing. Some rocks remain wet; moss grows, soft to the touch, vivid green and pungent.

So it is with memories of listening – significant moments sitting in memory like deeply embedded rocks, their place in our personal narratives changing shape over time. Maybe the rock moves a little as we come to understand ourselves better with age. At the end, all the rocks are dislodged, washed downstream. Others may find and collect them, examine them, take them into their own minds.

The past is always now, chronology and continuity broken into pieces, scattered by the pressure of living within depths of time. Images appear, flashes in darkness, maybe imagined: conscious of lying in a pram in the hallway; finding a toad in the neighbour's garden; a boy on top of me, bigger, stronger, holding me down, the boy my parents tried and failed to foster after his mother died; the cattle market at Waltham Abbey, pigs screaming; on my parents' bed, transfixed by the swirling wood grain of the headboard.

Hearing is more elusive. My first memory of a listening experience comes from a walk, a regular journey during my early childhood. I was born on the Fifth of May, 1949, in Enfield, suburban north London. My parents, both north Londoners, lived there with my maternal grandparents after World War II. Seven people – my grandmother, my mother's stepfather, stepsister and brother, my mother, father and sister – all living together in the same small house must have been claustrophobic.

Finally in 1949, just after my birth, my parents – Leslie John Toop and Doris Ada May Purver – bought their own modest house, three upstairs bedrooms, two rooms downstairs, a tiny kitchen and a long garden, in a small town called Waltham Cross.

This would have given them a great sense of achievement at that time, when ownership of a house became a realistic possibility for working class and lower middle class people. In the early 1950s Waltham Cross was still quiet and relatively rural despite being only twelve miles from the City of London. I could see fields from my tiny bedroom, a brook trickled along the lane and at the end of the road, across the railway line, lay mysterious marshes and the River Lea, traditionally a canal route for transportation from the Thames River into the borough of Hertfordshire. Many families moved into this area immediately after the war, hoping for the tranquillity and stability promised by suburbanisation.

Things could have been very different. My mother's father and older brother died in the great flu epidemic after the First World War of 1914-18. Her mother came close to death from the same illness, so she and her younger brother were placed in foster care, a traumatic experience that my mother would sometimes speak of in a guarded way, as if her brother had suffered some unmentionable harm during that time. My father was a soldier during World War II and took part in the Normandy Landing. While he was away in Europe, a V2 bomb dropped on a house in Enfield, directly across the road from my grandparents' home. The force of the explosion threw a long spike of glass onto the pillow between my mother and sister Angela as they were sleeping. "I always remember the windows were blown out, the cat disappeared," my mother once told my daughter. "My husband's photograph was in the room. Everything was broken but this photograph stood. It didn't move and I remember looking at it and saying, 'You'll come home.'" This is how close we come to not existing.

To visit my grandparents when I was a child we would take the bus from Waltham Cross to Enfield, then walk from the centre of the town to their house in Bush Hill Park. The walk took us close to the railway lines. This was the early 1950s, so prefabricated housing had been built there, homes for those who had been bombed out of their houses by German planes and rockets aimed at the nearby munitions factory. I was fascinated by these small, flimsy buildings with their gardens of vegetables. There was a sense of privation and disaster but also the optimism of starting life again.

Shortly before the railway bridge that took us over the tracks into my grandparents' road the path was bordered on both sides by a concrete wall. The narrowness of this path meant that the walls reflected echoes from our footsteps very rapidly, an effect described as flutter echo by acousticians. Like the fluttering of a moth's wings, sound bounces back and forth rapidly between the two parallel walls to create a 'zing,' the illusion of a pitched note with a metallic quality. Sound came into focus as a phenomenon that could change according to physical laws (not that I understood this as a child, particularly since I had no aptitude for science). Then there was the complex relationship between sound, its causation, its environment and the active role of the listener. An 'active role' meant not just the realisation that listening is going on but the emotional connections to its circumstances, in this case family, the consequences of war, notions of home and the way in which something habitual – the walk from one destination to another – open out into the unexpected. A lifetime later the same effect of flutter echo resonates within deep memory as a flutter of the heart.

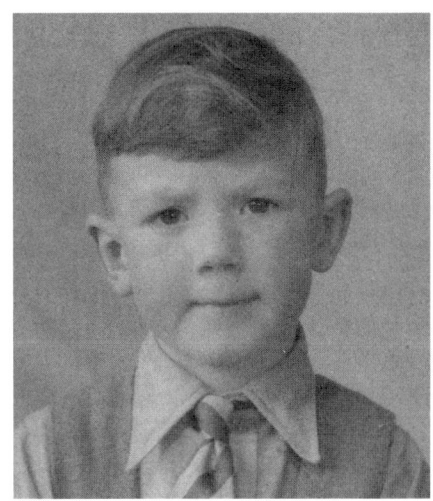

Early school photograph

David Toop & Terry in Waltham Cross, circa 1953

I heard the same effect again during my fifth trip to Japan; first of all in Nikko, the famous Naki-Ryu dragon voice of Yakushi-doh where a monk hit a wood block to demonstrate the strange transformation of its sharp impact bouncing between floor and ceiling; then in Tango, where Akio Suzuki built the Hinatabokko no kukan, his Space in the Sun, back in 1988, two parallel mud-brick walls constructed on a high hill on which cows now roam.

I have spoken to Akio-san many times about the significance to him of what he learned by building the walls, then sitting and listening within their space. Elsewhere, he has written: "On the day of the solstice I sat by the centre of the northern wall and was immediately bitten on the neck by several mosquitoes – it was an unexpected way to begin. In order to make my many supporters proud, I applied my entire body and soul into this moment – an irreplaceable experience in my life. Just when this point of all intersections felt like it was on the verge of breaking down, I heard the autumn insects call to each other and heard the cries of the mountain birds. It was then that I was enlightened to the idea that 'When humans listen to these cries, they replace them with words.' After this point, I acquired through this bodily experience, the skill to become one with nature like the trees that surrounded me."

His hope was that the mud bricks would gradually decay over time, eventually returning to the soil, but in 2017 the farmer demolished Space In the Sun without warning, no longer tolerant of this unique intermingling of art work and farm work.

DEPTHS (do the bathosphere)

These experiences feel to me like stepping stones in water, as if my first memory of being a conscious listener had created the rock from which my present life began. Then as I grew older I came across reminders, places on which I could step to give myself continuity across lengthy spans of time. Somehow it seems symbolic that my first memory of consciously listening to sound was so similar to Akio Suzuki's epiphany in Tango. What I have learned from him, and from my own listening practice, is that hearing can take place without sounds being replaced by words. This is very difficult to achieve – a life-changing moment, in fact. To compound the problem for me as a writer there was the question of how to listen without replacing the sounds with words, but then to use words to describe the experience of listening without words. This is almost impossible – my life's work, you could say – yet it comes from the humble experience of walking with my mother along a nondescript alley between two grey walls.

When I was a little older my mother would take me into London for day trips, indulging my curiosity about old buildings and museums. My parents were not cultured people. There were very few books in our home, no music except for easy-listening, military bands and light music on the radio, few signs of their inner lives. In either case, was there an inner life? Both of them were sensitive and intelligent in their way but they had no knowledge of arts, literature or the history of ideas and little patience with any of it. They were conservative in all senses. To them, most art was a form of delusion, an unnecessary madness to be kept at bay. Novels were pointless, my father once said, just made-up stories. Because of this I had no way to experiment with such ideas out loud. I imagine I must have been a perplexing child to them. While we fought in the 1960s over the usual banal issues of shoes (pointed), hair (long) and music (my father was not pleased that I listened to so much black music, the subject of bitter arguments during my teenage years), a condition of secrecy and silence grew up in me, a private place in which ideas and fantasies began to grow and slowly connect up through reading, drawing, daydreaming.

Creatures that live at great depths under the sea grow into strange alien forms. Despite a fear of deep water these peculiar fish, sea spiders and worms came to fascinate me, as did the notion of abyssal oceanic depths and the machines – the bathysphere and bathyscaphe – designed to explore them. With hindsight I realise that I was observing a projection of my own process of secrecy and the necessity to dive deep to retrieve all of the creatures developing within my psyche. As a compensation my imaginative life developed its own weird and exotic forms, each of them giving birth to new offspring.

David Toop ID photo for Hornsey College of Art, 1967

My Tastes In 1955:

Fess Parker, The Ballad of Davy Crockett
Dick James, Theme Song to the Adventures of Robin Hood
The Melodi Light Orchestra, Puffin' Billy

Memory is so slippery, deceptive in its construction of images, filling in the lost time that shreds history into rags. The strong feelings of my childhood were shame, alienation, curiosity, a creative energy, overwhelming shyness. If I look at my school report cards, still hoarded in a cardboard box as a reminder of failure, there is a pattern in both schools – a disturbing event followed by the collapse of scholarly achievement. Yet somehow there was a continuity of happiness based in small things. We had a dog named Terry, a Border Collie unwisely bought in the same year I was born. My mother often talked of trying to raise a puppy and take care of a baby at the same time.

An internal fantasy life grew inside me – a 'secret place of secret places' (boxes within a box) – drawing inspiration from places outside the civilised boundaries of home. There was nothing dangerous or wild about these places – maybe some bushes at the end of the garden or the unkempt alleyway that ran between the backs of houses – but with Terry I could pretend that they were forest, jungle, the American West, places in which I could become a fantasy figure other than myself. Sometimes I would even chant, the way that so-called 'Red Indians' did in the Westerns I watched. Even though this chanting imitated a Hollywood exoticisation of authentic Native American singing, it was an indication of my latent fascination for the music of other cultures, later developed through ethnomusicology and field recording.

For a child there is nothing unusual about this kind of play - a creative means of experimenting with possible identities, a place of escape from the limitations of the adult world – nor is there anything unusual for it to become the source of work in later life – the unconscious drive to construct a place that doesn't exist in the physical world, whether from sounds, words, lines, atmospheres. But there was something deeper, some need to penetrate further into the structures from which we have emerged as modern beings. This feeling was also connected with animals. My mother often told the story of when I was a boy of three-years old, seeing a skinned rabbit in the window of a butcher's shop and resolving from that moment not to eat meat or fish. As she was a very traditional cook this was a constant worry to her.

# FEAR

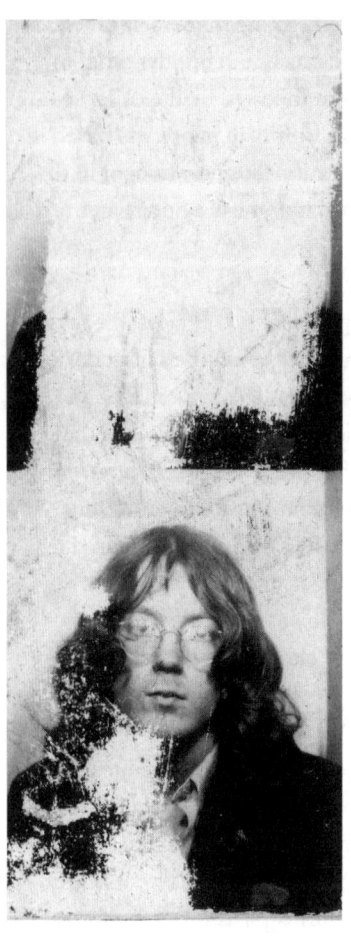

David Toop photobooth portrait, circa 1969

I felt, and feel, an empathy and fascination with the extra-human nature of animals, along with a desire to learn from their voices, movements and behaviour, but I was also attracted to horror, fear, aliens and monsters. Directly across the road from my junior school was a shop that sold sweets and newspapers. At some point in the late 1950s I bought a copy of an American magazine – *Famous Monsters of Filmland* – and through photographs of Roger Corman's versions of Edgar Allen Poe stories like *The Fall of the House of Usher* and *Masque of the Red Death* was drawn into the claustrophobic, hypersensitive world of Poe. My sister, Angela, bought me the Everyman edition of *Poe's Tales of Mystery and Imagination* for a present (still part of my book collection, nearly 60 years later) and so I became steeped in stories such as *The Tell-Tale Heart*, a narrative based on what I would now call 'paranoid listening', a listening so close to the smallest of sounding phenomena that there is no way to distinguish between sounds out in the world and auditory hallucinations coming from within the self. Macabre and claustrophobic, his writing scared me with its ornate, antique atmospherics yet compelled me to read deeper.

In Poe there was an articulation of something already experienced, an acute awareness of sounds heard when the cause of the sound is not seen, perhaps masked or hidden in some way, out of the line of sight or too distant. As a child in bed at night I would listen intently to the dark silence, fearful that each anomalous noise was an intruder, a nameless creature or phenomenon from beyond the world of humans. One night I lay still on my back in the darkness, convinced that I could hear a person moving slowly around the edges of my bed. If I avoided any movement, breathing as quietly as possible, then I hoped that this invisible being and its sounds (almost entirely a product of my overactive imagination) would move on to some other victim. Although the horror of the moment was overwhelming it was also an experience to remember, maybe even to enjoy in retrospect.

This taste for horror, in itself an almost masochistic need to feel the intensity of sensation, was ignited by a BBC television science-fiction drama series broadcast over six weeks in 1958-59: *Quatermass and the Pit*, created by Nigel Kneale. The story was complicated – a ruined alien spacecraft discovered during excavations in London, ostensibly supernatural phenomena and strange sounds emanating from the site, a disturbing transference effect, from human to insectile, finally a spreading invasive growth of alien life form that must be eradicated.

The anxieties embedded within the plot can be easily rationalised through hindsight as a fear of the other – the Cold War and nuclear escalation, race riots in Britain, the lingering trauma of World War II, even the post-war collapse of Empire – but to a child these were vague shadows transmitted subconsciously through the nervous talk of adults. The impact of the series was more visceral: an eerie atmosphere of the unknown, haunted and occult, heightened by strange electronic sounds – sine tones, echoed percussion and tape feedback produced by the BBC Radiophonic Workshop. One scene in particular implanted itself in my mind, a scene in which a man dismantling lights in the spacecraft is infected by the alien presence. As he runs through the street he is taken over by a weird insect gait; when he falls, the ground ripples, a movement echoed by uncanny electronics. This was how my generation came to hear electronic music for the first time.

Certain popular records of the 1950s could induce fear in me, seemingly innocent songs whose lyrics played upon the magical thinking to which children are prone. One was Alma Cogan's "The Railroad Runs Through the Middle of the House," for me a nightmarish vision of a home split in two by express trains. Another was Harry Belafonte's "Scarlet Ribbons," a maudlin lyric with something disturbing in its story of ribbons miraculously appearing in a girl's bedroom. At that time, my father's job, what was then termed a commercial traveller or travelling salesman, took him away from home for four or five days each week. The atmosphere of anxiety to which I was so sensitive perhaps conflated my father's absences with self-induced fear, the result of over-imaginative interpretations of song lyrics, science-fiction and Poe.

In March 2016, a few days after I became a grandparent, I dreamed of burning things in my parents' garden. From over the garden fence I could hear a record playing – "Great Balls of Fire" by Jerry Lee Lewis. Then I walked towards the house. A woman walked past me, a stranger. In the house I was trying to clean everything but the people sent to help me were teenagers, impossible to organise. It was as if my unconscious was adjusting to this new stage of life, trying to rid itself of antique memories and the strangers of history. As for the Jerry Lee Lewis record, that came from an actual memory of childhood, when the neighbours' daughter came home with a copy of "Great Balls of Fire" and played it over and over, maybe ten times in a row. It was number 1 in the UK in January 1958; I was nine years old, hearing the obsessional power of music through the connecting wall of our houses.

In memory, the emotional shifts of childhood are ungraspable, actually more of a freeze-frame of the place, the moment and its colours or only a feeling of looking or hearing. Faintly I can recall seeing a reproduction of Agnolo Bronzino's *An Allegory with Venus and Cupid* and experiencing a stirring of erotic sensation strangely mixed with guilt; from my aunt Jean's record collection, on breakable 78rpm disc, the mysterious but unmistakeable sexual charge and shamanic frenzy of records like Little Richard's "Long Tall Sally"; from my sister's record collection, also on 78rpm, the melancholy of Elvis Presley's "Heartbreak Hotel," so drenched in echo that the emotion of loss seemed transmuted into a tangible place; then there were pangs of loss and guilt from the death of our dog. After this I retreated for a time into solitude, culpable in my own mind for forcing him to run during our morning walk before school. Just before she died in the summer of 2008, drifting in and out of consciousness, my mother repeated this story, the memory of me retreating to my bedroom still vivid as her mind dimmed.

# GUITARS

Family is a casket of unseen pressures, tightening screws, shrinking boards. My paternal grandmother was agoraphobic. If she left the security of her house and garden she would vomit repeatedly as a symptom of her fear. My maternal grandmother rarely left her house, so crippled by arthritis that she spent her days in a wheel chair. I was aware that my grandfather refused to speak to my uncle, even though they lived in the same house together, only much later discovering that my uncle was gay and had been convicted of gross indecency at some point in the past. How do these examples of confinement and repression affect the mind of a young child?

My father was not an easy conversationalist. He could be taciturn and moody, often giving the impression that some inarticulate anger was held just under the surface of an argumentative silence. Perhaps that is one reason he loved to watch boxing. When I was very young I remember him getting up in the night to listen to the radio commentary on a big fight from America. That may also be why I shared his interest, despite our lack of common feelings, since I inherited some of his unhealthy tendency to mask strong emotions with the deceptions of silence, displacing them through violent sports and, in my case, the products of vivid imaginations. His tastes in music were more limited than my mother's; she spoke nostalgically about youthful dancing to bands of the swing era and in that gap between them there lay the gulf of difference so typical in many marriages of that type. Yet despite showing no interest in my musical tendencies, it was my father who guided the course of my later life by buying two guitars for me.

On the second occasion I was 21 years old. I had bought my first serious guitar – a blonde finish Fender Esquire (stolen in 1979 and never recovered; I replaced it with a Fender Telecaster) – with the aid of a loan from him. As it became obvious that I was unable to pay him back the £110 he rather grudgingly gave me ownership as a twenty-first birthday present. Funny to think that it would be extremely valuable now. The Fender Esquire replaced a solid-body electric guitar I made in school woodwork classes in 1964, basing its design on a rocket-shaped guitar made by Bo Diddley, shown on the back cover of his *Go Bo Diddley* album. My future brother-in-law, Gordon Stringer, played guitar. His tastes leaned more towards country music but for some reason he owned a copy of *Go Bo Diddley* and gave it to me, realising it was a record I would like. Perhaps it was with his help that I managed to source the necessary parts – fret wire, machine heads, rosewood for the fretboard and pickups – to make an instrument that worked, even though the height of the string action made it hard to play.

Paul Burwell & David Toop
Rain In the Face rehearsal
Ealing College, circa 1972

But my first instrument was an acoustic steel-string guitar, quite small, also with a very high action. A marquetry design was Inlaid into the yellowish wood by the sound hole. There was a magical aura to that image that makes me think of Chagall – an animal like a deer, maybe, and a moon (hard to remember exactly) – but the most magical aspect of the guitar was the way it was given. This desire for a guitar was sparked by rock 'n' roll singers: Elvis Presley, Little Richard, Bill Haley, Jerry Lee Lewis, Fats Domino, Buddy Holly. Like an electric shock, they jolted me into an awareness of the ecstatic energy of music; despite my young age I felt a compelling desire to enter their world even though I knew nothing about it. At some point in the 1950s my mother's half-sister, Jean, travelled to America in reckless pursuit of a man she had met at a London nightclub. The trip was a disaster but she returned with a stack of 78rpm records of rock 'n' roll, R&B and jazz, which I used to play when we visited her at my grandparents' house. I could be alone in the front room, away from the adults, their smoking and incomprehensible talk, picking out television theme tunes on the upright piano and listening to "Numbers Boogie" by Sugar Chile Robinson, "September In the Rain" by the George Shearing Quintet and Fats Domino's "Blueberry Hill," wondering why combinations of instruments, voices and emotive chord changes made me homesick for places I had never been. This must have been 1957-58 maybe. I was about eight or nine years old. After a turbulent life of breakdowns and ECT treatments my aunt Jean committed suicide in the 1980s, almost certainly unaware of the important role she had played in my musical education. I remember her after one of her ECT treatments. This was in 1967, when I was still living at home with my parents. My father had driven her to our house to recover. She lay on the sofa, seemingly asleep. I was playing a blues record, Johnny Shines maybe, quietly in the other half of the room. "Nice music," she said raising her head. I knew nobody else of her generation who showed appreciation for music like that.

My first guitar was either a birthday or Christmas present. I remember coming downstairs into the living room and finding an extraordinary tableau waiting for me. My parents had constructed a kind of tepee, probably out of a blanket and sticks. My sister, Angela, seven years older than me, was sitting cross-legged in front of it, wearing a feather in a headband and holding the guitar. I loved Westerns, one of the biggest cinema and television trends of that time – *Rawhide*, *The Lone Ranger*, *Wagon Train*, *Gunsmoke* – but when the feared and hated so-called Indians broke into a scene with their Otherness, I identified with them. My fascination with Native American culture deepened as I grew a little older, reading whatever historical information I could find and also drawing scenes that I imagined.

The only drawing of mine that survives from that period was called Gypsy Camp. Dating from when I was six years old, probably 1955, it depicts a gypsy camp, though the scene has elements of my own family – my mother, a black and white dog, and over by the fire a boy who could be me, cooking food in a frying pan, wearing a Davy Crockett hat. Davy Crockett was the big craze at the time and I had two of these hats, fake fur with a tail, supposedly racoon, hanging from the back. The idea of temporary structures and nomadic living attracted me: the prefabricated housing I noted during the walk with my mother, Native American encampments, gypsy camps and maybe even the log cabin in which Davy Crockett allegedly lived, according to the Disney television series based on his life. My secure life in suburbia was too fixed for me, even though I would have been frightened to leave it.

What do you want to be when you grow up? Adults always ask this question. During a class in primary school we were asked to draw a picture of ourselves in the future. I drew myself with a beard and check shirt, drawing cartoons in New York City. Even then as a young child I felt the allure of a bohemian life in America. Some of this came from westerns, then later on in my childhood it was intensified by television series like *Dragnet*, *Route 66*, *77 Sunset Strip* and *Naked City*. There was no television in our house until I was five years old. I remember sitting at the top of the stairs in my pyjamas, hearing the delivery of our first television set. I was consumed with excitement for this unreliable machine with its flickering grey and white images and soaked it up like a drug.

But the strongest attraction was music and this was predominantly American or American-influenced. Between my sixth and twelfth birthdays there was the wild aura of rock 'n' roll and rhythm and blues, then a cooler phase of guitar instrumentals by groups like The Shadows, The Hunters, The John Barry Seven and The Ventures – 1950s and early 60s music without words, its appeal based in the creation of simple atmospheres through reverberation, dramatic drums, mysterious melodies and electronic timbres. But certain records from childhood fully brought to life that nascent exoticism awakened by the guitar emerging from its Sioux or Cheyenne teepee, in particular the theme song to a television series called *Rawhide*, sung by Frankie Laine in 1958 with cattle herding and whip-crack effects. Percussive, echoing sounds, like the whip effects or Bo Diddley's technique of playing single strings and open-tuned chords on his homemade electric guitars as if they were drums opened up my physical connection to the guitar and its possibilities. The atmospheres of all these records, often associated with television series, films or photographs, is central to what I'd describe as a myth or imaginary ethnography lying tantalisingly just out of reach of whatever can be done with sound. This is about boundaries and the lack of them, sound that is as fuzzy and indeterminate as a Chinese scroll painting. The mystery of it lies at the outer edges.

How this gift-giving scenario came about is a mystery to me. My parents were not particularly imaginative, nor were they emotionally demonstrative. They struggled financially when I was young so it may be that they were compensating for not being able to buy me expensive presents. But the incident was highly unusual, so it glows in my childhood as a beacon of something unknown, outside normality. What it did, I can speculate retrospectively, was to make a link between anthropology and sound in a formative period of my young life. It also raised a question of how a deep experience might be stimulated by the setting of its presentation.

I was never given music lessons so a few years passed before the guitar became anything other than an object that occasionally made sound if I thrashed at it. In 1961 the first tune I learned to play was Jerry Lordan's "Apache," learned from a record by The Shadows. This was no coincidence. The boom in Westerns generated many recordings, particularly twangy guitar instrumentals, but it echoed that first encounter and reinforced the feeling within me that music was not only exotic but profoundly transformative. A space opened out as if in wide screen and Technicolor, a wide sky starlit, a dry desert out of which rose mountains so strange that they might have been built by giant ants. These were the visions that music created in my mind.

As a compensation for shyness and introversion as a child, I was compulsively creative, particularly in drawing, but often incapable of learning, usually uncomfortable and fearful socially. The physiological effect of hearing music at that time was a movement across divisions of thought, feeling, the physical body, ideas, environment, other people. I understood this early on, though I wouldn't have been able to articulate it. Music allowed me to project a presence into the world, rather than retreating into being a retiring, scared boy – all intensity with no outward expression. In a sense that still holds true. For all the writing and talking I do, the activity I value most is making music, that is to say, physically working with sound.

Music touches the emotions very deeply, moves the body, fills space yet has the invisible mystery of thought, scent, air, mind, sensations, the feeling of floating in the world of time. For this reason perhaps, music can become embedded in a person's sense of their identity, even though identity is complex, never reducible to a single image. By listening to music, many identities can be unearthed within this recognisable body called the self. In making music I have always felt that I am birthing creatures. These musical materials – the sounds and living silences – have their own lives. They begin to make decisions for themselves, finding their own forms, learning to exist with the other creatures that occupy their space but at the same time growing autonomously without any regard for others. In doing so they play a part in shaping the identity of the person who compelled them to approach. They are active and have the potential to be as powerful as the magical sound of the catalpa bow, the stringed instrument that compels the spirit in the Japanese Noh play, *Aoi no Ue*. Then this angry spirit is subdued by a reclusive holy man from Yamabushi who compels her to retreat with the sound of friction from his rosary beads, a sounding of words – the Middle Spell of Fudō – that strikes fear into the heart of the spirit.

David Toop, circa 1970

My Tastes In 1963–1964:

Sam Cooke, Another Saturday Night
The Ronettes, Be My Baby
Chuck Berry, Run Rudolph Run
The Rolling Stones, Come On
Doris Day, Move Over Darling
Beach Boys, Don't Worry Baby

Contact sheets:
David Toop & Paul Burwell
The Little Theatre Club

BLUES

*I wish I was a catfish, swimming in the deep blue sea*

In November 1963, President Kennedy was assassinated in Dallas. The radio programme I was hoping to hear was cancelled, replaced by sombre funerary dirges. Incidents like this helped me to realise the social and symbolic significance of music, the way in which music is entwined in our beliefs about the nature of society and the constitution of the world. Earlier that year I bought two 7" singles that shaped the course of my life in music. The first was Sam Cooke's "Another Saturday Night", the beginning of a lifelong passion for African American music of all kinds; the second was "Come On" by The Rolling Stones.

Somehow I was inquisitive about the origins of this latter track, a cover of a lesser known Chuck Berry song. This was the path that led me to the strange notion of authenticity. I bought the next few records by the Rolling Stones, even going to hear them live in concert in a 1964 UK package tour that also featured The Ronettes and Marty Wilde and the Wildcats. My first pop concert, it was memorable for the deafening screams unleashed by all the teenage girls in the audience as soon as the Rolling Stones hit the stage. My interest quickly shifted toward the original artists copied by British R&B groups, African American singers such as Muddy Waters, Otis Redding, Marvin Gaye, Bo Diddley, John Lee Hooker, Slim Harpo and Howlin' Wolf. This was the music I wanted to play and for much of my teens I felt that black music was superior to most white pop (though there were exceptions like The Beach Boys).

This curious, almost comical attitude of a white teenager from the suburbs of London idolising black artists from cities like Chicago and Detroit was commonplace at that time. Here was an obsession with music – emotionally intense, obscure, remote and replete with references to sex and violence – that was perfect at that transitional stage of my life. Despite being an abject failure in most subjects at my school – Broxbourne Grammar – and despite not knowing a single person of colour I found the confidence to give a talk on post-war African American migration from the south to the industrial northern cities and its impact on the sound of urban blues. The uncomfortable feeling of giving that talk still lingers – the other pupils at school were either baffled or indifferent – but these were first steps in analysing and contextualising music, then presenting the ideas to an audience.

Listening to music had a collective aspect, perhaps because music was taking on an almost religious significance for my generation, far more compelling to most of us than party politics, orthodox religion or sport. There were occasions on which friends gathered together to listen to significant records: one Sunday morning in the early summer of 1967, for example, we met to hear the newly released Beatles album, *Sgt. Pepper's Lonely Hearts Club Band*, earnestly discussing its merits and weaknesses as if we were a university debating society. We also gathered later in the same month to watch The Beatles perform "All You Need Is Love" for the first live global television link. These events felt like major cultural shifts and yet they were peripheral to my increasingly specialist interests. Already I was developing solitary habits – going alone to some films and concerts because I knew that they were best appreciated as a reflective, lingering experience, without having to discuss or defend them directly afterwards.

My first band was formed in 1964 with school friends, perhaps not friends exactly but we were a quartet of contemporaries with instruments, all of us struggling to imitate this new sound of British R&B. I played guitar, learning Hubert Sumlin's riff to Howlin' Wolf's "Smokestack Lightning," John Lee Hooker's "Boom Boom," Slim Harpo's "I'm a King Bee," Bo Diddley's "Mona" and "Road Runner." During a rehearsal one night (the band never progressed beyond rehearsals, never even gave itself a name) we were playing "Road Runner." Suddenly I found that the glass bottleneck I was using took on a life of its own, sliding across the strings in what later became known in the psychedelic era as a 'freak out.' Somehow I, or the body of me beyond conscious will, had crossed a line into the as-yet undiscovered territory of free jazz, improvisation and electronic noise. The other members were appalled. Our band survived only a little longer but the noise of glass moving freely across amplified steel strings was now established in my mind as a way of breaking the rules of music.

Two years later the next band was more serious, partly because I was becoming fanatical about musical knowledge, digging deeply into the history of the blues through scholars like Paul Oliver and Samuel Charters, through the Mike Raven Blues Show on pirate radio and the few records that were available and affordable at that time. We covered tracks by Otis Rush, Junior Wells and other hardcore urban singers from Chicago but by 1966 music was moving into a psychedelic phase and besides, what was a group of young white boys from Hertfordshire doing, singing songs like "Prison Bars All Around Me"? Vexed, complex questions of authenticity and race troubled me more than they did the others but none of us could avoid comparing ourselves to more gifted blues imitators. One night in November 1966 we went as a group to see The Paul Butterfield Blues Band play at Cooks Ferry Inn, Edmonton. This was the band featuring Mike Bloomfield and Elvin Bishop on guitars. Afterwards we sat in the car, almost speechless, knowing that what we had heard was far out of reach for us. Our band played only one live gig before its members dispersed. That was enough to realise that we were going nowhere, though I maintained a friendship with Peter Gallen, the bass player. With him I moved on to a more experimental kind of improvised music using home-made and amplified instruments. That duo failed to develop but for a few years we created light shows together.

My Tastes in 1965–66:

James Brown, Papa's Got a Brand New Bag
Ornette Coleman, This is Our Music
Beach Boys, Pet Sounds
BB King, Live at the Regal
Major Lance, I'm the One
Buddy Guy, First Time I Met the Blues
Martha and the Vandellas, Nowhere to Run

Paul Burwell & David Toop

David Toop artwork 'Violated Man', 1967

## LIGHT, SOUND, DESTRUCTION

David Toop artworks:
'Disappearing woman', 1967

'Woman Without a Body', 1967

My first experiments with light were probably in early summer 1966, first of all using a thick glass plate owned by my parents, refracting the beam of my father's slide projector and adding music, particularly Indian ragas, from the record player. I then tried this out with a small audience at school where I had the support of an art teacher named Michael Evans. Michael, an ex-Slade School painter, became interested in this medium himself and so we collaborated on Super 8 film projects to combine with the light projections.

By the end of 1966 I had seen light shows at rock concerts, notably at the Roundhouse (probably Gustav Metzger) and was developing an idea of combining pop art imagery with light manipulations and film. Peter Gallen, later a recording studio engineer and record producer for Uriah Heap, Osibisa and Colosseum, was interested in these experiments so we started working together. He concentrated on liquid lights, using concentrated acids and coloured inks while I continued with slides and film. Peter found us gigs at venues like the Fishmongers Arms in Wood Green (Pete Brown's Battered Ornaments, Keef Hartley Band) and in 1967 the Pink Flamingo in Wardour Street. The biggest thing we did was a chaotic show at Granby Halls, Leicester, in 1968 with The Who, Joe Cocker and Yes.

Inspired by Andy Warhol, Richard Hamilton and Eduardo Paolozzi I started using more provocative material – burned slides and defaced images, soft-core porn films on Super 8, horror film stills, short film loops and at one gig live maggots, overheated in the projector beam but throwing out huge writhing shapes before their death. I seem to remember doing this at a gig where the band was a soul group called Jimmy James and the Vagabonds. Unsurprisingly, the audience hated it. While studying graphic design at Watford College of Art in 1968 I was living in a house full of drug users and addicts (very typical of the time) and made Super 8 loops that reflected this environment. After showing one of them, an addict shooting up heroin, at a Roundhouse all-night concert I was told we could never work there again. At the time, incidents like these convinced me that this supposedly free psychedelic scene, awash with drugs, was inherently hypocritical; at the time it never occurred to me to interrogate my own desire to show this kind of imagery.

One of my inspirations was the light shows created by Peter Wynne Wilson for Pink Floyd in early 1967. I had seen them play at Enfield College of Technology in March of that year, then at the 14 Hour Technicolor Dream at Alexandra Palace in April. Wynne Wilson's sister was my English literature teacher at school – Ailsa Cregan – who put me in touch with him. After writing to him I received a reply (since lost) inviting me to the famous Earlham Street address where Syd Barrett lived. Sadly, or perhaps fortunately (considering my youth and the drugs I would have encountered), I never visited. I was also aware of light shows by Mark Boyle and Joan Hills through seeing Soft Machine play live but the biggest impact came in 1968, from seeing films by artist John Latham.

My first exposure to John Latham's work would have been in the Tate Gallery, where one of John's magnificent book reliefs – probably *Film Star* (1960) - hung alongside works by Jackson Pollock and Franz Kline. This was in the mid-1960s, so it would be dubious to claim through hindsight that I can clearly recollect the impact on my adolescent self, but I am convinced that this strange work of books held open by wire and plaster, like the upended floor of a bombed library or the mouths of fish gasping for air, made a profound connection for me between the textural paintings and reliefs of Italian and Spanish artists – Alberto Burri, Lucio Fontana and Antoni Tápies – and a deeper world of ideas which I barely glimpsed at that time.

Again, I can only speculate, but the sight of books transformed into instant hits of visceral, burnt-out information was wildly exciting. In the post-war period of reconstruction, destruction was a problematic concept, particularly when linked in

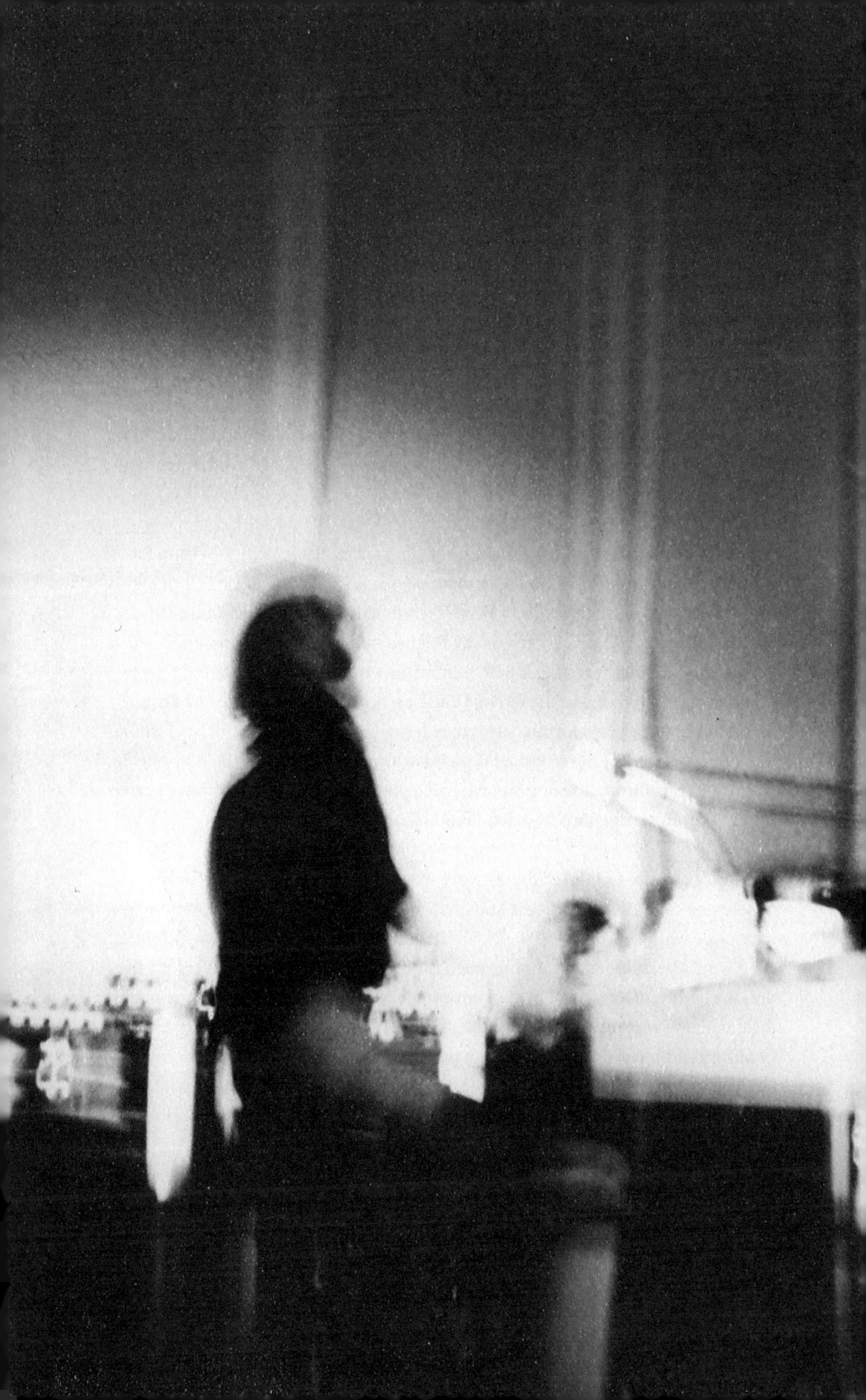

The Doors at The Roundhouse, London, 1968, photograph by David Toop this way to knowledge and, by inference, civilization. At the same time, destruction seemed inevitable and necessary. Growing up in the inertia and conservatism of London's outer suburbs in the 1950s, I could only respond positively to that which was radically other, that which was reduced to fragments or rubble, the outer edges of emotion, or to celebrations of noise and chaos. I was hugely attracted, then, by DIAS, the Destruction In Art Symposium held in London in 1966, publicized in the Auto-Destruction issue of *Art and Artists* magazine in that same year. In an atmosphere of nuclear threat and a growing awareness of vanishing species and environmental disasters, these ideas were in the air.

In May 1968, towards the end of my first year as a foundation student at Hornsey College of Art, the college was occupied by students and some members of staff for what became known as the Hornsey sit-in. A wave of unrest was flowing across the world at that time and this linked to a growing discontent over the future direction of higher education. As Lisa Tickner wrote in *Hornsey 1968: The Art School Revolution*, "The sit-in erupted when strains in the fabric of art and design education – related to and exacerbated by, the perceived needs of corporate capital and the British economy – were compounded by inadequate resources, poor communication and a lack of leadership in the college itself." This moment of choice – either continuing daily studies at an annex college or going to the main college building to get involved in the sit-in – was a pivotal moment of my young life. I chose the latter and benefitted hugely from being part of such a radical experiment, taking part in open discussions, seminars and lectures, DJing with my soul records (and being told my taste for Jimmy McGriff and Alvin Robinson was out of date), working in the kitchen, making my own Super 8 films, organising a concert and watching the strange cast of characters who stopped by at the college to see what was going on. John Latham's early 16mm films – *Talk* (1961) and *Speak* (1962) – were screened as part of the late-night film shows held in Hornsey's main lecture theatre. I can still recall my feeling of being overwhelmed by their visual and auditory power.

Also in 1968 I was in the audience for a performance evening called *Float*, held at Middle Earth, a psychedelic club located at 43, King Street, Covent Garden. The poster for *Float* advertised performances by seventeen artists, including Stuart Brisley, Peter Dockley, Bruce Lacey, and Carlyle Reedy, but I was most impressed by Latham's contribution. He was cutting up books with the kind of floor mounted electric saw used by timber merchants. As if the noise from this activity wasn't brutal enough, the body of the saw was amplified through a contact microphone. This noise attack was so thrilling that I picked up one of the book fragments from the floor and took it home. Reading through this sundered volume in a conventional manner generated fantastic imagery automatically. The book was a collection of philosophical ruminations written in florid style (*Prue and I* by George William Curtis, I later discovered through a Google search), and so nonsensical lines of overheated, exotic poetry flowed from its pages: ". . . the hissing of the owls came at full speed sounded almost instantly uproar had warned . . . a small card lay four tiny doll's heads . . ." These broken texts became songs, in some cases, and I read long passages from them into a cassette tape recorder, using a flat voice that gave no acknowledgement to the consistent ruptures of syntax and meaning.

Perplexing and convoluted as they were, John Latham's ideas about time began to intrigue me. At the Latham house in Holland Park, where he had fixed a life-size photograph of a front door onto the real front door, I listened to John talk on many occasions. We corresponded and I even worked as an assistant on his 1971 film, *Encyclopedia Britannica*, but whatever his meaning it was absorbed in a slow process of osmosis rather than direct understanding. Musicians find the notion of a world based on time-base and event, rather than object relations, relatively easy to assimilate, since time and immateriality form the foundation of their practice. I would describe John Latham as another mentor, like Bob Cobbing, and there were connections between the two artists. Cobbing was an organizer of events in which Latham took part, and his tape sound poetry had been incorporated into at least one of Latham's performance installations of the 1960s. From both artists, there was the attraction of destroyed syntax and scattered nouns, even though their intentions and methods were radically different.

This was a turning point for me. By that time I had read *Nova Express* by William Burroughs, and I was getting to know more about literary cut-ups and concrete poetry. I had also experimented with stream-of-consciousness writing, some juvenile examples of which had been published in the school magazine in 1966. A few years later I would be working in a trio with sound poet Bob Cobbing and percussionist Paul Burwell, my introduction to the world of sound poetry. Bob was a pioneer in this field, active in visual and performance poetry since the 1950s. During the 1960s he had managed the notorious Charing Cross Road bookshop and performance venue, Better Books, a hub of underground culture; he was also one of the organisers of the Destruction In Art Symposium. He knew everybody on this scene, so within a few years we met and sometimes performed with sound and concrete poets such as Lilly Greenham, Henri Chopin, Dom Sylvester Houédard, Jackson Mac Low, Jerome Rothenberg, Paula Claire, Sten Hanson, Gerhard Ruhm, Francois Dufrene and Ernst Jandl. There was an emergent context then, but I had discovered a way to write, as well as a way to speak and sing (and new subjects to speak and sing about).

Bob Cobbing, Paul Burwell and David Toop
Sound Poetry Trio

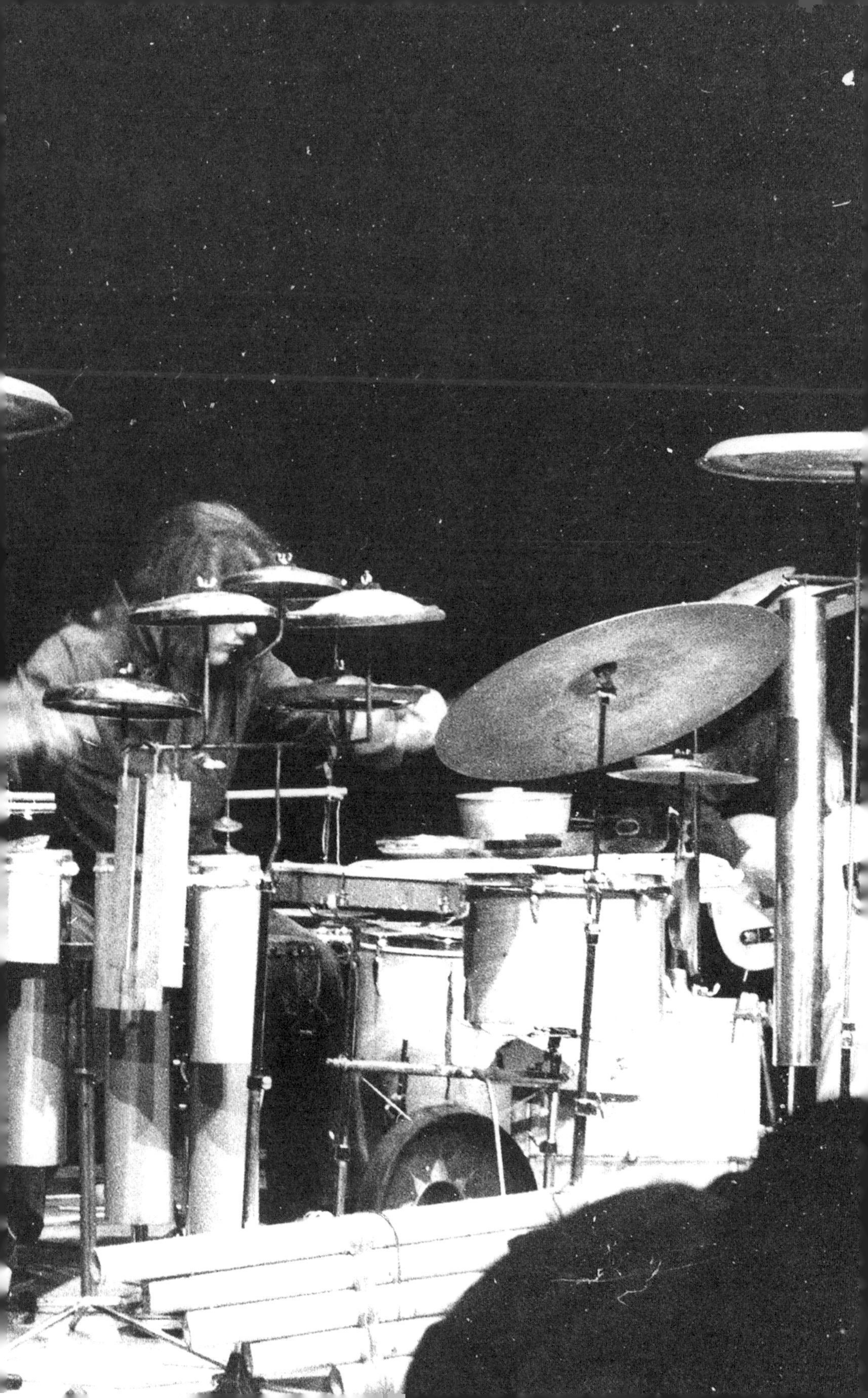

This page:
Recording at the BBC Studios
Opposite:
Almost Free Theatre

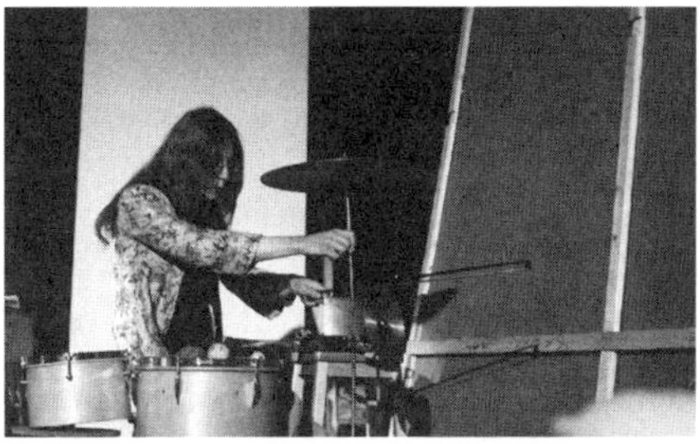
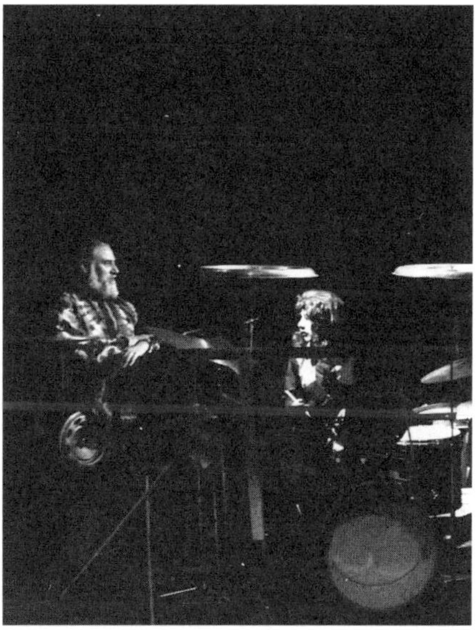
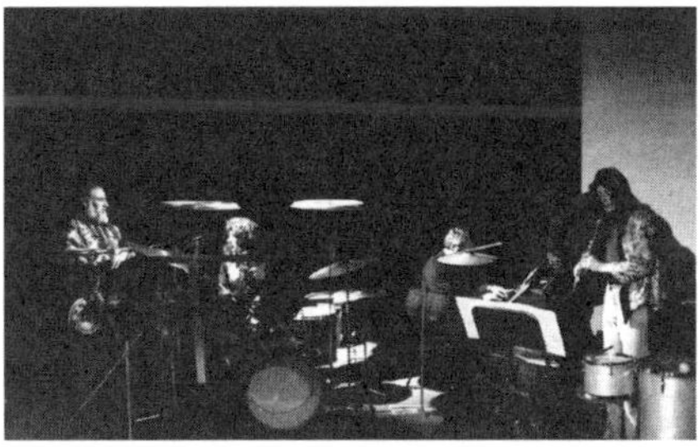
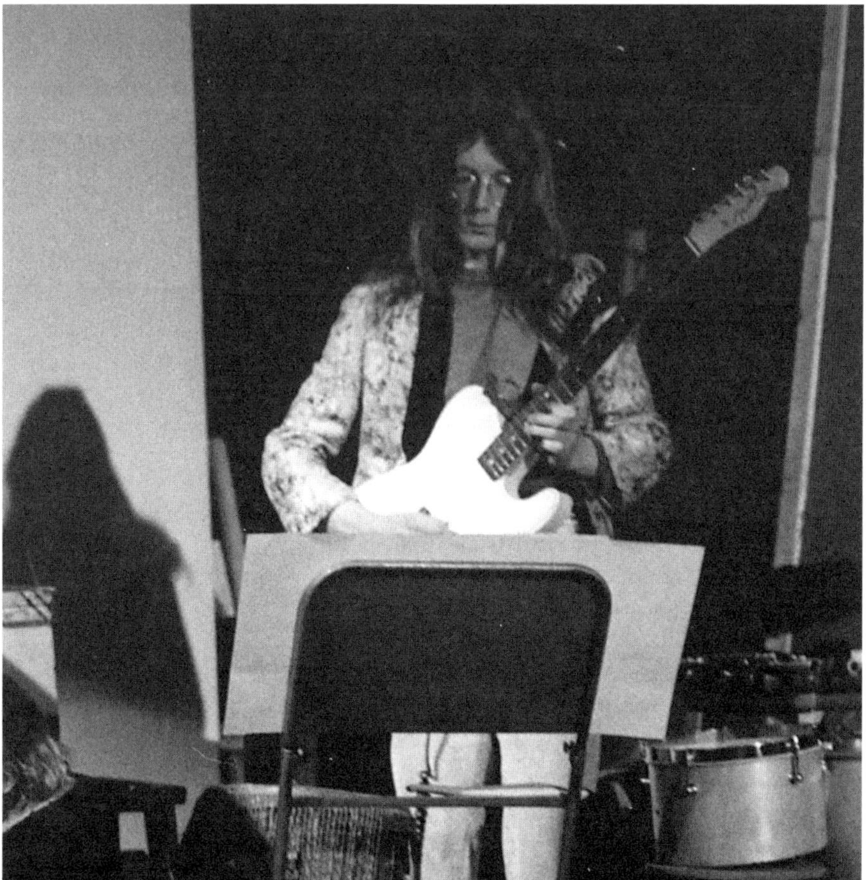

## FINDING A WAY

After the sit-in experience during my first year at Hornsey College of Art, my art school education gradually fell apart. I was accepted at Watford School of Art in 1968 to study graphic design for three years but left after one year. Some of the tutors were interesting artists who did their best to help me – Peter Schmidt, co-creator of *Oblique Strategies* with Brian Eno, printmaker and publisher Hansjorg Mayer and photographer Raymond Moore (whose influence I still see in my own photographs) – but I was not remotely interested in hot metal type setting and printing processes like photogravure. Drugs were rife in the town at that time, The flat where I lived was an inter-tribal crossroads of hardened heroin addicts and methadone users, skinheads up all night fighting and gobbling huge quantities of speed, hippies taking acid to a soundtrack of the Incredible String Band and bank robbers living upstairs. Music was more often at the centre of my thoughts than anything else but this turbulent, often violent atmosphere was not conducive to sustained work or mental clarity. One night we were raided by the police. Poleaxed by liquid cannabis and still recovering from a dramatic out-of-body experience earlier in the evening, I was in no state to go anywhere, least of all Watford police station, but that was where I ended up, barely knowing who I was. I was fortunate not to be charged.

Beginner Studio, Cologne, 1979

My visual work was confused, still influenced by pop art but wrestling (often literally) with issues of violence, sexual difference and identity. On the one hand I was making large prints of photographs, reversed out, taken from American magazines like *Wrestling World*. There was nothing conscious about reversing these images of absurdly exaggerated hyper-masculinity but now I read it as an ironic comment on a phenomenon that was already on the edge of camp, a faked, operatically melodramatic war between good guys and bad guys. On the other hand I was making drawings and prints of women with their faces obscured or replaced by light fittings and other objects. What comes through now, embarrassingly plainly, is both unrealised homoeroticism and an unacknowledged fear of women. A course that taught typography, calligraphy and photogravure was clearly not the environment in which to explore these adolescent struggles. I decided to try fine art, again at Hornsey, and was accepted. This turned out to be a further mistake: the course offered very little of what I was seeking and most of the tutors were unhelpful and obstructive. 'You should make pornographic paintings on big canvases,' a painter named Mike Tyzack told me. Maybe it was good advice, at least in the sense of being a provocation, but certainly not what I needed to hear. Social life opened up in unexpected directions, however. I met my partner and collaborator of the next five years – Marie Yates – and a number of friends and future collaborators, notably Max Eastley.

Outside of social life I was moving between music gigs, cinema, jazz and blues record stores like Dobell's, first in Rathbone Place, subsequently in Charing Cross Road, and Colletts in New Oxford Street, book shops like Better Books and art galleries, notably The Robert Fraser Gallery in Duke Street (Andy Warhol's floating silver balloons), Kasmin in New Bond Street, the ICA in Dover Street, the Lisson Gallery in Lisson Street, the Rowan Gallery in Bruton Place (Andy Warhol's Most Wanted paintings), David Medalla's Signals in Wigmore Street (Gerhard von Graevenitz kinetic sculptures) and the Cork Street galleries (anything from Paul Wunderlich to Jean Tinguely's motorised wall pieces flailing to the point of self-destruction). Finally, in 1969, I decided to give up visual arts for music. 'Give up' may be too strong a description of the process – I continued to draw and at the same time searched for a new form, somewhere in the interstices of music, sound, text and visual arts – but there was a dramatic shift of emphasis. Sound became ascendant. Dropping out of Watford College meant that a year of my grant was used up. I had to survive the first year at Hornsey by working, so at the weekends I had a job at the Roundhouse, bringing drinks from the cellar to the bar and serving ice cream during rock concerts. Barbiturates had become the drug of choice. I had tried them myself occasionally, usually ending up in absurd or dangerous situations, too stupefied to cope. This was the feel of audiences there, semicomatose and barely able to function, an atmosphere that may have intensified my desire to lift myself up out of this torpid scene. When the venue closed for the evening some of us started regular jam sessions that lasted all night, playing rock improvisations in the freezing cold. A tenor saxophonist/flautist named Geoff lived and made jewellery in a tiny platelayer's hut behind the Roundhouse. He seemed to know a limitless supply of beatnik conga drummers so the music we played often settled into ragged grooves vaguely reminiscent of Dr. John's *Gris Gris* album. One night we played for so long that we were still on the stage when Ginger Johnson and His African Drummers arrived to play a Saturday morning kids' show, so we just carried on jamming with his group.

At one of these sessions Paul Burwell showed up with his drum kit. When the beatnik conga players headed back to Devon Paul and I discovered a mutual drive, intensity and ambition to make music that set us apart from the others, not that we knew at that immature stage of our lives how this would develop. Paul and I became close friends soon after we first met. By visiting each other, rehearsing, going to gigs and films together, talking and looking through our respective record collections and books we were amazed to discover that we shared similar tastes in music. There were differences between us – he found my love of soft soul and Charlie Parker baffling, I liked Led Zeppelin, he liked Black Sabbath – but we were both fanatical about Sun Ra, Albert Ayler, Bongo Joe, One String Sam, the Johnny Burnette Trio, raw blues, free jazz, Indian ragas, Scottish pibroch bagpipes and the first records of improvised music emerging at that time, particularly AMM's first LP, the Spontaneous Music Ensemble's *Karyobin* and the duos of Derek Bailey with Han Bennink and Evan Parker with Paul Lytton. We also shared a desire to go beyond existing frameworks of music, to think more deeply about sonic experience (particularly through anthropology) and to build instruments that could produce unprecedented sounds.

During a terrible holiday job in 1967, toiling in a cement factory in debilitating heat and enveloping dust clouds, I was asked a question by one of the Irish men who endured this work on a regular basis. "What do you want to do with your life," he said as both of us shovelled gravel onto a moving conveyer belt. I told him I planned to be a filmmaker. "I don't think you'll do that," he replied. I was annoyed by his dismissal of my ambition at the time but he turned out to be right. Films such as Kaneto Shindo's *Onibaba*, Akira Kurosawa's *Seven Samurai*, *Throne of Blood* and *Rashomon*, Kenji Mizoguchi's *The Life of Oharu*, *Repulsion* by Roman Polanski, Yoko Ono's *Four*, Alfred Hitchcock's *Psycho*, *Hiroshima Mon Amour* by Alain Resnais, Anthony Harvey's *Dutchman* and Henning Carlsen's *Hunger* affected me deeply in my teenage years. One of the more interesting aspects of art school education in the 1960s was the opportunity to see examples of American underground cinema by film makers such as Kenneth Anger, Ed Emshwiller and Stan Brakhage. During my first year of college, in 1967, I saw *Seven Samurai* for the first time, the room of the film society fogged by cigarette smoke, so that Kurosawa's rain-drenched battles and misty morning skirmishes were seen through eyes so irritated by smoke that they streamed with tears.

Inspired by the way these films used music I was intrigued by the possibilities of combining moving images with sound. As Toru Takemitsu once told Peter Grilli, when asked why he wrote music for film: "Writing music is like getting a passport – a visa to freedom, a liberty passport." Only the technical difficulties and expense of making films stopped me at that stage; since then I have composed some music for film and television but I prefer to think that all of my work, including writing, is enriched and transformed by cinema, sometimes in ways I barely understand. To give one example, the unusual structuring of Wong Kar-wai's films of the mid-1990s – *Chungking Express* and *Fallen Angels* – suggested ways of organising the material of my book, *Exotica*, published in 1999. As Takemitsu did, I watch many films, sometimes five or more in a week now that hard-to-find films can be found on YouTube, always with the thought that cinema conveys more about the dark and often violent motivations of humans than any other medium.

If Hornsey College of Art had felt able to support my interest in light and sound in 1970 then I might have followed this course. As it was I was told by the head of college that there was nothing they could do to help me. For a few years Hornsey had been a leader in experimental light and sound; now it was turning back to more traditional media. The inference was that I should concentrate on making big paintings, a form of art in which I had diminishing interest and little talent. In disgust and bitterly disillusioned, I walked out of the college, got drunk and started a new life, concentrating instead on trying to develop a new type of free rock music with Paul Burwell and any other musician who would play with us. None of them lasted long; our vision was too experimental, too elusive even for us – we would spend many hours of rehearsal discussing ideas that felt just out of reach or play brief sessions with bassists, singers or saxophone players, only to find that they were hoping for something more structured and predictable.

Finally we found collaborators outside music. All of them came at the same time. Along with Bob Cobbing there was a Japanese Butoh dancer who had performed *Barairo Dansu* with Tatsumi Hijikata and Kazuo Ohno in 1965 – Mitsutaka Ishii – who danced in a wedding dress and ate raw fish on stage; Carlyle Reedy, poet, artist and founder of Monkey Theatre, and Marie Yates, an artist who had switched from poetic sculptures made from neon to a practice based on the atmosphere of place. Later, in 1976, we played music live for Steven Berkoff's production of *Agamemnon* at the Greenwich Theatre. Visible to the audience, we were set up on one side of the stage close to the actors. From that vantage point we produced all the sounds for the play with drums and flutes. Working with Steven was an education. Although text was vital to his vision of theatre he began with movement, voice exercises, the drama of bodies in space. English critics were intolerant of his unique approach but the way he conjured expansive effects out of simple means was invigorating.

As a duo Paul and I called ourselves Rain In the Face, after the Native American Lakota war chief who contributed to the defeat of Custer at the Battle of Little Big Horn in 1876. This choice of name came from my obsession, going back to childhood, with Native American history and culture, but also the transient, delicate sensation of feeling rain on the skin of the face and how that connected to the kind of improvised music we were trying to develop, a music that openly expressed the intensity of being alive in the moment.

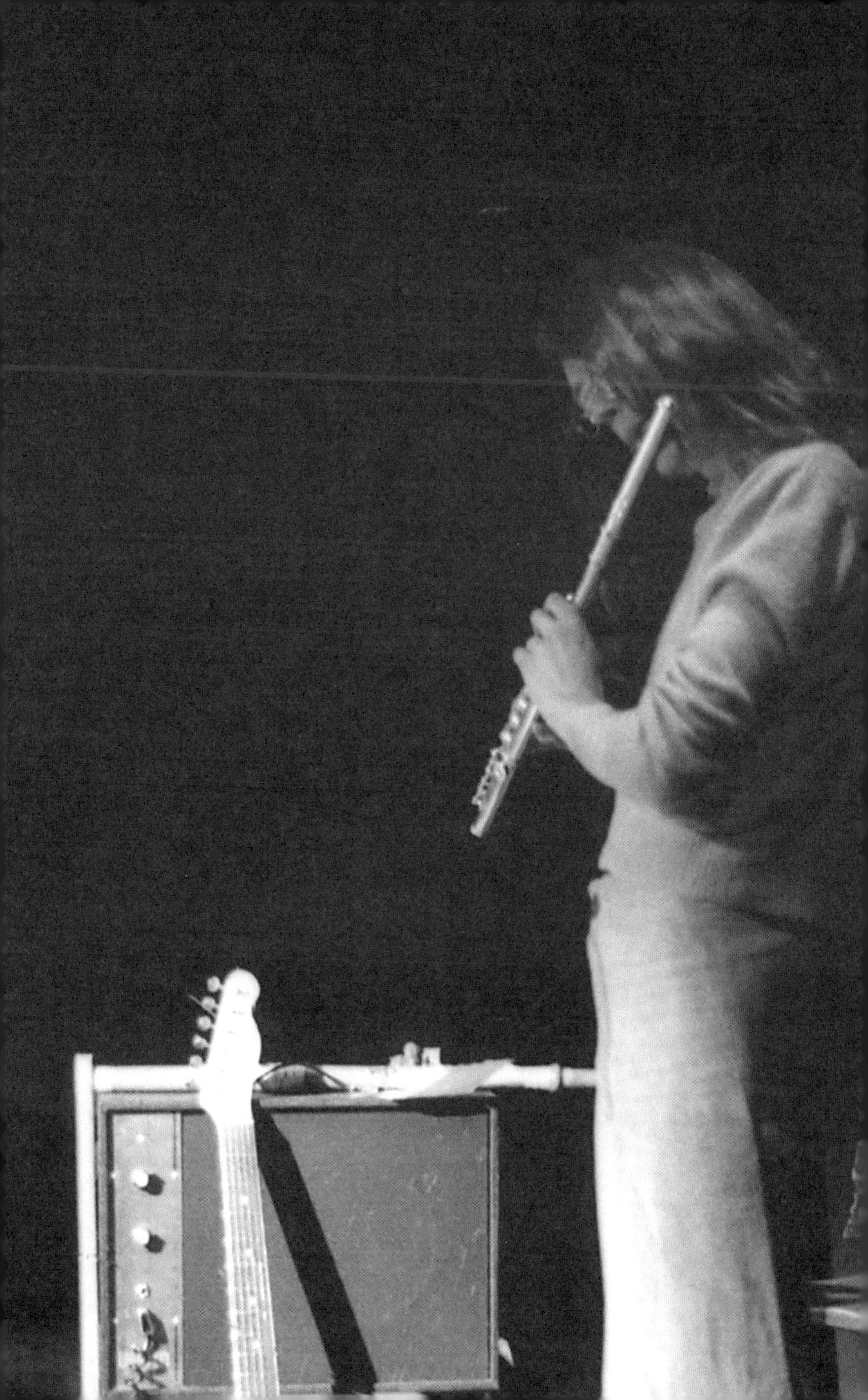

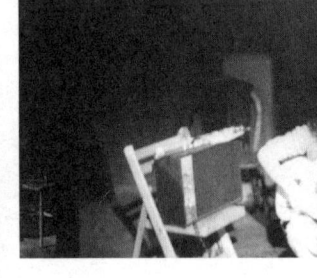

This page:
Paul Burwell & David Toop
at The Little Theatre Club
Opposite:
Mitsutaka Ishii, David Toop
& Paul Burwell

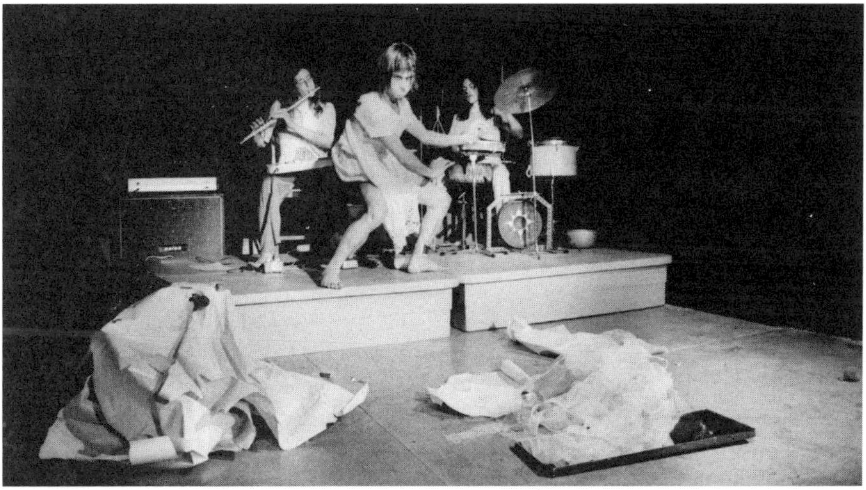

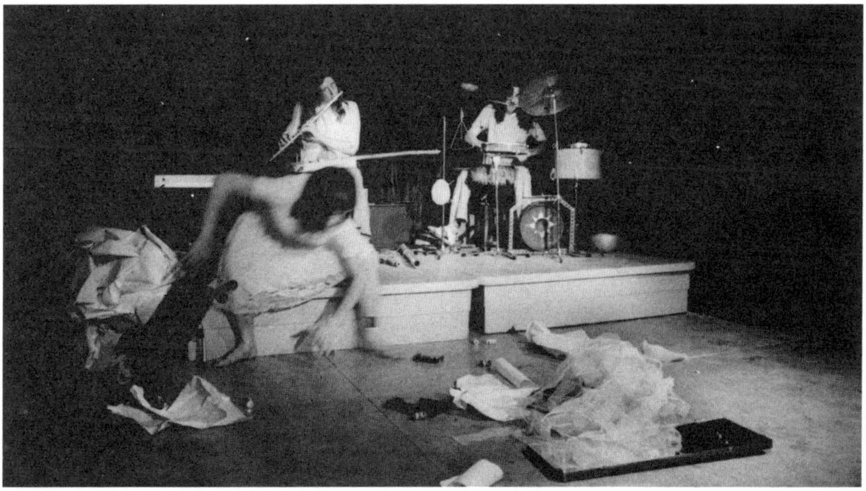

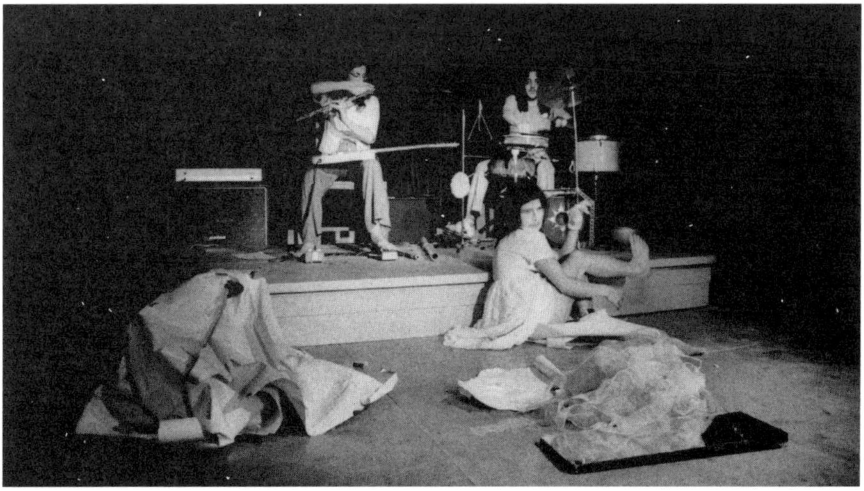

## WORD AND SOUND

Bob Cobbing, Paul Burwell and I began working together in 1971, in circumstances coincidental enough to invite disbelief. Unbeknownst to Paul, his partner at the time – Sheila – was Bob Cobbing's daughter. Her pregnancy led to an awkward meeting between the three of them in which they talked about anything – art, music, poetry and the possibility of collaboration – rather than discuss Sheila's pregnancy.

As Paul wrote in 2000: "We have never touched on the subject from that day to this, but instead talked about Bob's work and how he was attempting to get at the sounds of words themselves, to liberate words from the tyranny of semantic meaning. He was examining them for what they were, not what they were symbols of . . . He explained that he was frustrated with playing tapes at live readings, and had been learning to reproduce these sounds, with sub and high frequencies, rumbles and so on, with his own voice. The tapes of his own voice were used to extend the possibilities of that same voice . . . This approach had similarities with the work David Toop and I were engaged in at the time as Rain In the Face: an interest in the microstructure of sounds, dissecting sounds and structures, and trying to decondition ourselves from unconsciously acquired preconceptions of what sound, music, creativity and art were about."

I still have a cassette tape of the first meeting of Paul, myself and Bob in 1971, convened at the Maida Vale flat shared by Bob and photographer/dancer Jennifer Pike. Bob runs briskly through a number of his pieces – *Linade* and *Ana Perena* among them – presumably to give us something to listen to, to work out how we might approach them. There is another recording, a rehearsal tape made at Ealing College on May 3rd, 1972, that includes one strange piece of three silences and two unisons of loud noise. By this time the group had expanded to a sextet: Christopher Small on piano, Herman Hauge on alto saxophone, Lyn Conetta on voice, myself on flute and electric guitar, Paul on drums. Our first concert was on April 1972, at the Almost Free Theatre on Rupert Street. The original name of the group - ANA – was misprinted in *Time Out*'s listings as abAna, so it stuck. The sextet's performances were carefully planned, using each of Bob's pieces to vary the resources of the group. So for a BBC Radio 3 broadcast by the group on the 17th May, 1973: a trio for two voices and piano for *Ana Perena*, saxophone, wooden flutes and Lyn Conetta's voice for *I Paint His Face*, group voices for *Soma*, a trio of Bob, myself and Paul for *The Judith Poem*, whistles, bowed cymbals, electric guitar and voices for Paul Burwell's piece, *Memphis*.

None of these approaches could be described as 'settings' for poems; the aim was to integrate voices and instruments, to blur lines between word and sound. In retrospect, Bob may have found that his ideal form for sound poetry was compromised by our more musical approach, though in an interview from 1999, he said this: "The interesting thing is, with Paul Burwell and David Toop particularly, they are very definitely performing the text through their instruments, very close interpretation of the texts indeed."

Where the sextet was fairly disciplined, the trio had an anarchic edge which Bob relished and provoked. The music we played swung between being unpolished and violent or slow and quiet. A lot of alcohol went down, particularly during tours that took in Stirling, Aberdeen, Edinburgh, Sunderland, Swansea and Cardiff, the Stedelijk Museum in Amsterdam, the Sound & Syntax International Festival of Sound Poetry at Glasgow's Third Eye Centre in 1978, and, back down to earth, the public library in Whitley Bay. There was nothing luxurious about these tours. Making any money at all depended on taking overnight trains, Paul and I sleeping sometimes in shared beds in local B&Bs, cheap pub meals and beer then onstage in various states of inebriation. Subtlety and listening were vital but as video from the Sound & Syntax performance shows, we were also intent on dismantling performance precepts. Given Bob's background as a lay preacher, teacher and organiser he assumed a dual relationship with the audience: on the one hand pedagogical (which Paul and I would try to undermine); on the other hand, a shamanistic physicality in which repetition and mantra folded words back upon themselves, extended them into pure sound or picked them into their component parts.

Interpreting sound poetry with instruments was not straightforward. Was it mimesis, a reproduction of vocal sounds implicit within those letters, syllables and permutated nonsense words designed on a page? What about list poems or poems in which words and letter forms were buried in black ink? Were they graphic scores, read from left to right and downwards or were they non-linear, closer to painting than written and spoken language? Or was it a form of improvisation in which one person leads, the others follow?

There was something uneasy about the process, not helped by our inexperience or Bob's nervousness as a performer. He would fortify himself with sips from a whisky flask and at times, particularly when he felt himself losing control during a performance, that would go too far. I have vivid memories of our trio at the ICA in 1990: after a brilliant rehearsal in the afternoon, the first time we had played together for maybe twelve years, the evening performance was chaotic, sabotaged

Gigs Witnessed: 1964-68

The Ronettes, Rolling Stones, Swinging Blue Jeans, Marty Wilde And The Wild Cats, Creation, Little Richard, Thelonious Monk Quartet, Cream, Jimi Hendrix Experience, AMM, Ronnie Ross Octet, Pink Floyd, Paul Butterfield Blues Band, Frank Zappa And The Mothers Of Invention, Otis Redding, Sam & Dave, Booker T And The MGS, Eddie Floyd, Carla Thomas, Freddie King, The Doors, Jefferson Airplane, Roland Kirk, The Crazy World Of Arthur Brown, Graham Bond Organisation, Traffic, Charles Lloyd Quartet, Tomorrow, Geno Washington And The Ram Jam Band, Jeff Beck Group With Rod Stewart, Chicken Shack, John Mayall's Bluesbreakers, Pentangle, Quintessence, Soft Machine, Sam Gopal Dream, Ginger Johnson And His African Drummers, Etc.

by Bob abandoning the plan we agreed on earlier. Then there was a nightmarish performance by the sextet at the Poetry Society in the 1970s, Bob effectively creating a band within a band as he felt the music moving away from the poems, Paul Burwell standing in front of us at one point and shouting "Band!" in an attempt to restore unity.

All of these instabilities during our thirty-year collaboration were symptomatic of its intensity. As uncharted territory it had explorer-ancestors but no real precedent in our cultural context. What we learned from each other was incalculable, not least Bob's generous sharing of knowledge and resources. When Paul and I began making our own books in 1972, it was Bob who co-published us through his Writer's Forum imprint, helping us with everything from manufacture to distribution, invaluable for our later forays into independent publication, record production and collective organisation. Herman Hauge died in December 2014, Christopher Small in 2011, Paul Burwell in 2007, Bob Cobbing in 2002. I would like to think that the music we recorded, though only a fraction of what we produced, could be released while the memory of these two groups is still within reach.

David Toop in 'Field Working' performance
at Midland Group Gallery in Nottingham, 1973

## II. JOURNEYS, INSTRUMENTS, SOUNDS

Marie Yates and I started living together in north London in 1971. In the summer of that year we stayed for a few days in a roughly converted barn in Devon, on the edge of Dartmoor. Owned by John and Barbara Latham, the barn had been a mill with a water wheel and so the River Dart was diverted to pass underneath the upstairs living space. At night in bed I would listen to the water below and imagine I heard voices speaking in indecipherable tongues. In the daytime I made recordings of flute played close to this terrific force of water.

Because of our intensifying relationship, my growing fascination with environmental sounds was converging with Marie's turn towards a new approach to sculpture, in which walking to a destination, recording the conditions of place with words and photographs and making an impermanent sculpture from sticks gathered from the site, muslin, sometimes small bells, were all part of the work. One of the first of these walks took place on Dartmoor, in July, 1971.

Field Workings, Marie called these activities, and that is how they seemed – walking and working from within the self and under the sky, deeply private even though conducted on open land and documented. From this remove an intentionality or conscious method seems apparent but at the time it was all instinct, a response to the volition of unstoppable forces. At one point I took advantage of another boundary, hanging my microphone on a wire fence, then walking away as I played sounds that were snatched from me by the wind, as if by invisible hands. Later I listened to the recording and felt a shift away from the centrality of myself as singular humanity, beginning to hear sound as an ear, like a shell - the wind's course over rough land and stone walls, the rattling fence, the bleating of the sheep, all opening up and gathering together the sounds passing through, brushed away, dying away with my slivers of breath only a part of this flow of forces.

David Toop & Paul Burwell
Field Working Performance at Midland Group Gallery, 1973

During the same year I had been given access to the BBC Sound Archives by a BBC radio producer named Madeau Stewart. In response to a lengthy, very presumptuous letter I sent the BBC in 1971, urging them to broadcast programmes reflecting the loss of environments, animal species and traditional musics, she took a risk and invited me to make the first of three programmes for BBC Radio Three. This first one was called *Crossthreads*, broadcast in 1972, followed by *Language of the Sacred* in 1974 and *The Breath of Magic* in 1975. Many of the archive recordings were stored on 10-inch vinyl discs; surprisingly, I was given permission to borrow those that interested me, so I would take them home and record them onto my cheap mono cassette machine, connecting a cable to the loudspeaker terminals of the record player. The quality was poor but suddenly I was able to hear extraordinary and rare music from everywhere in the world: sacred flute music from Papua New Guinea and the Brazilian Amazon, suling flute orchestras from Bali, a Dogon bullroarer from Mali, Taoist ceremonies from Formosa, a Colombian snail shell flute, shakuhachi music from Japan, a Symondsbury Mummers play recorded in 1957, Gaelic songs about birds, Scottish spells, hill tribes from Laos, a Hindu tongue spearing ceremony, Gomera whistled language, strange voice disguisers from Africa, English church bells, snapping shrimp, ancient Korean Confucian music, wailing for the dead in Surinam and Papua New Guinea, a street musician playing "Loch Lomond" on spoons and whistle and wildlife sounds ranging from howler monkeys, gibbons, trumpeter swans, beetles burying a field mouse, a fight between a raven and peregrine, a mynah bird mimicking a frog and the brain fever bird or Indian common hawk-cuckoo, so-called because its repetitive song seems to become increasingly manic as it rises in pitch.

A similar brain fever affected me. My dreams were full of hissing birds, howler monkeys and monstrous sea snails. In winter 1972 I wrote down my memory of a dream in which I heard "a person playing a thumb piano kind of instrument — the sides of which were rubbed. It also had large teeth which were plucked. The sound was like whales and like a large, breathy Jew's Harp." A profound and lasting change had been set in motion simply by absorbing the sounds and structures of these recordings. In ways I barely understood they connected to the development of my listening skills as Marie and I walked through ancient landscapes. The pagan moor, its legendary mists and bogs, its standing stones and sombre horizons seemed to stretch away from twentieth-century roads and seaside towns to the edge of the world. We were walking and marking places as if building sculpture without form, Marie placing fragile sculptures of twigs and muslin, their life as short as the temper of the weather. I was marking invisible boundaries with flute sounds carried away by the wind. "A flute was played on Dartmoor," I wrote in a notebook in 1972. "Mist covered the distant hills. The presence of a cold wind meant that decisions with regard to breath control were regulated by an uncontrollable shivering."

This experience became a text composition called *Shiver Music*, published in 1973 in my second book – *the Bi/s/onics pieces*, then published a few years later in *The Educational Anthology* by Experimental Music Catalogue, run by Gavin Bryars, Michael Nyman, Christopher Hobbs. This tiny book was comprised of only four text scores composed between May and September in 1972 – *Lizard Music*, *Shiver Music*, *Oracle Music* and *Sleep Music*. Intended for players of any ability, they betrayed an uncertainty about free improvisation – was it broad enough in its possibilities? – and at the same time there was a genuine desire to expand the scope of improvisation, to level hierarchies still prevalent in music and to make explicit links between the practice of music making and all other aspects of living.

The text of *Sleep Music*, for example, presupposed a performance context and duration that would have been almost impossible to organise:

sleep music: music is played

until all the participants fall

asleep. on waking, the piece

continues with a recounting of

the dreams remembered. the

piece might be expanded by

recounting dreams experienced

during previous performances.

As for *Lizard Music*, this was based on watching large lizards in London Zoo, gazing at their stillness and the way they would change position so rapidly that the human eye could barely register the transition. Was it possible, I asked myself, to apply the same kind of stasis and sudden change to the performance of ensemble music?

Influenced by Jerome Rothenberg's ethnopoetics, John Stevens' improvisation workshops and perhaps (somewhat reactively) to the intuitive scores of Karlheinz Stockhausen's *Aus den seiben Tagen*, the *Bi/i/sonics pieces* was a more practical book than my first – *Decomposition As Music Process*. This was published the previous year and even now I find it hard to understand what I was trying to do in its twelve pages. It was an attempt to develop a theoretical approach to sound and performance but never directly expressed. Everything was articulated through found scientific texts, cut-ups taken from the novel I had taken from John Latham's performance at Float, hand-coloured drawings and photographs (a diver, the image of his body distorted because the camera lens is both under and above the water line) and the beginnings of ideas that would preoccupy me from that moment on. A page was devoted to one of the Field Workings with Marie Yates, the sheep, wind and fence incident of 1971; another page documented two of my strange dreams. I also wrote about breath, sound and atmosphere, all typed on John Latham's typewriter. Buried within the book are themes that would resurface twenty-three years later in *Ocean of Sound*, yet then, when I was twenty-three years old, I could only express them through obscure and oblique metaphors. I was stumbling in the dark, yet with an almost mystical conviction that just beyond my limited thinking there was something I had to find.

From childhood I had been mixed-handed, writing with my left hand, playing instruments right handed, in cricket bowling left handed and batting right handed, eating with a spoon left handed, knife and fork right handed. Growing up at a time when left-handedness was still regarded with some suspicion meant that I would sometimes feel confused about whether I was performing mechanical tasks correctly. I also lacked the single-minded dedication to perfect motor skills. I would practice the guitar but not in a systematic way or for long enough or obsessively enough. To add to this there was insufficient belief in the system I was supposed to be learning and not much aptitude to absorb the necessary information.

The musical instruments I played at that time – electric guitar and flute – seemed too much an expression of equal temperament and fixed pitch for sounds created in Neolithic sites or in what Barbara Hepworth had called the "barbaric and magical countryside" of West Penwith, the south-westerly peninsula of Cornwall that leads down to Land's End. I wanted my music to be closer to bird song, bat echolocation and the sound of voices I had heard in the River Dart. So I began to make flutes and other instruments, the house where Marie and I lived often pungent with the smell of burned bamboo. Many of them based on drawings made by Karl Gustav Izikowitz for his book, *Musical and Other Sound Instruments of the South American Indians*, these long flutes often played only a few notes. For variation they needed to be overblown or played into water but the beauty of these single notes reminded me of wind blowing across the moors or on the clifftops.

Between 1971 and 1975 Marie Yates and I spent some time each year in St Ives in Cornwall. Marie's mother worked at the Leach Pottery so we would spend Christmas with Bernard and Janet Leach, meeting other local artists such as Patrick Heron and occasionally catching sightings of Barbara Hepworth. All of them were connected within this strange, somewhat insular community. I knew very little about the legendary status of Bernard and Janet, nor did I know anything about ceramics in general, so my interactions with them were naïve at best. I took them at face value: Bernard had a gentle, patrician air about him, otherworldly and from another era; Janet, thirty years younger than him, was formidable, lively and combative in her opinions. They were living separate lives, as far as I could see, but tied together through the Leach Pottery and its demands. When I learned Bernard had spent time in Korea I told him about my passion for Korean court music. In response he presented me with three LPs he had been given during one of his visits, records of Korean traditional music pressed on transparent green vinyl. I still have them, still play them.

A little later we accommodated Japanese artists with a connection to the Leach Pottery – Toshio Sekiji and one of Shoji Hamada's sons – in our house in London. The connection between Cornish clay and ceramics, an art form grounded in the earth, was clear; it was less straightforward to find ways for sound to articulate this place that I was growing to love. But the sight of the ocean, the dripping of water in sea caves and wind whistling on the moors opened up a feeling for the oceanic nature of sound within which the ears themselves were caves. In a text written at the time, Marie wrote about our collaboration as "a composition in time and space of everything, a continuous ritual to which from time to time we return." I wanted to compose the sound of things and the sound of not-things, she wrote, whereas she wanted to compose the spaces in between everything. This was close to the Japanese concept of ma, of course, though it would be many years before I discovered the term.

My Tastes In 1967–70:

AMM, AMM Music
Dr. John the Night Tripper, Gris-Gris
Sounds of The Serengeti, Wildlife Sound LP
Junior Wells, Hoodoo Man Blues
Velvet Underground, White Light/White Heat
Scott Walker, Scott

Ilhan Mimaroglu, Agony
The Soft Machine, Volumes One and Two
John Coltrane Quartet, A Love Supreme
Laura Nyro, Eli and the Thirteenth Confession
Son House, Father of Folk Blues
Nico, The Marble Index
Spontaneous Music Ensemble, Karyobin

David Toop & Paul Burwell
at Logos Foundation, Gent, 1977

# SLOW TIME

Time is a convoluted passage of circles and cycles, maybe a single moment in which an entire lifetime unfolds in order to twist back on itself and vanish. Through the discovery of gagaku music from Japan, Korean Pomp'ae chanting, the floating harmonics of Chinese guqin, Tibetan Tantric Buddhist ceremonies, the banshee wail of Joujouka rhaita and drums (as recorded by Brian Jones) and Javanese gamelan from the Sultan's palace in Jogjakarta I felt myself drawn into regions of time that were radically different to those with which I was familiar. Their slowness, music suspended over deep silences, themes whirling, receding and returning, was far closer to my own inner experience of time's relativity, its elasticity.

This slowness was a quality that Paul Burwell and I encountered in the improvisation workshops given by drummer John Stevens at Ealing College in 1971-72. Hoping to escape a life of menial jobs (he had worked as a gravedigger, gardener and as drummer in a strip club), Paul applied and was accepted as an art student at Ealing. He befriended Christopher Small (the author of books such as *Musicking*), then Senior Lecturer in Music at Ealing, and so we came to join the improvisation workshops led by Stevens and hosted by Small in one of the college classrooms. The exercises Stevens was developing through his pioneering works in group improvisation have been collected together as a handbook called *Search and Reflect*. They included *Sustain Piece*, in which we would play a note for as long as an outbreath lasted, and Click Piece, in which we had to find the shortest possible sound on our respective instruments. These four elements formed the irreducible foundation of his method: sustain, click, the capacity to listen (search) and the capacity to respond (reflect). Though much of the British improvised music of this time was a restless web of rapid sounds – insect music, some called it – there was also an undercurrent of slowness; in part this was inspired by a moment in the 1960s when Stevens first heard Japanese gagaku music on a recording of *Karyobin*, in which the magical kalavinka beings dance in paradise, leading him to wonder what life would be like if humanity slowed down to that tempo.

John Stevens could be loud and belligerent but he was equally capable of sensitivity to what was happening with younger musicians, taking the trouble to listen and give advice. One day we were speaking on the phone. I was despondent about being so broke all the time. "I'd rather be grafting," he said. In other words, it was better to be active doing something you hated than constantly worrying about poverty. Neither of us followed that advice but it was at least a sign that somebody cared. Thanks to John, the first public appearance of Rain In the Face took place at the Little Theatre Club in 1971. Martin Davidson reviewed one of our first gigs in the *Melody Maker*. "Their youngness precludes any advanced togetherness," he wrote, "and there is no cliff edge in sight; but they could well work towards that."

In the centre of London's theatre district, the Theatre Club, as it was usually known, was one of the most important venues in the early history of British free improvisation. At the top of a tall building in Garrick Yard, the club was small and intimate with perfect acoustics. Usually we played to very small audiences, sometimes two or three people, but at the age of 22 or 23 we felt we had landed at the heart of London's experimental music scene. Usually we would play opposite other groups or solo musicians, such as the SME of John Stevens and Trevor Watts, Dave Panton or OMU, a trio of Terry Day, Davie Payne and Charlie Hart. Usually these were valuable opportunities to meet like-minded players and forge long-term friendships though on one occasion John Stevens put us on the same bill as the Tommy Chase Trio, a straight-ahead hard bop group playing tunes like "Surrey With the Fringe On Top." Notoriously aggressive, Chase didn't like our music and used the threat of physical intimidation to shut us up. It was a case of Stevens trying to please both ends of the spectrum, the jazz players who were part of his social world and the young experimentalists like us who were beginning to redefine the improvising scene. Most of the time the Little Theatre Club was a perfect setting in which to gain experience. Anything seemed possible there. One night we were playing in a festival. Almost everybody in the club seemed to be playing at full blast, whether they were standing on the stage area or in the banked seating. At one point a policeman appeared. He had heard the din from the street, come up to investigate and stood at the back in a state of amazement, holding up his walkie talkie so his colleagues could hear the extraordinary noise.

Our method we developed in Rain In the Face, a consequence of our early efforts to establish a new kind of free rock, was to play simple pieces, perhaps a few notes or a specified instrumentation to establish moods for improvisation. "Cold As Breath Ocean," for example, was an extremely slow piece for flutes, gongs and cymbals, its title alluding to the oceanic sensations that I encountered in Cornwall. The title of "Barra da Tijuco F.S. goes towards ocean at tremendous speed" – was taken from one of George Adamski's 1950s books on UFOs and alien visitations. At the time I was reading books on subjects such as occultism, anthropology, mysticism, psychoanalysis, mythology, trance, even Scientology, not from the point of view of belief but because I was searching for an independent understanding of music's potential as social ritual and performing art. So I read about UFOs, not because I believed in their existence or the obviously faked photographs but because Adamski had written about their sound in *The Flying Saucers Have*

*Landed*. Witnesses, he wrote, have been ". . . overwhelmed by the beauty, the serenity and the silence" (having made these claims he then had to explain the awkward contradiction of a machine flying so quickly yet so silently).

A lifelong sceptic, I have no particular interest in flying saucers other than as pulse quickening symbols of cosmic loneliness. It was the poetic image of a silence on the other side of noise that fascinated me; this was typical of the way I was turning to all sources for ideas and information about listening. So my piece, composed in 1972, called for "invisible sounds (i.e., short becoming of no duration, thin becoming of no substance, such passages might be interpreted as silent by listeners)." Along with a composition called "Barbastella," this was also influenced by recordings of the echolocation signals of bats, ultrasonic clicks that were then shifted down to a pitch audible to humans. So I would use a rare and extreme distortion pedal called the Wem Rush Pep Box, allowing me to play short electronic clicks through the guitar while Paul played drum rolls and fast cymbal sounds.

Another piece was titled "Cloud Studies number 2", in which I used two distortion pedals, the Rush Pep Box and a Zonk Machine, their effects fighting each other. I also masked the sound of the strings with the kind of crocodile clips used by electricians. In the BBC Sound Archives I had come across recordings, particularly of African music, in which the sound of acoustic instruments – drums, xylophones, flutes, thumb pianos, trumpets and voice disguisers – had been altered in various ways, maybe by attaching bottle tops that clicked and rattled or spider egg sac membranes that buzzed. Because of the two distortion pedals there seemed to be an equivalence in those two methods of distortion. At the same time I had come across Javanese gamelan, particularly Robert E. Brown's recording of *Ketawang: Pusp*åwårna in Jogyakarta, released on Nonesuch Records, and John Cage's prepared piano pieces, notably *Prelude For Meditation* played so beautifully by Jeanne Kirstein. The thought occurred to me that I might be able to do something similar to the guitar, finding a way to prepare the strings to make it sound more like tuned gongs or bells. I tried crocodile clips and they worked really well. They were cheap, they could be attached to the strings in a stable way, you could move them easily and they turned the guitar into a sort of gamelan, albeit one you could only play slowly.

In 2016 I saw Carlyle Reedy again, this time in an exhibition called The sun went in, the fire went out, curated by Karen Di Franco and Elisa Kay at Chelsea Space gallery, London. The show featured work by Carlyle, Annabel Nicolson and Marie Yates, three women whose impact and influence on me at different times of my life was profound, both in relation to feminism and the making of art work. Speaking about the Rain In the Face duo she said, "Each one had what the other lacked." The expression – one started fires, the other dampened them down – would be an accurate description of our working relationship. Paul would play drums with overwhelming energy and passion, building the music up into a giant climax while I would be more analytical, trying to cool him down, thinking about how to understand and develop our music, trying to contextualise it within all other musics. Like many such relationships, its dynamism came from opposition, held together in fragile balance until something comes along to destabilise it.

# MASKING

Improvised music had a hunger for new sounds, sounds that bypassed the tempered scale and the regularity of standardised manufacture. With his amplified springs and 'Feelie Boxes' – assemblages of variously textured materials amplified by contact microphones – Hugh Davies was one of the pioneers of a movement dedicated to expanding available sounds by building instruments. Incidentally, he was also an ecological thinker, a proponent of invention through recycling. In response to this I edited and co-published a little book called *New/Rediscovered Musical Instruments* in 1974, featuring the inventions of Hugh Davies, Max Eastley, Evan Parker, Paul Lytton, Paul Burwell and myself. My contributions included two examples of sound masking: one was the Shell Hat, a hat made of stones and a large sea shell, designed to mask the singing voice; the other was the prepared guitar. In 1973 Henry Cow drummer Chris Cutler was in the audience for a Rain In the Face performance at the Architectural Association in London and invited us to play at one of Henry Cow's Explorer's Club nights at the London School of Economics. After seeing me play prepared guitar that evening, Fred Frith started using the technique. When his first solo album came out on Virgin there was a close-up of the guitar prepared with crocodile clips and from that moment an army of guitar preparers was born. Fred has always been very generous and open about the fact that he got the idea from me. In fact Keith Rowe was using crocodile clips on the guitar with AMM before I did it. I attended a lot of AMM gigs from 1966 onwards but they always played in the dark so I could never see what Rowe was doing. The enveloping, cloud-like quality of the music was what I enjoyed. It never occurred to me to think about the way it was made.

A third contribution to *New/Rediscovered Musical Instruments* was the Wasp Flute, a bamboo flute with a small bamboo chamber attached. The chamber was ventilated with holes and closed at the top with a lid, the idea being that I would attract a wasp inside with something sweet, close the lid then play along with the drone of its buzzing. The instrument was conceptual, more of an idea than a practical technology, though its origins lay in an instrument called the live beetle jew's harp, another BBC sound archive recording in which a man from Papua New Guinea held a live sago beetle close to his mouth, then adjusted the size of his mouth cavity to resonate and emphasise different frequencies in the insect's drone.

All of these ideas had their origins in an intense period of research into animal languages, mythology, occultism, shamanism, anthropology and ethnomusicology. Notebooks from that time are filled with laboriously copied passages from books on birdsong and the sounds of mammals, fish and insects, symbolism and dreams, sacred and ritual music and human imitations of animal sounds and spirit voices. It was as if I had been struck by a posthumanist vision of a world in which humans were no longer dominant or even necessary. The desire to communicate across the boundaries between species was to some degree an apocalyptic fantasy, a nostalgia for paradise, but that didn't diminish my conviction that humans should understand themselves as being an integral part of a complex ecology entangled with what we call nature, rather than being separate and superior to nature.

Barely out of my teens I bought an unlikely record — *Sounds of the Serengeti* — released on a budget label called Music For Pleasure. The atmospheric recordings of Tanzanian animals such as lions, baboons, elephants, hippos and hunting dogs were made by Grahame Dangerfield. At that time, records of this type usually followed one of two templates, either produced as scientific documents or radio programmes. In the case of *Sounds of the Serengeti*, the radio model was followed, each sound clearly identified by the voice of conservationist Peter Scott. Soothing as it was, his narration was an irritant to me. I wanted to hear more creature sounds and those that really excited me were not those of the big mammals but strange back-and-forth duets by Tropical Bou-Bou Shrikes and Crowned Cranes. There was something mysterious in the way their voices moved in and out of synchronisation, as if distilling the bare essence of social relations into audible cries. They reminded me just a little of the way Albert Ayler played with his brother, Donald Ayler, and yet there was another quality within them, extra-human and unfathomable. This was something I began to seek out, hearing some ghost of it in African horn and flute ensembles, khene mouth organs from Laos, Vietnam and Cambodia, and flute duets from Papua New Guinea and the Amazon region of Brazil.

Whatever was engendered as I reflected on these listening experiences, the breakthrough came on the third of January, 1971, when I created a conceptual work that through its mysterious convergence of mental and auditory images came to inform much of my subsequent thinking and musical approach. Did I even understand it myself? *Bionic Rock*, as it was called, was simply a text typed on a single sheet of paper with some added ink blots. The substance of the text was a reference to bionics (the science of systems based on living things), the ultrasonic signals of Pipistrelle bats (with reference to the BBC record on which I had first heard them – *British Mammals and Amphibians*, BBC Wildlife Series), the Wem Rush Pep Box and a page number for an early 1960s book by Vitus B. Dröscher, *Mysterious Senses*, all these four disparate subjects linked under the title *Bionic Rock*.

## UNKNOWN DEVICES

There was a bringing together of electronic technology, field recording, bioacoustics, research and the limits of human perceptions. Only now, by buying a copy of the Dröscher book, am I able to fully understand my thought processes back in 1971. I was fascinated, for example, by the opening chapter – Beyond the Five Senses – which he began by describing a party during which the host showed that moths could be made to drop to the ground (a defensive measure against the ultrasonic echolocation of bats) simply by running a dampened cork around the rim of a wine glass to produce a high-pitched sound. The page number I quoted in *Bionic Rock* referred to the echolocation abilities used by hunting bats to detect fish swimming underwater. As with the diver in *Decomposition As Music Process*, his head in the air, his body under water, I returned again and again to this trope of being able to exist in different mediums. "Perhaps we can learn from the animals how it is done," wrote Dröscher. This was my first exposure both to bionics – to me a twentieth-century scientific development from ancient shamanistic arts such as music and dance based on animal sounds and movements - and to the notion of ultra-senses, those animal senses capable of perceiving a world beyond the fiction of human 'reality.'

2012: Objects on my floor: an eight-string steel guitar (out of tune in the way that percussion instruments are 'out of tune'), small Marshall amplifier, volume pedal and lead, two lengths of copper pipe of different diameter, two steel bars, some lengths of bamboo of varying diameter, a thimble, a serrated stick, a child-size violin bow, two eBows, a collection of picks and crocodile clips, rough stones from Dorset and Cornwall. To collect objects is to accumulate time, building an increasingly complex instrument that has no edges, no boundaries. The amplifier, for example, was used by my daughter when she learned to play guitar at school. When she decided to stop playing she returned the amplifier to me so now her short history with an instrument becomes part of my longer history. The stones, of course, are mementoes of journeys, walks during which music is floating through my mind, waiting to be realised, just as the stones lie on the ground, waiting to be sounded.

Here, also, in my possession since 1974 or 75, mottled, almost green with age, is a circular pellet bell hung with four metal rings that at one time I identified (mistakenly) as *ekiro no suzu*, a kind of horse sleigh bell used in kabuki for certain dances. Here also, placed next to the mistakenly identified *ekiro* because they are in relation to each other through organological classification and sound type, are the two circular pellet bells of a Hmong shaman rattle from Laos. The two parts are worn, old, pitted, like two overcooked doughnuts tied together with the distinctive red ribbon always seen on such rattles.

2011: On the dusty main street of Nong Khiaw, a man was selling antique things from a glass case set out by the road. For the rattle he wanted US$70; after haggling for a long time we settled on $50, quite a large sum of money in rural Laos. The same day we take a boat to Muang Ngoi Neua, karsts towering over the Nam Ou, trees clinging to their steep sides, some growing almost parallel to the surface of the river. Buffalo ruminate on the banks or soak eye-deep in the water. Beyond the village is forest leading to caves reached by rough steps cut into the mountain, a steep climb of pulling on tree branches and unstable bamboo rails.

Tham Kang cave's entrance is narrow, only accessible by climbing over a rock. Inside is dark, dry and completely silent. With the aid of a torch I can see the conical interior, an opening some way up one wall allowing in a little light. At the back sits an oval rock, glittering in the torchlight. As the village lay on the Ho Chi Minh trail, these caves were used as shelters to protect Laos people from America's covert bombing campaign during the Vietnam war. Standing alone in relation to such silence, contained within an eerily dry yet vibrant acoustic, I feel I must record something. The Hmong shaman rattle is still in my backpack, wrapped in newspaper so I take it out, sound it in the tranquil air, distant to the world, distant from human presence, close to the archive.

That night, far out in the distant dark, a huge explosion wakes me. The conical mountain is blurred by purple-grey mist, its shape a mysterious inverted pyramid, blacker than the black night sky. The atmosphere is eerie. Unexploded American bombs lie everywhere in this country, waiting for an unsuspecting child, a buffalo, some other creature to step on them.

A few days later I sat on a balcony in Luang Prabang. A still night, just a light breeze. Just after 4.00am, I heard a single drum sounding distantly from over the Nam Khan river, answered from this side of the water to my right by a more complex drum pattern, then further to the right a double gong. More join in over the next fifteen minutes. Spread like an invisible web over the impenetrable darkness, they draw a map of sound, ghosts travelling ahead of their own shapes. More and more drums and gongs pulse loudly from the many Buddhist temples in and around the city. Gradually the sound subsides until the sleeping city falls quiet again. Lao men are still drinking just up the street; a woman sweeps the road in preparation for the day; a fisherman glides by, lighting the water with his torch. In the room, a gecko sings, loud and melodious.

## SUIKINKUTSU

1993: my first visit to Japan began in Kobe. Nobuhisa Shimoda invited Max Eastley and I to play at Xebec Hall, also helping us to organise a tour in which we performed and lectured in Hiroshima, Yokohama (where we performed with Minoru Sato) and Tokyo. Having dreamed of visiting Japan since my early twenties I felt that a gap in my life had been filled suddenly with impressions which were both strange yet somehow familiar: Itsukushima Shrine at Miyajima, the nocturnal lights of Shibuya, the Great Buddha of Kamakura, traffic jams during Golden Week, the Peace Museum in Hiroshima, Japan's beautiful intimate light and its unique aesthetic.

In Kobe, sound recordist Yoshihiro Kawasaki played me extraordinary recordings of the Shunie ceremony, the Omizutori held in the Nigatsu-do of Todai-ji, in Nara. He also played me something I had never heard before – lengthy tapes of an Edo-period suikinkutsu. The suikinkutsu, which translate as water koto cave) was a buried pot into which water dripped from a basin above ground. With Kawasaki-san's help I visited Kyoto to experience the remarkable dry garden at Ryoanji and hear the uguisu-bari, the famous nightingale floor of Nijo Castle. The highlight of this journey was the opportunity to get close to the suikinkutsu in the private garden of Zuishun-in. The quality of each sound, water falling slowly in individual drips into an underground chamber, is hypnotically fascinating but what impressed me profoundly was the timing of each sound, random of course but endlessly compelling in its slowness and unpredictability.

## LIVING BEINGS

2015: on my shelves, a temple bell from Thailand, small bells (in the shape of a mouse, a bird, a cat) from Japanese shrines, metal and wooden cow bells from China, ceramic water whistles in the shape of birds from Beijing, and from the same city, a pigeon whistle and tiny friction drums made from clay, shaped like the heads of mice; a Basque pan flute; a bullroarer from Papua New Guinea, from Seoul a wooden temple block, a pair of shaman cymbals; a Burmese kyeezee spinning gong; a Balinese bamboo angklung; a Karen hill tribe rain drum from South-East Asia; three battery operated Buddha boxes from Chinese temples; a handmade metal chime given to me by Toshimasa Matsumoto either in Hiroshima or Tokyo, 1993; two pellet bells in the shape of shisa, from Naha, Okinawa; from America a Cherokee gourd rattle; a Tibetan conch shell trumpet bought in Hong Kong in 1989; a Japanese sho (no longer in working order); from Tokyu Hands, a battery-operated cricket that lights up and vibrates its wings as it sounds; from Beijing a wooden box in which to keep singing crickets; from Central Africa, a one-stringed instrument; from China a ceramic whistling pot. These are the objects of my language, collected over 46 years, each saturated with its own time, each one part of an orchestra without people, without a form. Each one of them is present in my music like a living being, either in live improvisation or mutated unrecognisably in the digital domain. Each sound, all sounds are living, growing beings, independent of the human sphere. Like animals, they move through the world as if humans are obstacles.

# HAIKU

Circa 1965. The English translation for Mukai Kyorai's seventeenth-century haiku begins: "Which is tail? Which head?" With my school friend, Peter Sinclaire, I took a hitchhiking journey, not so long after reading *On The Road* by Jack Kerouac. We got only as far as Hertford, a distance of roughly twelve miles, where the museum displayed a two-headed chicken and other weird exhibits. In the public library I found a copy of Kyorai's poem, never to be forgotten: Which is tail, which head? Unsafe to guess, given a sea slug. Even this pathetic adventure by two teenage boys revealed a precious truth, that journeys themselves, no matter how mundane, raise these questions: which is beginning, which end? Where do they begin, where do they finish (if ever)?

Sometimes I was reluctant to leave the house; even now I can feel sadness at the beginning of a journey, as if a journey is the ending of a fragile illusion, the security of home. Many of my early journeys were created in the intensity of imagination. Inspired by books, television and music, they were the writing of a script for physical journeys of the future. As a boy I drew jungle animals, a gypsy camp, Native Americans, believing that I could summon such journeys into being with pencil lines and colours.

Perhaps it was Christmas 1972, Compendium Books, until its closure in 2000 the best independent book shop in London: I bought a copy of *Shamanism: Archaic Techniques of Ecstacy*, Mircea Eliade's classic study from which I learned about shamanic imitations of bird and animal sounds, a language based on secret words, mystical sounds and words that only animals and spirits can comprehend. "We might speak of a new identity for the shaman," Eliade wrote, "who becomes an animal-spirit, and 'speaks', sings, or flies like the animals and birds." This adoption of a new identity through transformation and the acquisition of a secret musical language was what I longed for.

By 1975 my relationship with Marie Yates was breaking up. I was devastated by this separation. It began a long phase of chaotic drunkenness and promiscuity which continued through to the late 1970s. Change was inescapable but I felt numb with shock, often out of control, and the performance nerves that I suffered early on in my career escalated to an ungovernable anxiety that profoundly affected my ability to play music live. The most pressing problem, however, was finding some employment. For five years I had earned almost no money. It was a shaming thing to realise how inadequate I was at earning a living or surviving without Marie's financial and emotional support. Now on my own and in the impossible situation of still living in the same house as her I had to find answers to multiple problems. That year I found a job as a bookseller in a central London university bookshop called Dillons. Very quickly I fell into the atmosphere of the shop. Most of the departments were staffed by young university graduates, highly intelligent and knowledgeable but also intent on enjoying themselves both during and after work. We drank during the day and all through the evening, showed up in the morning with hangovers and treated the shop as our personal library.

After stumbling through stints in departments like Engineering and English-as-a-Foreign-Language I was promoted to manager of the record department, an opportunity to establish a shop that represented my tastes in music. Racked alongside the classical music I was obliged to stock for the shop's regular customers were LPs of gamelan, Japanese Buddhist chant, Afrobeat, dub reggae, electronic music, free improvisation, soul and salsa. Many musicians dropped by — John Stevens, Derek Bailey, Evan Parker, Brian Eno — but among our regular customers was A. C. Graham, the famous Sinologist and translator of Chinese Poetry and Taoist texts. He was fanatical about Balinese and Javanese music to the exclusion of all else and would often walk the short distance from the School of Oriental and African Studies to buy whatever new records of Indonesian music I had in stock. When the French

Recording Yanomami Shamans, Dayariteri, Amazonas, 1978

Yanomami Shamans, Dayariteri, Amazonas, under the influence of ebena

Amazonas listening to playback of recordings

Galloway label became available to UK shops, an overwhelming glut of sumptuous Asian music LPs, most of them recorded by South East Asian specialist Jacques Brunet, Graham was so excited that he invited me and my colleague, Nestor Figueras, to his house in the suburbs. Upstairs in a converted loft space he had built a man cave dedicated to gamelan. His capacity for alcohol was as prodigious as his enthusiasm for gamelan. Drunk as I was I found myself observing the scene with detached bemusement, remembering reading his delicate translations of late T'ang poets like Li Ho, Tu Fu and Li Shang-Yin when I was in my early twenties: "Never let your heart open with the spring flowers / One inch of love is an inch of ashes." (Untitled poem, Li Shang-Yin, *Poems of the Late T'ang*, Penguin, 1965).

Nestor Figueras was a Venezuelan performance artist then married to an English woman. I met him while he was working in the Foreign Language department at Dillons. During a holiday in Spain he got himself into an altercation with a policeman, was imprisoned for a short time and then found his job had gone to somebody else when he returned to London. There was a vacancy in the record department and I was impressed by his knowledge of Latin music so fixed it for him to work with me. We became friends, drank together, occasionally performed together (as on the LP with Paul Burwell – *Cholagogues*, released in 1977 on Bead Records) and gradually formed a plan to record Yanomami shamanism in the Amazonas region of southern Venezuela. In 1978 Nestor went back to live in Caracas with his new partner, Odile Laperche, the two of them organising a journey that would take us along the Orinoco and Ocamo Rivers into the heart of Yanomami territory.

EMBRACE OF DARKNESS

So it was in 1979 I found myself lying in a hammock under a roof with no walls, sticky from the heat, sleep made fitful by the fervency of night insects. The last shooting star blazed across a fading dark to signal ending and beginning. As if a curtain was being slowly raised the light grew dominant and so I came awake to the eerie overture of potoos, owl-like birds with gaping mouths. Night-feeders, they sit in monkish immobility on a branch all day, feathers camouflaged to merge with tree bark and leaves, their long slitted eyes apparently closed in meditation yet seeing all. A slow, descending diatonic scale or glissando – oy – oy – oy - potoo calls sound like men shouting or whistling from some distant unearthly place and so they are associated in Brazilian and Caribbean folklore with unrequited love, the mournful voice of an unhappy person who has been reincarnated in non-human form, wandering ghost-souls of condemned criminals or the hairy dwarf with backward pointing feet known as the curupira, protector of the forest. I had heard this weird sound on record, on Jean C. Roché's record, *Oiseaux du Venezuela*, without knowing quite what it could be; now I was in Venezuela, on the edge of the Orinoco and about to embark on our journey in search of Yanomami shamanism.

In the village of Tayari-teri we found a group of men about to take the hallucinogenic drug they call ebena. Another man was sick, needed healing, and so they were preparing to take command of the spirits inside their chests, do battle with those malevolent demons that were causing this sickness.

Headphones on I sit close to them with my tape machine. Nestor squats beside me, Odile takes photographs as the scene unfolds. At first there is talking, laughing, bodies slapped to deter the tiny biting mosquitoes that abound in this area. As the drug takes hold, they vomit from its effects. A chant builds up, other men still chatting and laughing, women and children looking on with only mild interest. I am transfixed by the escalating tension, the way that songs emerge from nothing, fade away again.

Then out of these passages of the everyday, intensity flares like flames caught by a gust of wind. There are climaxes, but no climax. Images and sensations seem to collect slowly, invisible to me but nonetheless powerful agencies of Yanomami belief. Men shoot imaginary arrows against their enemies with invisible weapons, invoking and calling under control the hekura spirits which live within their chests. Then the older shaman picks up real weapons – a bow with its seven foot arrow, a large machete, finally an axe – and starts his dance, marching back and forth, chanting rhythmically, voicing the sounds of spirit animals and birds, transforming into the supernatural beings that exist on the plane of the hekura spirits. The rhythm erupts into chilling screams, growls, grunting, fierce roaring, cries and ensembles of apparent anguish that evoke the tortured shades of hell depicted by great painters such as Bosch, the scream of Artaud's Theatre of Cruelty.

One arm in the air as if holding up an invisible creature by the tail, he shapes his body into extreme angles, walking the path of the shorori, described by anthropologist Jacques Lizot as "water demons and masters of subterranean fire". The hazards of this journey break through into our world. He rolls in the dust, rubbing his body as the demonic heat burns his skin. His chant to the motoreri, the whirlwind spirit, breaks down in shrieks, tailing off in an eerie, quavering falsetto. Just as the voices of Yanomami shamanism reminded me of collaborations with sound poets, so this extreme body movement recalled performances in London with Mitsutaka Ishii in the early 1970s. Ishii had been a student of Tatsumi Hijikata, one of the founders of the post World War II Butoh movement in Japan. Hijikata was said to have been guided by shadows, his dance an embrace of darkness. "Inside this one body," he said, "there are various mythic things that are still sleeping intact. The work is how to excavate them at the actual site. I would like to see something where such things float up like departed spirits."

As the ebena takes its full effect, the other shamans join in with the chanting – glassy eyed, spitting, retching, vomiting loudly, long strands of green snot hanging from their nostrils and streaking their chests. Some of them run to the other side of the shabono, tearing at the ground, striking at the high palm-screen walls, their shouts and high-pitched screams signalling a state of near-hysteria. Mutual massage follows, as they calm each other. All aspects of this hekuramou are symbolic. The mucus is not wiped away, for example, because this is said to be the excrement of those hekura living in the shaman's chest. Demons are thieves who are sent by enemy shamans to steal the noreshi, or spirit parts of human souls, especially those of children. As sorcerers who can voyage through the four levels of the universe, plunging into actualisations of myth and history, floating in free space and mythic time, the shamans undertake the burden of responsibility within their community to retrieve these souls.

Healing is an intense psychodramatic theatre in which the sick embody a battleground for the gruesome antagonism of tamed and malevolent spirits. Skin burns or oozes blood, the wind blows up havoc as the spirits move about. This is a world of jaguar, toucan, hummingbird, spider monkey, anaconda spirits, made visible by ebena, and so the shamans massage their patient, drawing out malevolent entities through an extremity and throwing it or vomiting it far away. Clustered around him in groups, they grip his neck, lift his arms, fight for his soul. A way of life is revealed in which the intensity of relationships between the body, the voice, the natural world, social formations and the spirit world is shockingly alien yet absolutely the opposite of sensational within its own context.

One of the most affecting experiences during this trip came suddenly and unexpectedly in a village on the Ocamo River. The Yanomami are endocannibals, meaning they consume a soup made from boiled plantain mixed with the ashes and ground up bones of a cremated corpse. The gravity of this rite of ancestral communication was so intense, the sense of being an intruder so marked, that I wanted to disappear into the shabono wall against which I pressed myself. Recording would have been unthinkable, unquestionably dangerous for us, but a part of me regrets having no record of the collective weeping and sobbing that formed an integral part of the rite, an eerie cloud sound rising up in sorrow to meet the gathering dusk.

Finally, this was what I had been searching to find through all my studies, performances and writings; this was a measure of what could be possible for music as a central element in the workings of society, the body and all that interpenetrates them both and makes them one. The effects of this trip were profound and permanent. For some time after arriving back in London I experienced attacks of claustrophobia and panic. In hynagogic states I would be jolted awake by the sensation of crawling things under my skin. Gradually those feeling subsided but they can still return, four decades later.

Gigs Witnessed: 1969–71

Rolling Stones, King Crimson, Family, Alexis Korner And Third Ear Band At Hyde Park, Blind Faith, Jethro Tull, The Move, Marc Bolan, Edgar Broughton Band, Pink Floyd, Led Zeppelin, Love, Ivor Cutler, Magic Sam, Earl Hooker, Clifton Chenier, Juke Boy Bonner, Rory Gallagher, Soft Machine, Sun Ra And The Intergalactic Research Arkestra, Sonny Terry And Brownie Mcghee, Groundhogs, The Who, Yes, Joe Cocker, Keef Hartley Band, Pete Brown's Battered Ornaments, Kevin Ayers And The Whole World, Moby Grape, Fleetwood Mac, Roy Harper, Frank Zappa, Christian Wolff, Johnny Winter, It's A Beautiful Day, Fairport Convention, Donovan, The People Band, The Blue Notes, Keith Tippett Group, AMM, Etc.

## III. DO THE BATHOSPHERE

In 1974, Brian Eno phoned me at home. I had sent him a copy of *New/Rediscovered Musical Instruments*. He had read it and wanted to tell me about a record label that he was planning. The label was to be called Obscure Records, distributed in the UK by Island Records. Brian came to hear Rain In the Face and Max Eastley play live, fell asleep (diplomatically, he said this was a compliment) and then invited us to record an LP for the first batch of four due to be released in 1974.

At that moment I was having serious misgiving about the Rain In the Face duo with Paul Burwell, experiencing a strong urge to work in a more personal way. A film was made for a London Weekend television arts programme called Aquarius, based on the book and featuring all of the contributors. In one respect this was a kind of miracle for such avant garde music to be shown on television but the experience of being filmed felt like a violation of our music. I was hypersensitive, not emotionally strong enough to withstand exposure to the way things were done at this level and so it adversely affected my viewing of the final film. After seeing it I cried and in this mood of over-reaction decided to end the group.

This was a betrayal of sorts on my part, not the first time nor the last that I would be troubled by this feeling or cause hurt in this way, but I had visions of a music that brought together composing and improvisation, based closely on the researches of the past five years. The duo with Paul was holding me back, or so I believed, even though many of my ideas were being developed in our regular private sessions of playing. Shortly before the record was due to be made I broke up our duo. As with any kind of relationship, collaboration can entail intensely hurtful negotiations between the selfish needs of the individual and the patterns established within a partnership or group. This was an opportunity I wanted to seize on my own.

As it transpired Paul was sufficiently forgiving and generous to play on my side of the record, in an ensemble comprised of percussionist Frank Perry, Hugh Davies on live electronics, myself on prepared guitar and home-made stringed instrument (a cross between a large Indian khamak friction drum and one of Futurist Luigi Russolo's early 20th century noise instruments, the intonarumori) and Brian Eno on prepared bass guitar. The music of this piece – "The Divination of the Bowhead Whale" – was inspired by bioacoustic signalling of bats and whales, particularly those too high and too low to be heard by humans, and the slow, extended tones and temporal percussive markers of Japanese gagaku and the Korean court styles of A-ak and Hyang-ak.

The night before the main recording session I prepared by listening to John Levy's recordings of Korean court music – Tang Ak, Kagok and Confucian A-ak - as if to slow myself down and immerse myself in a world of unfamiliar time. One important aspect of this piece was a twice-repeated silence. I asked Frank Perry to strike one of his Japanese resting bells – the keisu – hard. That would be the signal for everybody to stop playing. The sound of the keisu took nearly a minute to die away; we would all listen closely to this 'silence' and when finally it faded completely we would resume our playing. Of course the effect of this was somewhat lost on the noisy vinyl but it was a sign that listening was as important to me as music, the point being that silence is full of sounds, we simply have to listen more closely. This was a theme to which I returned many years later, during the research for my book *Sinister Resonance*.

For the other two tracks, "The Chair's Story" and "Do the Bathosphere", I composed short songs, sung in the high strained falsetto I was using in the duo with Paul. The lyrics, written with the same cut-up method I had discovered after witnessing John Latham's performance at Float in 1968, were personal expressions of the past five years of studying shamanism and the unconscious mind. To some extent this seriousness was masked by humour. The lyrics of "Do the Bathosphere", for example, not only alluded to my reading of Jung and Freud, particularly Freud's notion of oceanic religious sensations as a blissful return to the amniotic environment of the womb. They also referenced dance craze records like "Do the Boomerang" by Jr. Walker and the All Stars, "The Loco-motion" by Little Eva and "Twine Time" by Alvin Cash and the Crawlers.

My invented word 'bathosphere' was derived from bathyscaphe, a vehicle for diving into the depths of the ocean, but bathos is another kind of descent, from sublimity into absurdity. There was another reason for the reference to dance crazes and the use of simple song forms. At that time I conceived of my music in relation to popular music. Even though the Rain In the Face duo had failed in its attempts to develop a free improvised rock music, leaving only one option open to us – to join the experimental music scene - I wanted to give the impression that I was making pop music, albeit a type of rarefied pop music that not many people liked.

A joke at my own expense and yet deadly serious, it was another manifestation of masking. I have come to realise that this masking has been consistent throughout my life; much of what I have done is hidden in some way – jokes or esoteric allusions - from the direct gaze of outsiders, as if I am too ashamed, self-conscious or unconfident to expose myself completely. And yet if I listen to them now, these two songs feel startlingly exposed, my lack of courage turned in on itself to reveal some inner manifestation of the self that even I find alien.

The release of the Obscure Record was important to me for a number of reasons, coming as it did at a low point in my life when many ties to the past had been cut. Suddenly my music was being reviewed, albeit sparsely and with some incomprehension, and through the label I became associated with Brian Eno, Gavin Bryars, and Michael Nyman. The production of the record was disappointing, however. *New and Rediscovered Musical Instruments* was incorrectly labelled, the vinyl pressings were noisy, even the notes I had written for the sleeve were misprinted. There were concerns over payments also, relating to the copyright owners – E.G. Records (notorious for Robert Fripp's lengthy legal battle over alleged unpaid royalties) – and at one point a number of us, including Michael Nyman, met in the offices of E.G. in an attempt to resolve the situation. We were naive of course. It was very easy for E.G. to explain that costs (including the use of Island Records' big and expensive Basing Street studio) outweighed income and so I only received mechanical royalties (for each copy pressed) and songwriting royalties, even though the record was in catalogue for many years.

Many years later, re-mastering the record for CD release on Virgin I was able to hear the music in pristine detail for the first time since the original recording sessions in Island's Basing Street Studios. For the vocal tracks I sang into the strings of a grand piano to add natural reverberation to my voice and, at the same time, mask it by singing into the wood frame as if it were a deep, resonant cave (a memory of one particular walk with Marie Yates in which I sang and played bone trumpet in a Cornish sea cave at Clodgy Point, St Ives). Now it was possible to hear that the rock group recording in the studio next door was also audible through these same piano strings. The effect was uncanny, almost a scene from films like *Blow Up* or *The Conversation*. There was no way to identify this unknown band yet their session on that Saturday afternoon bled into my song, leaving a faint trace, a murmur from history.

REVELATIONS

Aged sixteen at home in my parents' house, playing records and wishing I could be at the International Poetry Incarnation, Royal Albert Hall, June 1965, listening to "Mama T'ain't Long Fo' Day" by Blind Willie McTell, suddenly hearing in his slide acoustic guitar those notes between the notes, hearing scales outside the tempered scale. Aged twenty-two, evening, lying in a hot bath, transistor radio playing classical music. Suddenly, unexpectedly, Erik Satie, *Trois Gymnopédies*, a music I had never heard before, simple, clear, serene, as drowsy as my mood in the steam and the heat, evoking an emotion that has no name, somewhere between nostalgic melancholy and bliss. Over time, the disruptive impact of such moments is lost as the strangeness of the music becomes normalised through familiarity.

December 1966, aged seventeen, I stand at the edge of the stage for a Cream concert at the Roundhouse and hear improvising group AMM as if by accident. Struck by a thunderbolt, I realise that fragmented, disruptive noise is a legitimate musical undertaking. Seven days after my eighteenth birthday, May 1967, the Jimi Hendrix Experience at Bluesville, a small room above the Manor House pub in north London. Feedback at the climax, Hendrix scraping his guitar across the Marshall stack, a roadie (probably Lemmy) braced behind it to prevent the entire rig crashing out of the first floor window onto Seven Sisters Road. I realise that noise can be thrilling, visceral, glamorous.

Aged circa twenty-three, a sultry summer evening, French windows of the bedroom open, walking into the garden, followed by the cloud sound of Javanese court gamelan from the Pura Paku Alaman, Jogyakarta (Robert E. Brown's recording from 1971). The flash of realisation that music like this is a field of complex temporality whose stickiness of individual objects holds the entirety together to give the illusion of a single sound object.

Aged twenty-one, hearing sacred flute music from Papua New Guinea and Roger Payne's recordings of humpbacked whales on BBC radio programmes, feeling close to formlessness in sympathy with these sounds floating in the oceanic aether without clear boundary. Of course, each sound possessed its own shapes but these were shapes closer to lights in mist, smoke in darkness or the spread of coloured inks in water that we see at the beginning of Masaki Kobayashi's film, *Kwaidan*.

Aged twenty-two, hearing "Time" by Sly and the Family Stone on John Peel's radio show, feeling that the layers of time in music, their cycles and discontinuities, hold endless potential for opening up the self, even changing society. Aged twenty-six, winter, sitting alone during a period when my relationship with Marie Yates was ending, looking out at snow in the garden, listening to shakuhachi and hochiku records by Goro Yamaguchi and Watazumi Doso, feeling the whiteness and purity of these bamboo sounds, as if they were stabilising my troubled emotional state, showing me that inner life can be like bamboo itself, capable of bending but immensely strong, able to withstand any disaster. This burst of utopian dreaming that took place within a few short years was close to a religious experience (though lacking in gods of any kind).

From that point on, whenever I felt lost, estranged from my purpose or losing my identity, I could invoke that period of my life, listen to the same music, attempt to re-enter its atmosphere. There is a clear danger here of succumbing to nostalgia for what was a formative time of my life but I would describe this period as a passage of unknowing, almost a deconditioning process pushing at ingrained habits and learned behaviour.

Nostalgia is a form of longing for past experiences based on the simplification of complex history. Like most people I do experience nostalgia from listening to music but these invocations I am talking about have always seemed closer to a re-immersion in the complexity and uncertainty that I felt on hearing these sounds for the first time. To read anthropology was to understand how cultural forms embody environmental, social, spiritual and political relations but to listen to music deeply over time, almost by entering into and becoming its structure, was a physical absorption into this lesson, an intimation of how authoritarian and repressive aspects of society might be shifted, even transformed. Was this possible? The only way to test this was to write about these experiences, not an easy task because music, sound and the act of listening all resist description. Most of all, the best way to test it was to play.

My Tastes In 1971–75:

Sun Ra, The Heliocentric Worlds of Sun Ra, Vol. 1
Terry Riley, Persian Surgery Dervishes
La Monte Young and Marian Zazeela, The Black Album
John Cage, Music for Keyboard 1935–48
Alice Coltrane, Universal Consciousness
Olivier Messiaen, La Nativité Du Seigneur
Evan Parker & Paul Lytton, Collective Calls
Yamaguchi, A Bell Ringing in the Empty Sky
Joni Mitchell, Court And Spark
Edgard Varèse, Intégrales
Minoru Miki, Music for 20-String Koto
Johnny Burnette, Rock 'n' Roll Trio
Claude Debussy, Images/Estampes/Deux Arabesques
Han Bennink/Misha Mengelberg/John Tchicai, Instant Composers Pool 2
Sly And The Family Stone, There's a Riot Goin' On


Gigs Witnessed: 1972–78:

Spontaneous Music Ensemble, Derek Bailey, Evan Parker And Paul Lytton, AMM, Tony Oxley Quintet, Brotherhood Of Breath, Derek Bailey And Han Bennink, Gagaku, Tibetan Monks from Gyutö Monastery, Steve Reich – Drumming (in the Hayward Gallery's Mark Rothko Exhibition), Olivier Messiaen's Et expecto resurrectionem mortuorum, Muddy Waters, Henry Cow, Sonic Arts Union, The Scratch Orchestra, Toru Takemitsu Piano Works, Dagar Brothers, Keiko Nosaka Plays Minoru Miki, Globe Unity Orchestra, Cecil Taylor

## IV. PASS THE DISTANCE

Ask three individuals to recall the circumstances of an event from thirty-five years ago and each account will be different. This is my recollection, wrong as it turns out: one evening in 1969, the group of musicians who gathered for all-night jam sessions in the Roundhouse, Chalk Farm, played a small gig in the Enterprise pub across the street. Afterwards, Paul Burwell and I were approached by a man who asked us if we would like to play on a record by an artist he was producing in his studio in Belmont Street, also opposite the Roundhouse. The man was Vic Keary, the artist was Simon Finn, the studio was Chalk Farm Studios, launched in the same year by Keary and his business partner, the owner of Blue Beat and Melodisc Records, Emil Shalit.

Now better known as the inventor of specialist studio equipment with his company - Thermionic Culture - Keary was trained as a technician, followed in the footsteps of Joe Meek by working as an engineer at Landsdowne Studios. Records he worked on included Acker Bilk's "Stranger On the Shore" and "What Do You Wanna Make Those Eyes At Me For" by Emile Ford and the Checkmates. Later he recorded many Jamaican artists such as Prince Buster, Laurel Aitken, Desmond Decker and Joe Harriott, then built his own studio in Chalk Farm, a state-of-the-art 8-track with home-made valve mixing desk. Vic had just released the first LP on his new business venture - Mushroom, a label specialising in progressive rock, jazz and what we would now call world music - and was planning to record an album with Simon Finn.

Although Paul and I recognised kindred spirits in each other, we were not yet committed to a musical career, nor was it clear that we would work closely together. The opportunity to record an album in a studio was a gift, far beyond our financial means. Nor was it just one session but a series of sessions in which we rehearsed with Simon, watched Vic at work in his tiny control room and

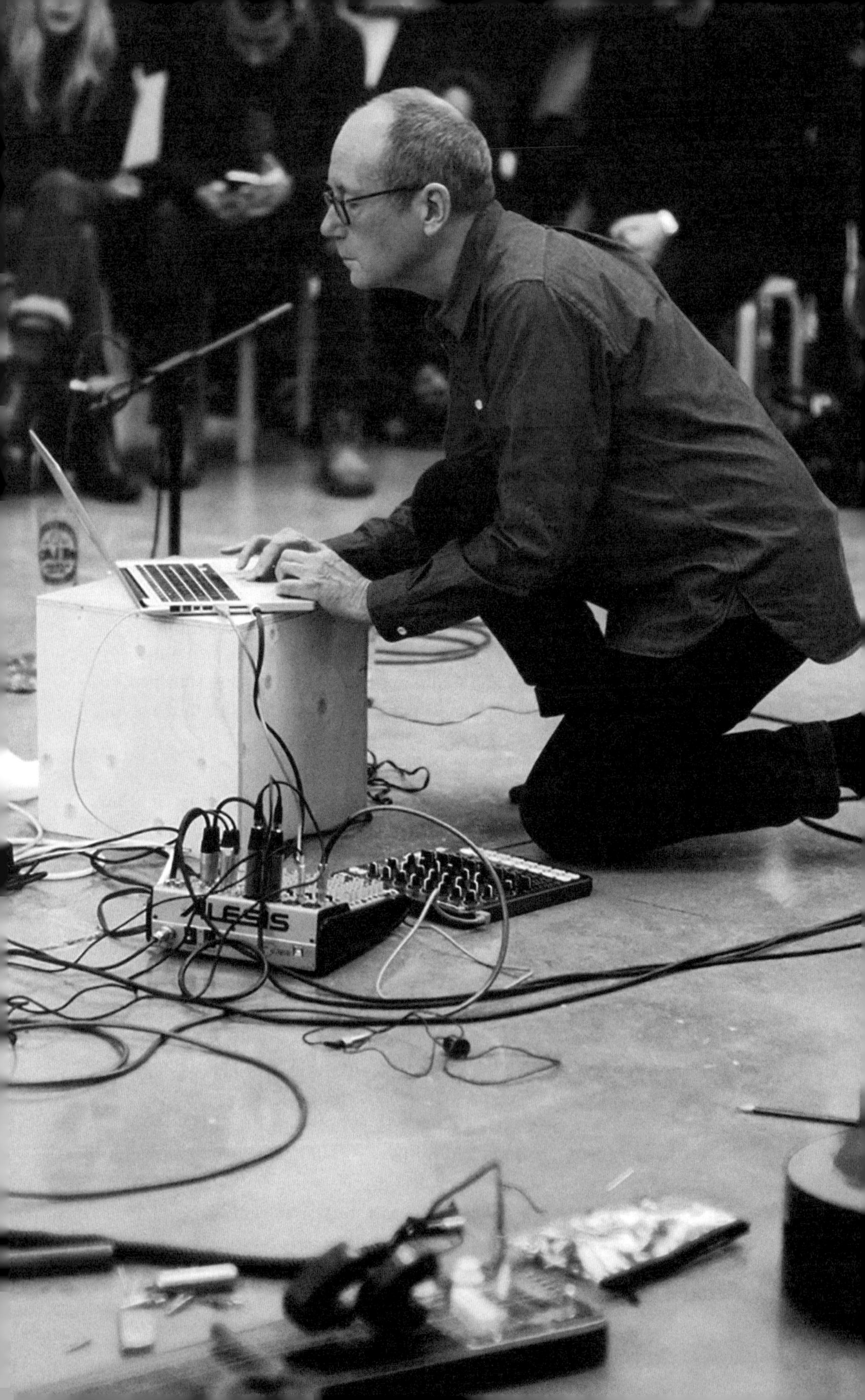
ALESIS

experimented with arrangements and instrumentation for each song. Even though I was out of my depth much of the time, inexperienced and still learning to play, Vic and Simon were almost perversely open to whatever I did.

Life changed. In 1969 I moved into a flat in north London with Sally, my ex-girlfriend from school and her new husband, watching with a sense of growing disturbance as their relationship quickly deteriorated into a grotesque episode of self-harm on the part of the husband. Marie Yates and I began a relationship; I left art college with uncertain prospects and no income. Meanwhile, the sessions for *Pass the Distance* continued. As the album came near to completion I was invited to create cover artwork. The title – *Pass The Distance* – reminded me of an advert for children's shoes, a brand named Start-Rite, that was iconic during the 1950s and 60s. I copied the image – a boy and girl hand in hand, seen from behind walking along an empty road, life stretching ahead of them. For the reverse side of the cover they were returning, their heads now terrifying fright masks, all around them darkness and hallucinations, monsters and war. Vic and Simon loved what I submitted but it was a mistake to use it. Almost immediately after the record was released, the Start-Rite company demanded the record be withdrawn. There was no money for a new cover and so Simon's debut album became an instant rarity.

Thirty years later I was in Tokyo, exhibiting and performing with Max Eastley at ICC in an exhibition – *Sound Art – Art As Media* - curated by Minoru Hatanaka. During interviews by Japanese journalists, I was puzzled to be asked questions about *Pass the Distance*. One writer showed me a bootleg copy. It was as if a ghost had suddenly appeared out of the distant past. This growth of a cult, partly exacerbated by the extreme rarity of the LP but also based on its oddity, seemed to accelerate after 2000. I was contacted by David Tibet of Current 93, who had become obsessed by the record, particularly Simon's "Jerusalem". He wanted to contact Simon, maybe reissue the record on his Durtro label. I had no idea where Simon had gone, whether he was still alive even, so I was unable to help. Not so long afterwards, as email communications proliferated and people found they could track down old friends on the internet, I was contacted by Simon, then living in Canada.

White Cube Gallery, 2015

The outcome of that email conversation was the reissue of the record, Simon's return to England and a revival of his career as a singer and songwriter.

In 2007, he released *Accidental Life*, in some respects a follow-up to *Pass the Distance*. It was strange to be in a studio again with Simon and Vic but also sad because Paul had died earlier that year. In 2015 Simon asked me to play steel guitar on two songs at an upcoming gig at Cafe Oto in London. We rehearsed together at my flat but then during the week of the gig I came down with flu and felt too ill to play. I have no desire to repeat or relive the past (even if that were possible) but this continuity of connections, looping across more than forty years, is an endorsement of chance meetings. Since then we have played together twice, both of them enjoyable experiences, and the record is due to be reissued for the third time.

## V. BURIED DREAMS

Since I moved house in 2013 my studio changed dramatically. Previously I was in a large room at the top of a house with a view that stretched far over north London. I felt up in the sky with the birds, particularly the screaming swifts in summer. From there I was able to look down on my garden, watch foxes at night, feel detached from the city. Now I have a tiny studio at the end of my garden which I rarely use. It's part of the garden and weather, existing as a remote ideal, maybe, a place of refuge where I can go to enter into another state of mind if the weather is not too bad. That section of the garden is like a Japanese dry garden – gravel, three stones, a tsukubai water basin and black bamboo – which symbolises water and islands.

On summer evenings it can be beautiful, dark and mysterious. The trope of the ancient Chinese scholar's studio resonates with the appeal of a detached room conducive to quiet study. Through a book of supernatural tales - *Strange Stories from a Chinese Studio*, by a 17th century writer – Pu Songling – I discovered a way to ease the transition from one studio to another. Chinese scholars surrounded themselves with objects, materials, images and instruments that stimulated the imagination, assuming that inspiration would take effect from the creation of a personal aesthetic environment. That has always been my guiding principle. Studios of all kinds represent an imaginative space or field in which miraculous objects can appear, complex sound works or books. All of the buried dreams of a human being can emerge through this instrument if the setting and conditions are in alignment.

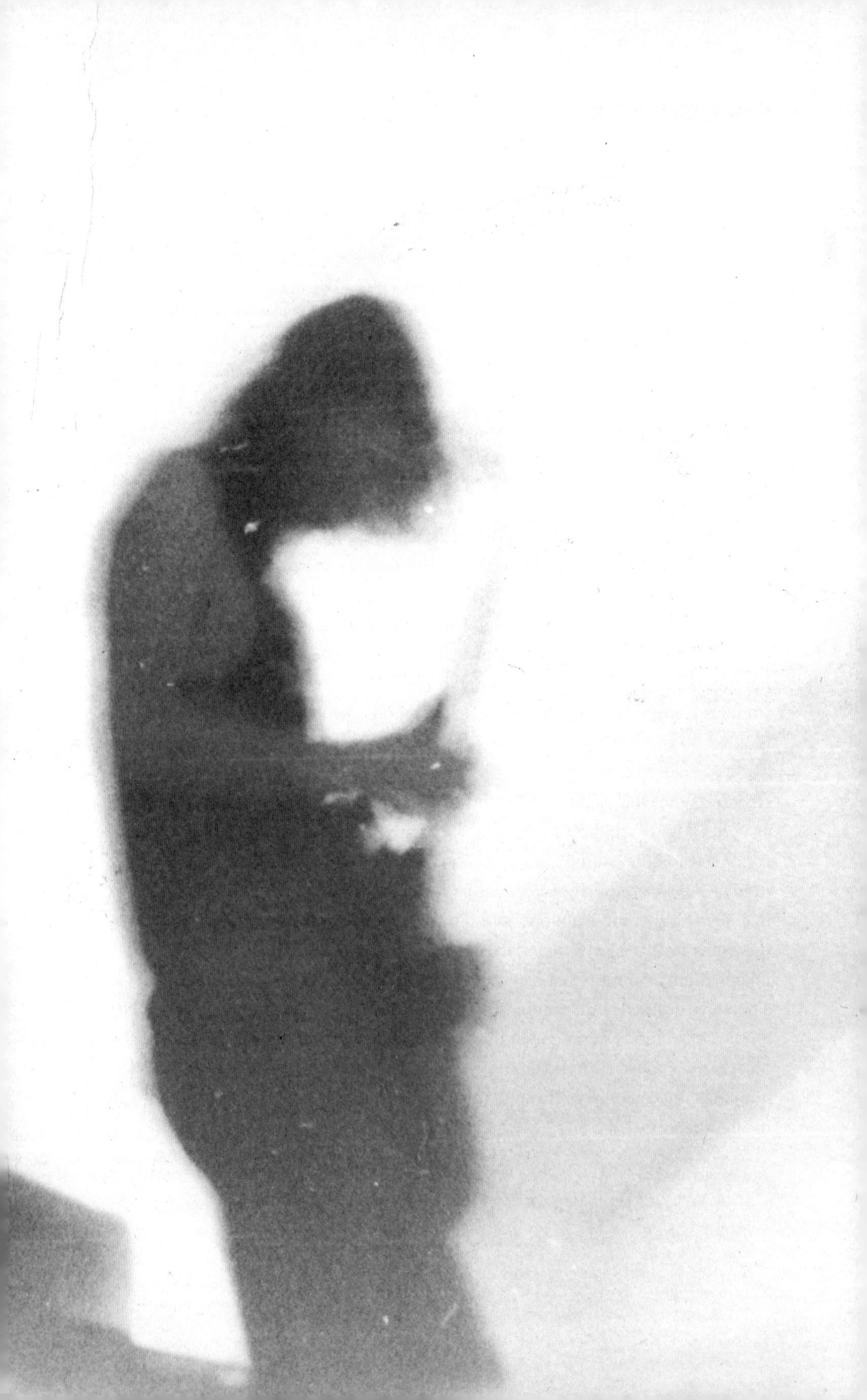

FANTASTIC TERRAIN

One of the lasting benefits of the Obscure record has been an ongoing collaboration with Max Eastley. Max and I met at Hornsey College of Art in 1969, both of us fine art students. Though I had dropped out of college I went back to see final year shows by Marie Yates, Max and other friends. Max's show was incredibly mysterious, like an alchemist's laboratory of strange kinetic sound machines. At the time I was fascinated by kinetic sculptors such as Jean Tinguely, Pol Bury, Li Yuan-chia, David Medalla, Liliane Lijn and Gerhard von Graevenitz, particularly the sound produced by their pieces almost as a side effect. Pol Bury's works, in particular, invoked a kind of second life, the infinitely slow growth of a near imperceptible sound world that in my mind suggested a posthumanist approach to composition.

Although I had included examples of Max's self-made instruments in the book - *New/Rediscovered Musical Instruments* - and we were given one side each of the Obscure record in 1975, our first performance together was not until 1976, when Max invited Evan Parker and myself to play solos (Evan playing soprano saxophone, me playing alto flute) with his mechanical instruments at the Serpentine Gallery, London. The experience of playing alone with machines in the resonant space of the gallery was extraordinary, being conscious of their inexorability and indifference and working within that limitation.

Many of Max's instruments were based on circular processes, rotations or the vibration of strings by air. These themes came together in 1977 after a dramatic performance at the London Musicians Collective by Paul Burwell. Paul swung two Chinese cymbals on long lengths of elastic, an effect that was dangerous for us in the audience yet sonically thrilling, the cymbals crashing into the floor, each one spinning on its own axis, their shimmering sound fluctuating as they whirled through the space. Immediately afterwards, Max proposed a performance composition solely for whirled, twisted and rotating instruments and soundmaking devices. This became a piece called *Whirled Music*, revealed for the first time in February 1978 by Max, Paul, Steve Beresford and myself, later recorded for a release on my Quartz record label, performed on many occasions until 1986 and reissued on vinyl by Oren Ambarchi's Black Truffle label in 2018.

Max's vision was of a performance so dangerous that the audience would have to be protected by a net and we, the performers, would need to wear masks in case we were struck on the head by one of the larger instruments. These wicker masks, made by Max's partner, Pamela Marre, gave the performance the look of a strange ceremony, a feeling intensified by the improvised sound-field structure of overlapping, random and continuous events, none of which led to the climaxes or resolutions of more conventional musical forms. 'Without means to place sound sources visually the spatial sense of sound is intensified," Annabel Nicolson wrote in her review of that first performance (*Musics*, no. 17, May 1978), "resonances and the relations of air movement to space become more evident . . . the sound sources were in constant movement since all the instruments were sounded by whirling and there were no fixed points of stillness to relate them to. Performers and instruments were caught in their own momentum . . . Nothing escaped intact or silent in the continual displacement of air."

Live performance, David Toop & John Butcher, 100 Years Gallery, 2014

## SILENTLY WRITING

Max Eastley and I often talked about the field in which we worked as a terrain or map of discovery, a journey into landscape, but the landscape we were talking about was a very broad definition of that term: rural and urban landscape, intricate maps of the mind and imagination, the fantastic terrain of hidden, unknown and fictional places that could be conjured up through sound.

Life is equally convoluted, never a straight line of orderly events. Elements of the narrative overlap each other, fall backwards, branch sideways or leap ahead into the future, echoing back and forth like the flutter echo of my childhood. In 1989 I contributed a computer composition ("Cat versus Rat", with spoken narrative by Kazuko Hohki) to *Clocks of the Midnight Hour*, a documentary film of Max's work. At the time I was working as a music journalist, frustrated by the job and desperate to find my way back into playing music.

One of the positive consequences of becoming a music critic came from buying an Atari 1040 ST computer in 1987. Writing for newspapers like *The Times* meant I needed to progress from electric typewriter to computer word processing and the Atari was an appealing option because of its inclusion of MIDI ports for electronic keyboards and drum machines. I was inspired by the extraordinary explosion of avant-gardism in dance music – "Acid Tracks" by Phuture and "Washing Machine" by Mr Fingers being two of the most significant example – but one record in particular made me want to explore MIDI sequencing for myself: Model 500's "Night Drive (Thru Babylon)", produced by Juan Atkins.

I had flown to New York in August 1987 to interview Jellybean Benitez for *The Face* magazine. The evening I arrived I went straight out to buy records, heard this track playing in Downtown Records on 6th Avenue and rushed up to the DJ to find out what it was. As it turned out I knew Juan Atkins' music from his previous group, Cybotron, though I had yet to discover the richness of Detroit techno. In my mind I had grouped Cybotron together with the New York electro hip hop of Afrika Bambaataa's "Planet Rock", The Jonzun Crew's "Pack Jam" and Warp 9's "Light Years Away", the kind of tracks played by Jellybean at The Funhouse in Manhattan and the music that persuaded me to write *Rap Attack* in 1984.

Records like Ryuichi Sakamoto's "Riot In Lagos" and Haruomi Hosono's *Video Game Music* conjured up another kind of landscape, melting away into images, virtual zones and dreams: the dystopian science fiction environments of films like *Blade Runner*, *Stalker* and *THX 1138*, or novels such as *Nova Express* by William

Burroughs, *Neuromancer* by William Gibson, *High Rise* by J.G. Ballard, *Time Out of Joint* by Philip K. Dick and *My Life In the Bush of Ghosts* by Amos Tutuola. All of these intimations of a future world were reinforced by changes within my own life. Shortly after returning from researching *Rap Attack* in New York in early 1984 I was invited to write a feature on electro for *The Face* magazine. At that moment they were looking for a monthly music columnist; my electro feature was accepted, liked and published as a cover feature in May 1984 and so they asked me to write a trial column.

This column, along with many feature articles and interviews for the magazine, turned out to be a long-term job for me, lasting well into the 1990s. For nearly fifteen years I had been close to poverty, struggling from one poorly paid gig to the next, moving frequently from flat to flat, at times having nowhere to live. On holiday in Cornwall with my partner at that time – music writer Sue Steward – I suddenly realised that my knowledge of African-American music history was an invaluable asset, a means to research and better understand the origins of hip hop. I loved the early records – 12 inch singles by Funky Four Plus One More, Sequence, Kurtis Blow and Grandmaster Flash and the Furious Five - but more to the point I understood something of their origins in rhythm and blues, gospel, soul, jazz, radio DJs and African American oral traditions.

The short journalistic pieces I was writing up until 1984 were not enough to lift me out of the stagnation of my life. A book was more substantial. If I could find a publisher then the anxiety of living on an economic edge might be lessened, if only because it could create new possibilities. Though lacking in confidence I wrote a synopsis of what I thought the book would be, posted it to a small selection of likely publishers (a business of which I knew next to nothing) and waited. To my surprise I had two offers. Both were from small independent publishers but I was content with that – it was a world in which I felt comfortable. I went with Pluto Press, signed a contract with my editor-to-be, Pete Ayrton (later the owner of Serpent's Tail, publisher of my next three books), then wondered how to start.

My first step was to go to New York. Knowing it would be freezing in January I bought a warm coat and booked a return flight. A photographer I knew through *Collusion* magazine – Patricia Bates – already had experience of photographing in the New York City club scene. I stayed in her Manhattan apartment and together we set up a packed itinerary of interviews, me asking the questions, her taking the photographs. We fixed meetings in the mornings, then went out until the early hours of the next morning. In two weeks we went to clubs like The Loft, Broadway International, the Funhouse (where I met Paul Simon in the DJ booth with

Jellybean), the Copa Cabana, Danceteria and The Roxy and recorded interviews with many artists - Grandmaster Flash, Afrika Bambaataa, Spoonie G, Lotti Golden of Warp 9, Double Trouble, Arthur Baker, The Fearless Four, Kurtis Blow – along with record label owners like Aaron Fuchs, the notorious Paul Winley and the legendary Bobby Robinson, a veteran of the R&B business whose labels had included Enjoy, Fire, Fury and Whirlin' Disc.

It was the second time I had been to New York but this time my fourteen-day return ticket meant there was little opportunity to do anything other than focus on hip hop. It was a fascinating time to be observing the scene as an outsider, a time of change as the second phase of hip hop (five years after hip hop had become known to the wider world through records like "Rapper's Delight") came to an end. Artists like Grandmaster Flash were trying to regroup, disillusioned by the way they had been cheated out of money and lost position to other members of their own crews. The music was in its electronic period but Run-D.M.C. were coming up. For all I knew, hip hop might disappear, just another brief fashion running its course. In fact it began to grow to enormous proportions, almost before the book was published, and by 1985 it had moved from small clubs to stadiums. Of course I had no idea of this at the time and certainly never envisaged having to write a second version in 1991 and then a further update in 1999 (by which time I decided that three versions were enough).

It was also an interesting time for research because of the access I was given. Most of the records were released by small independent labels run from tiny offices. There were no public relations people to stand in the way or make it difficult for me to speak to artists. We would show up at Arthur Baker's studio, for example, and rappers would come by. Many years later the situation was totally different. Successful rappers often felt no need to talk to the British press so made themselves inaccessible. But in 1984 it was a novelty to speak to a white person from England, particularly one who was prepared to listen to their stories in detail.

Back home in London I gave myself three months to write the book, just long enough for the money from the advance to last. Looking back at that time I think of it as an apprenticeship, a crash course in learning how to write at book length, at speed, to process a lot of information in a short time and write it in such a way that it held the reader's attention.

I was 34 years old. The decision to write *Rap Attack* had come at the point when I was exhausted by the struggle to survive and felt an overpowering need for more security. Having been involved in the collective, avant-garde, penniless and

Cover of Rap Attack

In the DJ booth with Grandmaster Flash, 1984

extremely unglamorous improvised music scene for many years I was suddenly thrown into book publishing and from there straight into the world of *The Face*, at that point one of the most influential, fashionable and visually innovative magazines on the planet. Although *The Face* didn't pay well – it was, after all, another independent magazine surviving from month to month with very high production costs – it gave me a regular income and opened the door to an unexpected career in music journalism. Being a regular contributor of columns and features to the ultra-fashionable *Face* meant I was commissioned to write for publications that wouldn't have given me a second glance in other circumstances, from *Elle*, *Vogue* and *Tatler* to the *Sunday Times Magazine* and American magazines like *Interview* and *Spin*. In most cases I wouldn't have given them a second glance either but suddenly I was a music critic, whether I wanted it or not.

In partnership with Steve Beresford I was also producing a group called Frank Chickens in 1984. Originally three Japanese women living in London, they based their first performances on enka music, singing over karaoke backing tracks. Kazuko Hohki had been a friend since she first arrived in the UK with Clive Bell, a brilliant flute and shakuhachi player I had known since the mid-1970s. I went to hear the trio play one of their first gigs in a club in Hammersmith, west London.

They were funny, the concept was original and as an act it was hugely appealing but I imagined something more daring and contemporary, a more confrontational fusion of Japanese tradition with hyper-modernity, exactly the kind of aesthetic designed for Ridley Scott's *Blade Runner*. Steve was keen to try this approach and the group were in agreement, though one of them dropped out in the early stages, leaving Kazuko with Kazumi Taguchi as a duo.

For the first record – "We Are Ninja (Not Geisha)", backed with "Fujiyama Mama" and "Shellfish Bamboo" - we crammed in as many of our obsessions as we could: the New York funk/electro of The System and Planet Patrol, rockabilly by Wanda Jackson, dub tracks by Sly & Robbie and African Head Charge, traditional Japanese music, songs and folk stories, Akira Ifukube's music for *Godzilla*, video game music and exotica, even the Mike Leander production of Gary Glitter and the Glitter Band's "Rock and Roll Part 2". For the cover artwork, Kishi Yamamoto's photograph showed Kazuko and Kazumi in kimono but with punkish hairstyles, headphones and Sony Walkmans. The record's novelty factor appealed to UK audiences (John Peel loved it) but at the same time it was a strong feminist statement and, like Yellow Magic Orchestra's first LPs, a witty counter-attack against stereotypical representations of Japanese people.

Overleaf: David Toop interviews Afrika Bambaataa, Arthur Baker's studio, South Bronx, NY, 1984

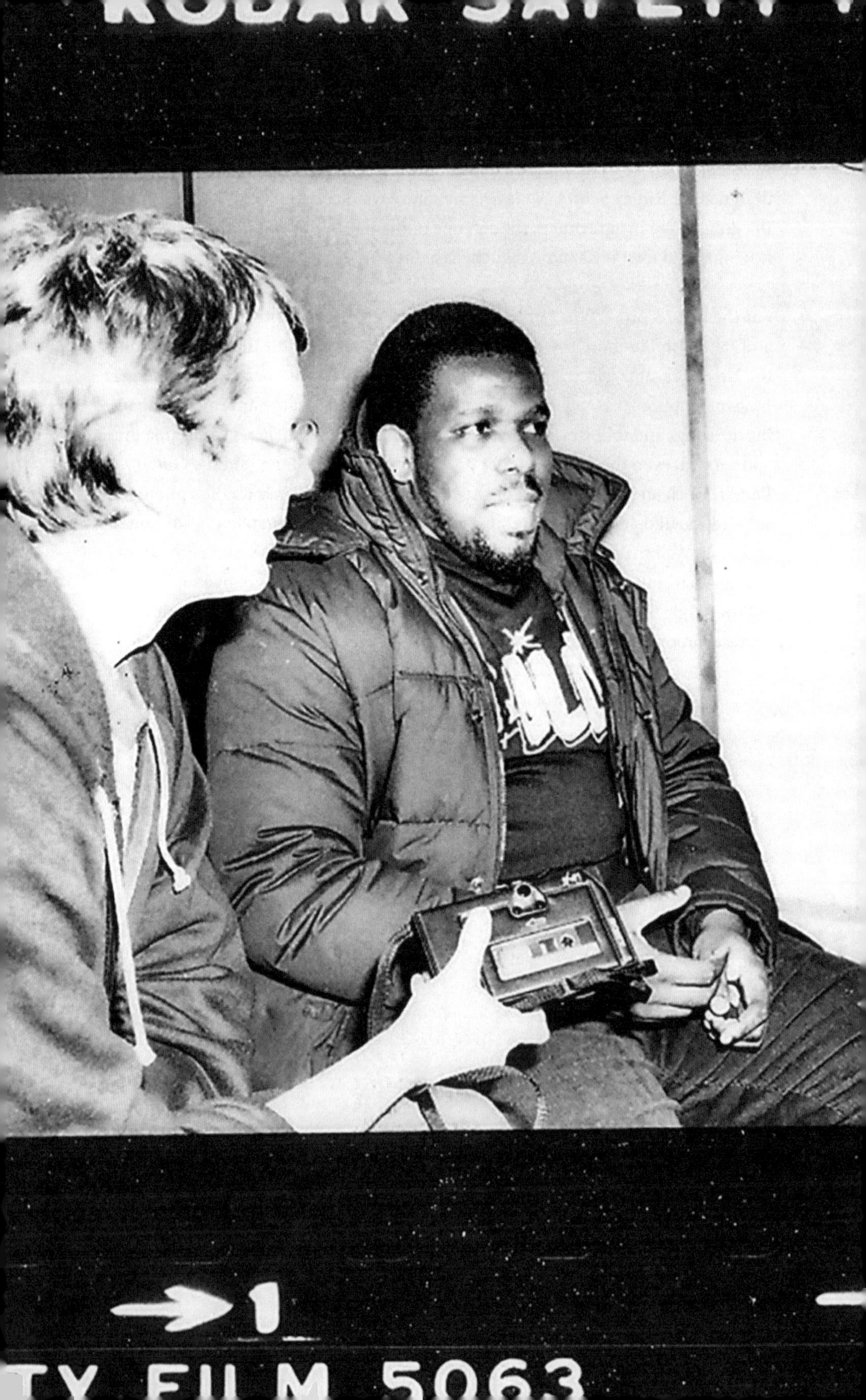

1
TY FILM 5063

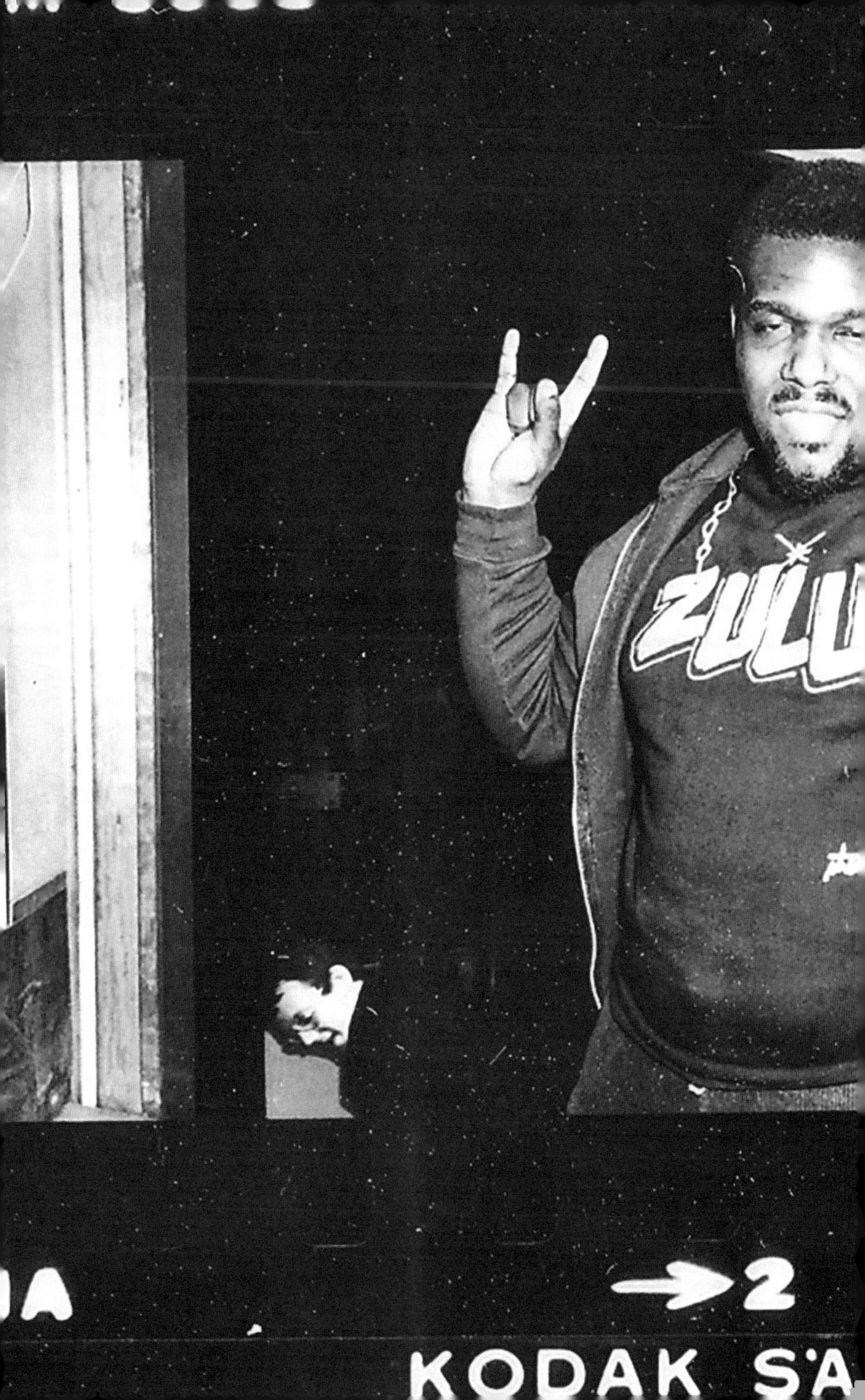

ZUL
2
KODAK

TELEMATIC NOMADS

Music technology was beginning to allow more plasticity, a more sculptural approach in which time could be out of joint, tradition clashing with futurity, at the same time that it was generating the kind of personalised listening and cross-genre cassette playlists that anticipated a future of digital downloads and mp3 players.

All of this futurology came together at the beginning of the 1990s, when Max Eastley and I began discussions for a CD length recording named *Buried Dreams*. My first thought had been to form a performing group. I was desperate to get back into music. Even though it had helped to make life easier, after seven years of full-time journalism I wanted to extricate myself and return to what I loved doing most. Max was one of my oldest and closest friends. When it came to discussing sound we had a real understanding and sympathy so he was the person I turned to. We even drew up visual images of what the stage set-up would be, a combination of Max's instruments with my electronics and Kazuko Hohki on vocals. Maybe this was too big a step after being so immersed in journalism, plus the cultural scene was suffering after so many years of Margaret Thatcher's reactionary, anti-art Conservative government. Instead we started playing small improvised music gigs as a duo. The gigs were frankly depressing – small groups of men huddled together to hear a music that had been starved of oxygen during the 1980s - but gradually I felt myself regaining some confidence as a player.

*Buried Dreams* was to be a sonic theatre of images and signs, an auditory cinema of imaginary landscapes, which would combine all our experiences of the past twenty years. We were both using computers and digital samplers to create music, alongside modified and self-invented instruments (amplified and bowed Arc, prepared guitar, etc.), instruments such as flutes, guitars, keyboards, as well as taped documentation of Max's invented instruments played by wind, water, mechanical motion and recordings of bioacoustic phenomena (Max's from Tennessee, mine from Amazonas and Bali). Our ambition was to merge the very different possibilities of organic, mechanical, meteorological, electronic, historic and future.

Our *Buried Dreams* discussions encompassed studies of abyssal geography, the fragmentation and distribution of postmodern signs, journeys of the imagination, chaos and complexity, folk musics absorbed into a network of pulsation. Some of the material was prepared beforehand, particularly those tracks in which I composed rhythm tracks, bass lines and keyboard harmonies using the Atari, but we also made 'scores' that were more like film storyboards. For example, I wrote this paragraph: "And now:

diurnal and nocturnal rhythms, the sounds of human and nonhuman agencies, the helpless noise of machines, the volatile responses of electronic sensors, stimulated vocalisations from humans and beasts barked into air, meteorology, a foot on the pedal, a hand on the dial, messages sucked out of the heavens into a dish, metal grinding on metal, bass vibrations from the passing of an underground train send faint shimmers through fallen leaves."

Recorded by engineer Dave Hunt (also the engineer for the Flying Lizards, Frank Chickens and many other projects over the past thirty-five years) modified over a three year period and rejected by various record companies during that time, it was finally released on a Birmingham based label called Beyond. I had sent some of my techno tracks to Mike Barnett, who ran the label. He asked me if I had anything else so I sent him the tape of *Buried Dreams*, not remotely confident that he would be interested. Instead, he was really excited by it and helped us to produce a release that closely fitted our original concept, using Max's drawings and my science fiction stories as part of the packaging.

After the frustrations of this long delay it came as an almost unbelievable surprise and relief to see it voted third placed record of the year, behind Portishead and Massive Attack, in the 1994 *Wire* critics poll. "Their alignment of environmental sound-sculpture and electronically-sourced music simultaneously finds a new intersection point for artistic and scientific methods, while providing a powerful lever into the subconscious," Rob Young wrote in the same magazine. "*Buried Dreams* is symptomatic of music's new aura: it is not a music that you can sink into, or project fantasy and fear onto, but rather it projects its aura onto the listener, making you the observer/wanderer/prisoner in someone else's lucid dream."

Coming as it did during the rise of ambient music, the record generated a lot of press attention by our modest standards, though many reviewers were ambivalent about its disquieting, dystopian atmosphere. Some even said it frightened them, something that Max and I found amusing. Finally we played the record in concert at London's Southbank, supported by Scanner. Despite all my personal problems at that time, I experienced a wave of euphoria. Finally, I was able to perform and produce music that made some impact.

Though an accident of circumstance, the release of *Buried Dreams* in 1994 was timely. The record dwelled on information overload, image saturation, the growth of mega-cities, the emerging communications revolution and transmissions over long distances. I picked up the term 'telematic nomads' from a 1988 essay called *Invisible Design* by Claudia Dona. Dona wrote of the overlapping of the artificial with the

natural, which reminded me of bionics, but she also talked about a new relationship to time, the telematic nomad being able to be everywhere and in one place at the same time: "The Telematic Nomad is equipped
for ubiquity."

This was something of a prediction of what was to come, the world wide web. At an ambient music event in the early 1990s I met Paul Sanders. His company – State 51 – was working on interactive music and media technology. One evening in his office in Brick Lane he switched on the computer to show me the internet, in itself a revelation in 1993, but he was full of other ideas. Many of them I couldn't grasp but with hindsight I realise he was anticipating social media, digital file sharing and blogging, though he lacked the desire or resources to develop them fully.

At a time when powerful music business people were oblivious to the potential of the internet, his company was one of the first in the UK to conceive of ways in which record labels could use online platforms to sell their music and establish a less passive relationship between artists and their fans. Paul suggested that we should put all of the extras of *Buried Dreams* – the images and stories – online through the State 51 website. This was so unusual at the time that MTV Europe broadcast a story about it. For one heady moment, *Buried Dreams* seemed to inhabit the imaginary landscape that we had created in the studio.

Gigs Witnessed: 1976–81

The Fania All-Stars, Bob Marley And The Wailers, Alvin Lucier, Bobby Womack, Johnny Guitar Watson, Dagar Brothers, Ram Narayan, The Slits, Adam And The Ants, Steve Lacy, Frank Wright, Chuck Berry, Toots And The Maytals, Sister Sledge, Chic, Milford Graves, Derek Bailey And Anthony Braxton, Bow Wow Wow, Black Uhuru, Tito Puente


My Tastes In 1976-79:

Dr. Alimantado, Ride On Brother
Marvin Gaye, I Want You
Syreeta, Stevie Wonder Presents: Syreeta
Richard Maxfield, Electronic Music
Cachao, Y Su Descarga '77, Vol 1
Bobby Womack, Looking For A Love Again
Little Beaver, Party Down
Walt Dickerson Trio, Peace
Oiseaux Du Venezuela (Recorded By Jean C. Roché)
Dadawah, Peace And Love
Evelyn 'Champagne' King, Shame
Chic, I Want Your Love
Johnny 'Guitar' Watson, Ain't That A Bitch
The Slits, Cut

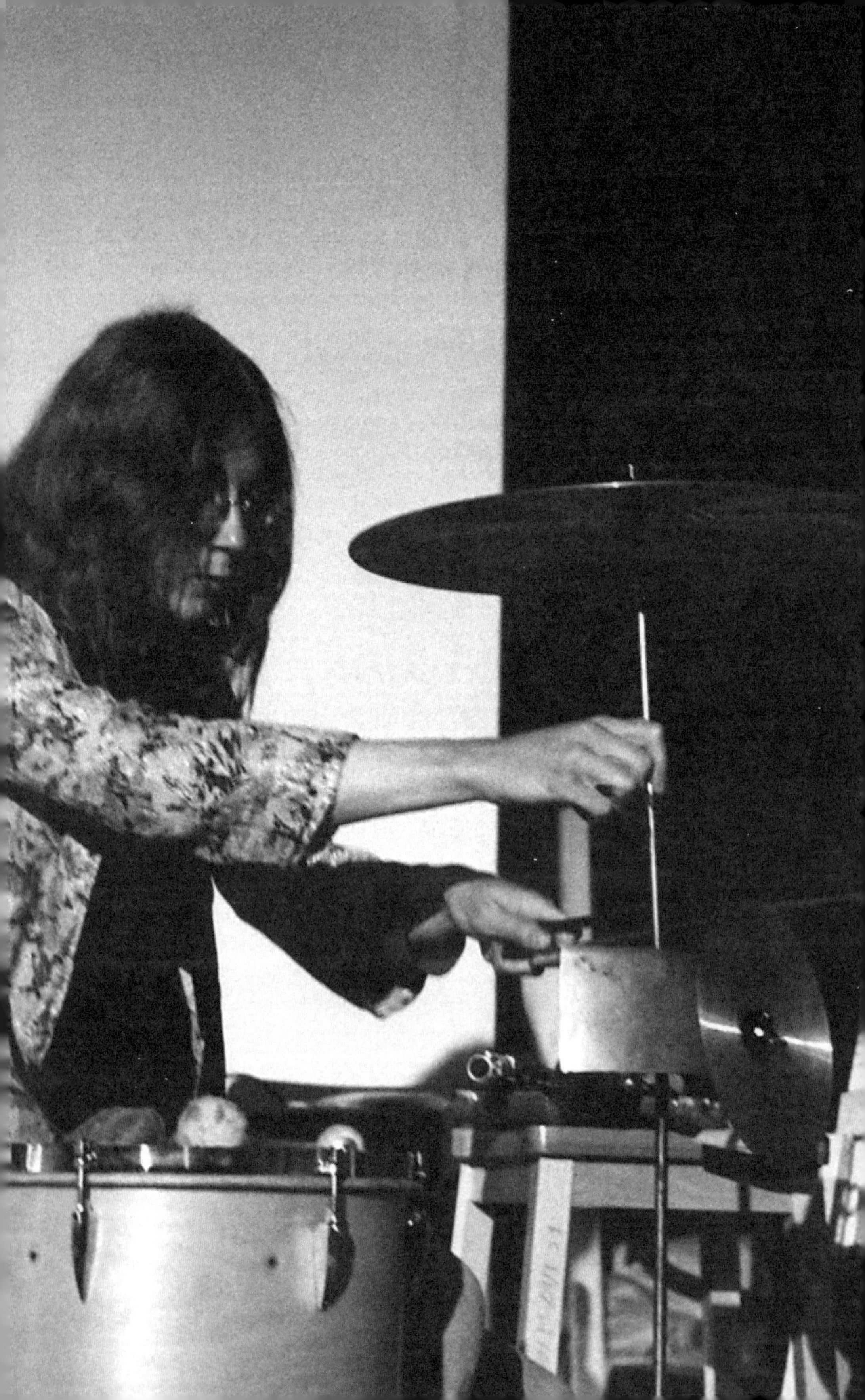

## VI. GROUPS IN FRONT OF PEOPLE

"Clear voice," was the comment written by the music teacher in my school report of 1957, my overall mark in music a C, equal in mediocrity to mathematics in which I was described as a "slow learner". Faint praise then, but on the strength of it I was persuaded to join the choir at Holy Trinity, an imposing nineteenth century Anglican church sited at the end of the road where I grew up.

Coincidentally, the hall attached to this church is where Britain's first rock 'n' roll star, Cliff Richard, sang along to records in 1956 with his first group, The Quintones. I was too young to have any knowledge of this, though my sister was at school with him at Cheshunt Secondary Modern (Harry Webb didn't change his name to Cliff Richard and enter public consciousness until 1958). But in retrospect, the church was significant for my later career in music. The Sunday morning hymns were uninspiring but I enjoyed the starker atmosphere of psalms sung at Evensong, and on special days – Good Friday and Christmas – the ritual elements of incense, procession and (on Good Friday) the austere solemnity of spoken psalms was deeply affecting. Christianity held no appeal for me but there was a heady pleasure in realising the potential for music when combined with profound convictions, ceremonial and a reverberant building. At school I had sung with other children in class and taken part in maypole dancing, a strange survival of English folklore with pagan associations, but singing in a church choir gave me a taste of what it was like to be a part of a group sound.

ALTERATIONS

*Groups In Front of People* was a clever title with two meanings, used for two of his LP releases on the Bead label by English improvising guitarist and field recordist Peter Cusack in 1979. On the one hand it emphasised the centrality of live performance for improvised music; on the other hand it suggested (with slightly sinister overtones) that collectivism should take precedence over the individual.

Free improvisation was a group music, created without composers, conductors, leaders or a score. For my generation, the second generation to follow the pioneers of the 1960s, it was logical to continue their strategies of collective self-organisation and musician-run record labels into the 1970s. Paul Burwell and I had learned about independent publishing from Bob Cobbing and his Writers Forum small press imprint. This was how I came to publish my own little books in the early 1970s: *Decomposition As Music Process* (1972), *The Bi/s/onics Pieces* (1973) and *New/Rediscovered Musical Instruments* (1974); it was also a direct route into the independent publishing of magazines and records that grew out of the improvised music scene.

In early 1975 I was contacted by Evan Parker. I was one of a number of younger musicians he was inviting to a meeting. Because of the lack of coverage given to improvised music in the music press and mainstream media there was a plan to start a magazine. A group of us, including Evan Parker, Mandy Davidson, Martin Davidson, Paul Burwell, Phil Wachsmann, Steve Beresford and myself gathered together in Wachsmann's flat to discuss what we wanted to do and how we could do it. This led to *Musics* magazine, a collectively edited and produced magazine of 23 issues published between April/May 1975 and November 1979. Naturally, the content of the magazine expanded to contain the diversity of ideas within our community, very quickly going beyond the original aim of being a voice for free improvisation.

Inevitably, this led to tension and numerous squabbles, people walking away from the magazine collective and arguing within its pages, either through combative articles, the letters pages or through comments inserted by the typesetters (I was one of the main typesetters and plead guilty to this misdemeanour). At that first meeting I noticed that Steve Beresford was carrying a copy of a Junior Walker and the All-Stars LP. This was an unusual sight in improvised music circles, most of the players at that time being either serious jazz musicians who were often disdainful of popular music or progressive rock fans who denigrated soul music as superficial. After the meeting I told him I liked Junior Walker's music. "I should hope so," he replied. At that moment I could have taken offense at such an abrupt response. Instead I laughed. It was typically abrasive but absolutely right.

That conversation was the beginning of a long association with Steve Beresford. Though interrupted for many years by the kind of self-immolating estrangement which seems to blight friendships within improvised music, it continues to this day, a collaboration that included many groups and projects: Alterations, General Strike, The Flying Lizards, Frank Chickens, The Promenaders, The 49 Americans, Ivor Cutler, John Zorn, *Collusion* magazine, recordings with Prince Far I, Toshinori Kondo and Tristan Honsinger, and releases on labels such as Touch, Sub Rosa, Y, Canal, Piano, Nato in France and Pinakotheca Records in Japan.

The real genesis of this very productive musical collaboration came from Peter Cusack. Peter had been living on a houseboat in Amsterdam and trying to form a regular group that could take advantage of the touring possibilities in Europe. In 1978 he proposed a quartet – the two of us plus Steve Beresford and Terry Day. On paper it looked like a disastrous stylistic mismatch but from our first gig in Norwich it was clear that the music was extremely free, quite different to anything else in improvised music at that point and frequently very funny. This looseness set the tone for a lot of the projects that followed.

Timing was crucial. All four of us had unusual backgrounds for improvised music and our relationship to the scene was committed yet seditious. Perhaps this was more imagined than real but there was the perception of an orthodoxy that threatened to smother the freedom out of which the music had grown. By the 1970s, unspoken taboos militated against referring to other forms of music, playing melodies or regular rhythms unless these were either a direct development from the jazz tradition or some form of notated contemporary composition. Certain instruments were not approved of; this was also true for the resolutely non-masculine, 'unmusical' small sounds that we all liked – the empty tins, plastic toys, cardboard tubes, snail shells, duck calls and novelties that formed a part of our kit. None of us were jazz players, though Terry had begun as a modern jazz drummer before playing free jazz with the People Band and rock music with Ian Dury in the original line-up of Kilburn and the High Roads. Peter had a growing interest in environmental sound recording and from living in Holland he had become used to the Dutch approach to improvisation – extremely iconoclastic, disruptive and humorous. Steve's early groups such as the Four Pullovers with Terry, Nigel Coombes and Roger Smith, were a noisy (though at low volume), insistently percussive onslaught of small, often abject and absurdist sounds.

Artist Placement Group Project,
London Zoo, 1976

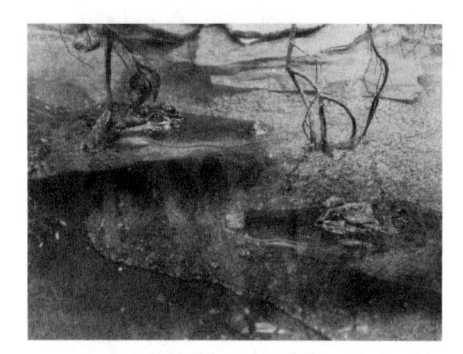

Crocodiles

Lizard

In Alterations, as the group came to be known, we were all working at the beginning with tiny sounds, provoking discontinuity and (as we discovered) open to almost anything. When the group started we were mostly playing acoustic instruments and Terry had given up playing drum kit, instead using small percussive instruments along with home-made bamboo reeds, tin cans, alto saxophone, mandolin and cello. Gradually our instrumentation expanded to include electric guitars and basses, electric organ and drum kit. By the time we recorded our last album of that period – *My Favourite Animals* – we had incorporated drum machines, Univox, Farfisa and Casio keyboards, pedal steel guitar and Peter's sampling instrument developed at Steim in Amsterdam, the Gatecrasher.

The music crashed its way through reggae, country, rockabilly, funk, fake jazz and cod classical, though if two of us were playing in any of those styles then the others would be doing something totally different, seemingly unrelated, often destructive. In the eight years the group lasted its strength lay in this capacity to accept a certain amount of chaos, to be able to focus while others were playing something contrary, disruptive or too loud, to be tolerant and open to change. In my opinion, the main reason the group split up was because we had lost our appetite for tolerating each other's idiosyncrasies.

Then in 2015 we performed together as a quartet for the first time in nearly thirty years. The music felt as strong as ever, only changed by the passing of years and the experiences each of us had accumulated during that long gap.

The formation of Alterations coincided with post-punk, an extremely open and creative period for live music. As a consequence we were able to play on the same bills as Jah Wobble and This Heat, also to perform at German anarcho-punk festivals *and* jazz festivals. Steve Beresford and I shared a love of everything from new American dance music, reggae, dub, rhythm and blues and jazz to Tibetan Tantric Buddhist ritual music and the John Barry Seven. Although Alterations made it possible to play our versions of these musics, the context remained experimental improvisation. In 1979, a huge change took place, first of all through being invited by David Cunningham to play on the first Flying Lizards album.

In 1976 I had been given a few days of teaching at Maidstone College of Art by video artist David Hall. Hall was a member of Artist Placement Group, an organisation founded by Barbara Steveni and John Latham in 1966. The purpose was to place artists as paid free agents within organisations such as industry or government departments. In the mid-1970s I undertook a brief placement within London Zoo, a reflection of my interest in bioacoustics and communications, later working with artist Ian Breakwell, electronic musician Hugh Davies and Audio Arts founder William Furlong on a project within the Department of Health, creating audio-visual reminiscence aids for elderly people suffering from the loss of short-term memory.

Work at the zoo was particularly relevant to my early interests in bioacoustics though my focus changed as I spent time there. Initially I took photographs of amphibious lizards underwater, recorded the sounds of parrots and sealions and presented an exhibition about sound-producing instruments with a connection to animals, for example pigeon whistles and horn trumpets, but mainly I was curious to learn more about humans in this setting, how they attempted to engage with caged animals, how they affected animals and the atmosphere created by such a concentration of otherness and entrapment. The animals could be described as unwilling or unwitting performers for an uncomprehending audience and so there were parallels to the uncomfortable relationship of experimental music to entertainment. Like much of my work it raised the question of whether this was research or music. In 2013, during a university interview for a professorship I spoke

## FLYING LIZARDS

about this problem and its relevance to the contemporary idea of practice-based or practice-led research within academia, referring back to my early work at the beginning of the 1970s. There was another way to think about making art. I was convinced of that. It lay somewhere between, in the interstices of art, writing, listening, oral history, philosophy, performance, study, the social and physical body. Many years passed before I began to understand this or felt able to put it into practice, either through art practice or teaching.

A financial lifesaver at a time when I was earning virtually no money, the opportunity to teach, even if only for a few days, came directly out of this network of associations with artists older and more experienced than myself, particularly those with connections to Artist Placement Group. I had very little experience of teaching and was barely older than those I was supposed to teach but one of the fine art students at Maidstone, in fact one of the only students who showed up for a tutorial, was David Cunningham. Already he had recorded a cover version of Eddie Cochran's "Summertime Blues" as a student project, with lyrics spoken by Deborah Evans (another Maidstone art student) in an exaggeratedly stiff, upper class English accent. In other words, the unique style of the Flying Lizards was established from the outset. He was also making connections in experimental music and when "Money" took off as a huge international hit he called on Steve Beresford to join him and Deborah for video and television 'performances' of what was essentially a recording studio creation.

The Flying Lizards sessions were very loose, more or less a working out of tracks in the studio. One of these became "TV", the group's third single; another became "Her Story" (years later sampled by The Roots), co-composed and sung by Vivien Goldman. "TV" was a relative failure, reaching only number

43 in the UK singles charts, but it rewarded us with two insights: how boring it was to shoot a video and how simultaneously tawdry, disappointing yet exciting it was to make an appearance on BBC TV's *Top of the Pops*. One excitement for me, felt ironically by this stage of my life, was that The Shadows also performed in the Top of the Pops studio on that day. Half-embarrassed, half-impressed, I shook hands with Hank Marvin, the guitarist whose version of "Apache" I attempted to emulate when I first started learning guitar. "Keep rocking lads," he said, at which we all cringed.

Just before appearing on *Top of the Pops* we also learned about tape switching. The Musicians' Union in Britain existed mainly to support and protect musicians who performed live in front of audiences in the traditional way. By the 1960s this function was complicated by new recording studio techniques. Some pop records – Phil Spector's tracks with The Ronettes and Righteous Brothers, The Beach Boys' *Pet Sounds* and *Sgt. Pepper's Lonely Hearts Club Band* by The Beatles – were impossible to perform on stage in a way that did justice to the original recorded sound. To add to this problem electronic keyboard instruments such as the Clavioline and Mellotron were seen as a threat to orchestral musicians because a single player could replace string and brass instruments.

In 1965, the Musicians' Union responded by launching a slogan: Keep Music Live. Television programmes like *Top of the Pops* were controversial because the demands of producing a weekly show with a number of disparate acts meant that it was easier for groups to mime to their hit singles. In 1966 miming was banned but groups were allowed to record a new backing track prior to the television appearance, so long as all the members of the group were present in the recording studio. In practice this meant a studio was booked, representatives from the record company and the Musicians' Union would meet there and go off for a meal, leaving the studio engineer to simply copy the original tape onto a new reel. This was then delivered as a new recording, with everybody involved fully aware of the deception.

Confronted by this strange collusive process The Flying Lizards decided to use the few hours of otherwise wasted time to do something productive. For us it was still a luxury to work in an expensive studio so we seized the opportunity to record a new track, a cover version of a song called "The Laughing Policeman". Originally a music hall song recorded in 1922 by Charles Jolly, this slightly sinister old novelty record was still played frequently on a BCC radio programme called *Children's Favourites* during our childhoods. Our version, vaguely ska in style and even more hysterical than the original, was offered to Virgin Records as a Flying Lizards track but they refused it so it was released as a single under the name of The Suspicions on Arista.

# GENERAL STRIKE

After the boom in punk independent labels it was possible to press 1,000 copies of almost any single in the late 1970s and sell them all through Rough Trade distribution. A friend of ours, Dave Ramsden, owner of a shop called Playback Records in Camden Town, wanted to start a label so Steve Beresford and I went into This Heat's Brixton studio with David Cunningham as engineer/producer and recorded two tracks: "My Body", and "Parts of My Body". For "My Body" I sang words taken from Michel Foucault's book, *Mental Illness and Psychology*. Retrospectively, the two tracks were typical of our strange perspective – romantic soul/disco chords played on toy piano by Steve, grainy, noisy rhythm loops made from my guitar playing by David Cunningham and on the b-side, a reggae rhythm played by Steve on drums, toy piano and euphonium, myself on bass and guitar, with me reading excerpts from Nicolas Slonimsky's *Lexicon of Musical Invective* along with texts on Tourette's Syndrome and torture.

We called the group General Strike, perhaps because the UK experienced widespread industrial action in 1978, or perhaps because Margaret Thatcher's Tory government had been elected in 1979, the beginning of an extremely conservative period in British politics. Along with dismantling labour unions, deregulating financial markets and privatising many industries, this was a government virulently opposed to everything it considered radical, left wing or avant garde. As one of the least popular arts, experimental music suffered badly from cuts in arts funding. Our move into a music that seemed, on the surface at least, to be a form of pop music, looks from the distance of hindsight to be an unconscious reaction to this political shift.

Other recordings followed the General Strike sessions – a Vivien Goldman session produced by John Lydon and Keith Levine with playing by Aswad's George Oban, Robert Wyatt, Vicky Aspinall from The Raincoats and Steve Beresford (my prepared guitar contribution never reached the final mix, though it did give me the opportunity to play with Robert) and then a dub album – *Dub Encounter Chapter III* - by Prince Far I, produced by Adrian Sherwood in 1980, Steve and myself adding incongruous instruments with Ari Up from The Slits dancing around in the studio giving us advice that we studiously ignored and Price Far I hunched up in the control room wrapped in a thick scarf even though Berry Street studio was like a sauna.

During the 1970s I was given cassettes of American exotica, recordings by Les Baxter, Martin Denny, Arthur Lyman, Yma Sumac, Esquivel, Dean Elliot, Ferrante and Teicher, Jack Fascinato and others, compiled by my friends Tom Recchion, Fredrik Nilsen and Kevin Laffey of the Los Angeles Free Music Society. Although this had been popular music in the United States during the 1950s and 60s it was barely known in the UK. Somehow it fitted the mood of the late 1970s and early 80s in which lost experimental pop oddities of the past were being rediscovered, boundaries between musical genres were breaking down and the notion of retro was fusing with electronic futurism. Latin and African music, jazz and funk had also become fashionable, partly due to a quirk of New Romantic style. All of these trends can be heard on the General Strike album, *Danger In Paradise*, but filtered through our own obsessions: doo-wop ballads, songs of outer space by Sun Ra, the fragments of Brian Wilson's unreleased *SMiLE* (beginning to emerge at that time through private cassettes and bootleg records), Chic, Ennio Morricone film scores, the Nigerian juju music of King Sunny Ade and dub records like *King Tubbys Meets Rockers Uptown*, *Pick A Dub* by Keith Hudson, *Africa Must Be Free by 1983 dub*, *East of the River Nile* by Augustus Pablo and *Super Ape* by The Upsetters.

The General Strike single gave us a glimpse of how much potential there was in our twisted pop music. Sessions for the album started in David Cunningham's tiny studio, once a meat storage room, now a bare concrete cell with no seats. Working with David was always unorthodox. For "Sea Hunt" (a tribute both to my original inspiration of twangy guitar instrumentals and to *Sea Hunt*, a television series starring Lloyd Bridges I used to watch when I was 10 or 11 years old) we recorded the underwater noises by splashing about in David's bath. Many tape delays were created by running long loops of 1/4inch recording tape around the room and part of the time during those sessions was spent discussing tape delay, studio echo and records by Lee Perry, Joe Meek, Legendary Masked Surfers, Phil Spector and Brian Wilson. Many of the rhythm tracks were produced by David making short recordings of small mechanical toys from Steve's collection, then looping and processing the tapes. Both Steve and I were using toys, duck and bird calls and small noise-making devices in our improvisations. For the General Strike recordings these became absorbed into an unorthodox way of thinking about pop music but in a circular process the techniques and arrangements that came out of these recording sessions were recycled back into our improvisations. For a brief (extremely brief) period it seemed as if improvised music was being drawn in closer to the musical mainstream.

# LONDON MUSICIANS COLLECTIVE

Before the internet, one of the major problems for marginal musicians trying to survive and connect in a complex major city like London was the lack of communication. In 1975, Steve Beresford invited a number of improvising musicians to his shared flat in the Finchley Road to discuss ways in which we could deal with this issue. Fairly quickly the conversation turned to one of the other major problems, that of finding decent venues in which to play.

Even though the music we were playing had grown into areas that bore little resemblance to the jazz tradition, we still found ourselves playing in rooms above pubs, jazz clubs or the occasional theatre. Whereas the first generation of improvisers – Evan Parker, Derek Bailey, Howard Riley, Tony Oxley, Trevor Watts, Kenny Wheeler, John Stevens and others – were treated with some respect by the more enlightened critics and promoters of the day, the second generation of which I was a part were frequently dismissed as jokers and incompetents. The only answer was to organise ourselves, produce our own press coverage, run our own interviews and develop theories in *Musics* magazine, put on our own concerts, design and print the posters and record and release our own records. Most of all we needed to find a flexible venue. As I wrote in 2000, for *Resonance* magazine: "Performances of music that involved dressing up in odd costumes, bowing balloons, swinging Burmese gongs in wide circles, playing Rachmaninov on a toy piano or scraping stones together in a bucket of water demanded a slightly more sympathetic environment than a brightly lit room above a pub."

Out of this first meeting, the London Musicians Collective (LMC) gradually took shape. The first LMC newsletter was printed in the late summer of 1976. At that time the organisation had no premises out of which to operate and no resources other than the energy and motivation of its members. In tune with the nature of improvisation and the cultural politics of the time, an organisation was founded on collective principles, with an open membership whose responsibility it was to decide policy and initiate activities through attendance at monthly meetings. At the end of 1976, the LMC was active in organising concerts in a variety of London venues.

By December 1977 the membership had grown to more than 100 and premises had been acquired adjacent to a space occupied by the London Filmmakers Coop at 42, Gloucester Avenue, Camden Town. Reached by walking up a metal staircase, it was a big and draughty room once used as a canteen by rail workers. The acoustics weren't good, there were big windows that had to be blocked and we had no separate office so this had to be built from salvaged wood over a weekend by those of us who could use a saw, drill and hammer. Despite its shortcomings as a venue (one of the most serious problems was that it had no toilet, a lack that generated much discussion but no solution over many years), this became the base for an ambitious programme of performances, discussions, workshops, festivals, book fairs and other events.

Once premises had been established as office headquarters and concert venue with Paul Burwell as our volatile but indefatigable secretary, the policy of open membership and collective organisation attracted a strange cross-section of musicians, live arts practitioners, instrument inventors, sound poets, sonic artists and leftfield pop and rock bands, all of them in search for a space in which to work, radical new directions in performance practice and a means of surviving outside the commercial criteria of the music business.

The first LMC members were improvisers. During the 1970s and early 1980s I played in a number of permutations of players who were either members of the collective or associated with it – with Steve Beresford, Paul Burwell, Georgie Born, Sally Potter, Lindsay Cooper, Clive Bell, Nigel Coombes, Roger Smith, Annabel Nicolson, Lol Coxhill, Evan Parker, Christina Munro, Nestor Figueras, John Stevens, Hugh Davies, John Zorn,

Nine (of twenty three issues) of *Musics*

David Toop compiling *Musics*, 1977

Charles K. Noyes, Max Eastley, Frank Perry, Jamie Muir, Toshinori Kondo, Tristan Honsinger and in Derek Bailey's Company concerts.

Some of these were regular and relatively long-lasting ensembles – I played with percussionist Frank Perry at his home every week for a period during the 1970s, for example – and others almost became fixed groups. In the spring of 1982 Steve Beresford and I tried a number of rehearsals with percussionist Jamie Muir. At the same time as playing in rock bands Jamie had been involved in the early free improvisation scene in London, notably playing in Music Improvisation Company with Evan Parker, Derek Bailey, Christine Jeffries and Hugh Davies. In 1972 he joined King Crimson, then left a year later to devote himself to Tibetan Buddhism at Samye Ling monastery in Scotland. In the early 1980s he reappeared. Most of his energies were devoted to painting but he was playing with Derek Bailey in Company and showed some interest in playing with other musicians. Starting as a trio with Steve Beresford on bass, me on guitar and Jamie Muir on a large set of Roto-Tom tuned drums, we expanded into a quintet with ex-King Crimson drummer Michael Giles and Slits guitarist Viv Albertine. The music had great promise – fluid, exotic and unlike anything else at the time - but temperaments, personalities and ambitions in the group turned out to be incompatible, so the experiment was short-lived.

From a musical perspective this seems a pity but successful groups frequently have a core of tension, conflict and contrasting personalities out of which the creativity and inspiration flows (The Beatles being an obvious example). The longevity of a music group is comparable to sustaining marriage or any other partnership over a long period – demanding constant attention to the dynamics and changes that take place over time, showing tolerance and openness but at the same time respecting difference and communicating even when things are going badly. From the beginning my preference has been to work in loose projects and flexible groupings. My duo with Paul Burwell lasted from 1970 until 2000, albeit with long intervening periods in which we chose not to work together. Alterations also lasted for a long time. At the end the music was still good but after too many years of touring in vans we were ready for a break from each other's behavioural and musical foibles.

# 49 AMERICANS

Quite early in its history the founding members of the London Musicians Collective began to notice a growing influx of younger musicians and non-musicians. Even though they were baffled by the arguments that took place in the monthly meetings and struggled to enjoy or understand a lot of the music they heard, the LMC was a place where they could experiment freely without all the problems that went with playing in rock clubs. Many of them were still at school, grown up with punk and pop but allergic to any notions of professionalism or careerism. In rock clubs they risked being bottled off stage but in the LMC they could do what they liked.

One of these younger musicians was Andrew Brenner; at the time he called himself Giblet. With schoolfriends he had recorded an EP under the name of the 49 Americans. Two of those friends – Nag and Bendle of Door and the Window, joined the LMC, followed by Andrew. In his autobiographical account of these times, *Permanent Transience*, Bendle describes his discovery of the LMC in 1978, after reading an article in one of the mainstream music papers about the Los Angeles Free Music Society and the LMC. "We attended a meeting which was very dull," he wrote, but nonetheless they joined. A handwritten message from pianist Akemi Kuniyoshi was pinned to the noticeboard, requesting musicians to share an evening at the LMC, so they put themselves forward. On the night they found themselves playing to a tiny audience of six or seven people, playing unintelligible noise through a guitar amplifier. One of them was Steve Beresford. "He enthused about our noise," wrote Bendle, "and especially about my naive approach to the guitar – don't EVER learn to play it, he directed."

In July 1979, just after finishing his A-level exams at school and preparing to begin architectural studies at university, Andrew Brenner took a trip to the Brighton Festival. His original intention was to see Ivor Cutler perform, then he decided to stay for the whole week. By coincidence, a large number of improvising musicians – Lol Coxhill, Steve Beresford, Paul Burwell, Peter Cusack, Max Eastley, Terry Day and myself – had been booked to play at the festival. The rooms given to us as performance spaces were small and depressing and we decided to play music on the beach. The sun was shining, people were sunbathing and swimming. The beach was a far better spot to play than a gloomy room with a small audience. The question was, what should we play? One of the things we did was to play drone pieces with composer Michael Parsons. Lol Coxhill knew an endless list of popular tunes from all genres and all eras so we set up as a kind of seaside dance band, Lol playing soprano saxophone, Steve working closely with him on euphonium,

WE SHOULD BE MORE IDEAL

Paul on drums, Terry on cello, Peter on guitar and Max and myself both playing bowed African stringed instruments amplified by contact microphones.

Played straight rather than for laughs (not unlike the Portsmouth Sinfonia) it was very English and very odd. Lol and Steve segued through bizarre sequences of tunes ranging from The Kingsmen's "Louie Louie" and Glenn Miller's "American Patrol" to the Sex Pistols' "Anarchy In the UK", Albert Ayler's "Holy Family" and Chubby Checker's "Let's Twist Again" while Max and I (the string section) sawed away on our one-string fiddles. Most people passing by on the beach thought it was absurd, some found it funny, so we repeated the performance, not just during that week but on summer days during the next few years. We gave ourselves a name – The Promenaders – and adopted 'stage names'. Mine was Steve Topp, take from an advert in *Melody Maker* in the 1970s, when my name was misspelled in exactly that way. In 1982 we recorded an album for Y Records and appeared on television dressed in identical white nylon roll-neck sweaters and cheap medallions, simultaneously a high point and low point of this comedic phase.

For much of the 1970s I was far from alone in feeling an intense mental struggle with a cluster of insoluble problems: how to reach bigger audiences without selling out; how to connect better with the small audiences we did have; how to make music that had relevance to the society in which we lived while maintaining its experimental spirit? Much of the exciting music at that time seemed hopelessly polarised — at one extreme so far out on the margins that it was both inaudible and invisible, at the other extreme in thrall to the excesses and naked commercialism of the record business. I loved improvised music and disco but what was worth listening to in between those two poles? There were long discussions about the problem in pubs, after gigs, during *Musics* magazine paste-up sessions and LMC meetings. Notoriously, there were fierce arguments with Scritti Politti and their entourage, who also drank in the Engineer pub, opposite the London Musicians Collective. In their view improvised music was reactionary self-indulgence. Only recently formed, they were on a path to the political strategy of entryism, whereby socialism and the Marxist tradition of continental philosophy would be infiltrated into wider society via seductive, big-selling pop records. I saw one of their early gigs, later formed an uneasy acquaintance with Green Gartside and admired some of their music and its interrogation of pop language but was never fully convinced by the politics. Having said that, those of us on the other side of the argument also failed to come up with effective answers. A long phase of right wing governance was about to dominate political life In the UK and USA and what we now know as neoliberalism was becoming savagely effective in subverting, absorbing or marginalising dissident culture. Finally it seemed as if the best way to get across our music was through humour, by being as silly as possible. After the high seriousness of the early 1970s it came as a relief and somehow fitted the loose exploratory mood of the times.

Like all modernisms, jazz was committed to the idea of progression, of surpassing the ancestors. So Charlie Parker and John Coltrane played faster, more complex solos than Lester Young or Coleman Hawkins while Dizzy Gillespie's harmonic sensibilities were in certain respects more sophisticated than those of Louis Armstrong. Musicians like Albert Ayler had created something of a break in that trajectory, but the first generation improvisers in Europe strongly believed in being as technically adept as their heroes. As an art school musician I had no such ambitions. It was more about the spirit of playing. Much as I loved jazz guitarists like Jim Hall and Wes Montgomery I felt closer to the raw force of Link Wray and Bo Diddley or the R&B minimalism of Jimmy Nolen with James Brown.

Groups like The Door and the Window were grateful for our support but failed to understand why we were so energised by their iconoclastic spirit. None of them knew much or cared about improvised music, let alone jazz or classical but that didn't matter. Their influences came from anarchist bands like Crass and so they shared the LMC strategy of doing everything themselves whether they were equipped to or not, playing musical instruments and singing whether they were competent or not. It felt like a continuation of my own attitude, just more radical and for that reason inspiring.

Andrew Brenner was one of the people who heard The Promenaders play on Brighton beach in 1979. Back in London he was very keen to include us in his group, the 49 Americans. There were some extraordinary performances at the London Musicians Collective, one of which had performers of all ages lined up on chairs in the stage area, all taking turns to play different instruments. We began to record very lo-fi sessions in our various bedrooms and living rooms. One of my favourite of these was with Andrew and Else Watt, an incredibly original and talented drummer who was still at school. We recorded a song called "Beat Up Russians" in my flat, sitting on the floor with my Sony cassette recorder right beside us, Else playing saucepans from the kitchen, me playing prepared guitar through a little amp, Andrew playing bass and singing. Else had the capacity to hit everything in an unpredictable order yet maintain uncannily perfect time. Though she was painfully quiet and shy she also played drums with incredible energy. Listening to her now I think what incredible potential she had and how sad that she took her own life a few years later.

Looking at my diaries of 1980-81 it's easy to see how my time was mainly divided between the Flying Lizards, Alterations, Whirled Music, The Promenaders and the 49 Americans. In July 1981 Alterations invited Fred Frith and Peter Brötzmann to play solos and perform with the group at the LMC; we also toured in England and Europe. Most of these gigs have disappeared from recall but some live recordings ended up on Alterations LPs and a few memory traces linger. On January 28th, 1981, for example, we played in Derby, in the north of England. After the concert we stayed the night at the home of the organiser, a lecturer at Derby College of Further Education, and his wife. We were asked to be as quiet as we could when we arrived at the house because their young children were asleep. In 2012, 32 years later I played in a trio at Cafe Oto with one of those 'children', saxophone player Seymour Wright, now grown up and one of the most radical improvising saxophone players in the world.

In 1979 Steve Beresford and I made a plan to visit New York City at the invitation of guitarist Eugene Chadbourne. At the last minute we were joined by violinist Nigel Coombes. We arrived in Manhattan in the evening and went straight to Giorgio Gomelski's club, Zu Place, where we played with Chadbourne, Polly Bradfield and John Zorn. At one point I looked behind the curtain at the back of the club and was shocked to find that there was no back wall. In my childhood and teenage years I had been saturated with American culture and imagery, particularly through music, television, art and books. Now in New York for the first time I felt I had stepped into a fiction where everything closely matched my imaginings. We went to see Robert Wise's 1949 boxing film noir, *The Set Up*, at the Museum of Modern Art with John Zorn and the harshness of the film seemed more intense for seeing it in a city that felt on the edge of decay and violence. One evening Steve and I were eating in a Japanese restaurant, only to see John Lennon and Yoko Ono come in for a meal. For a few days we visited Woodstock and took part in Karl Berger's Creative Music Foundation Workshop. Most of our very English ideas about improvisation were met with total incomprehension there but I felt the trip was worth it when I was warned about rattlesnakes after taking a walk in the woods.

Then in 1981 Alterations played in East Germany. Peter was the main driver on these trips with Terry taking over the wheel when the fatigue got too much. Usually we would hire a van, load it up with equipment and head for one of the ferry ports like Dover or Harwich. In this case we drove through Germany to Berlin, then crossed into the East via Checkpoint Charlie, border guards checking under the van with a mirror fixed onto a small trolley. All of this felt very romantic in a John le Carré fashion but underlying the strangeness was a lingering suspicion of why it was happening. Free jazz and improvised music seemed to be officially sanctioned at that time, almost the opposite of what we were used to. Years later there were stories of Stasi involvement in these improvisation tours but to what purpose exactly? Perhaps this kind of non-commercial, largely instrumental music was unwittingly drawn into a convoluted plot to suppress any desire to hear supposedly decadent, subversive pop

We played in Peitz, near the Polish border, and in East Berlin. Food and drink were terrible but it was fascinating to be able to walk around in such a secretive place. The cultural mix in our hotel in Berlin was completely different – Chinese, Mongolian, and African countries not usually seen in Europe. We were paid in East marks which had to be spent before our short visas expired, so this involved a hectic rush around a limited number of shops. The record stores were our first stops, buying up piles of birdsong and steam train sounds, Kurt Weill and Hanns Eisler, jazz and blues compilations and some cocktail lounge Cuban piano. Instruments and books were also possible. I bought posters of anti-Nazi photomontages by John Heartfield, a book on the AIZ magazine and three beautifully illustrated volumes on music from Asia, the Middle East and the Americas. The fee wasn't much yet it still felt obscene to be frantically rushing from shop to shop, spending money so randomly. With the clock ticking Steve tried to buy stationery, only to see the sheets of paper counted off one by one at painfully slow speed. Musicians who visited the GDR on a more regular basis looked for ways to circumvent this ruling. Some tried to buy flight tickets to Cuba but the system usually had ways to block their ingenuity.

Groups often come together through circumstances, accident, chance meetings or expediency rather than design. Their success is dependant on many factors: shared goals and compatibility at some level but also points of friction, contrasts, balancing elements, a willingness to take certain weights and the potential to break apart. Alterations was something of a mystery, the group least likely to endure, yet with hindsight it's possible to understand the way our individual character traits complemented each other. Peter was methodical and sensible. He did much of the practical work of finding us gigs, drove us around and maintained a quiet presence around which everybody else careened. As a player he was precise and thoughtful, often stubborn in the way he would stick to an idea but then good humoured when a particularly delicate, intricate guitar pattern he had set up would be obliterated by somebody else.

Terry was a true original in the way he spoke, his philosophy of life and his approach to playing instruments. His drumming was high energy but immensely subtle, particularly his cymbal work. Whichever instruments he picked up – alto saxophone, cello, mandolin or small percussion – sounded like nobody else. In the later stages of Alterations history he began to sing and read his poetry, making the group seem more like a strange rock band rather than an improvising quartet.

Steve was extremely volatile and restless in his playing, exploding with ideas, provoking both us and the audience. The pomposity, pretensions and delusions of classical and rock music were targets, so he would play grandiose improvised piano concertos or flail away at a plastic toy guitar as if he were in a progressive rock band. But as a musician he was brilliant, capable of picking up any suggestion of a chord sequence, a song, style or genre. As for me I felt drawn to disruption at that time, playing piercing sounds on bamboo and plastic flutes or the bass recorder I had bought in East Berlin. I used a metal plectrum on guitar (its hacked lines still visible on the scratchplate of my Fender Telecaster). Valves in my Fender Vibrochamp amplifier had to be changed regularly, blown by the overload of too many distortion pedals played at too high a volume. All of these different temperaments acted as both stimulus and homeostatic regulation within the group. On good nights, ideas flowed in a torrent but no *single* approach was allowed to become dominant. At its worst, Alterations could be noisy, chaotic and self-destructive but at its best the group exemplified the importance in free improvisation of maintaining an exchange balance between competition and cooperation.

# WE KNOW NONSENSE

Although there were LMC meetings, some writing and work on my record label, Quartz, and *Collusion* (the magazine we formed after *Musics*), my main focus was playing music. I had no settled place to live, earned very little money but in many ways my life was relatively uncomplicated, free and happy. Though we didn't live together I spent a lot of time with my partner, Sue Steward, one of the founder editors of *Collusion*. Argumentative as we all were, there was still a closeness between all of us, an atmosphere of mutual support and new ideas. All of the music was pleasurable but my growing involvement with The 49 Americans was completely liberating. There was no sense of self-censorship or any concern about what critics, audience or other musicians might think. One effect of the punk period was to sweep away the progressive rock/jazz fusion philosophy that you had to be a virtuoso instrumentalist to have a career in music. Andrew Brenner and I began a writing partnership, often working closely with Steve Beresford (who had far more knowledge about music theory than either of us). At first everything we did had a nonchalant attitude of making noisy, primitive music, though Andrew's lyrics were consistently funny, intelligent and idiosyncratic in the way they played with language.

>"Hope I be agile so fact don't catch me out
>
>Must I be worried? I yes I no in doubt
>
>Here I example as fumbling through the vague
>
>See me, I'm lying or just pulling your leg."
>
>from "Tendency To Lie", lyrics by Andrew Brenner

Gradually the music grew in sophistication as most of the original participants were replaced by full-time musicians. Even with this transition there was never any danger of it becoming a fixed group – everybody had other commitments. A young singer like Eddie Saunders might appear for a session, record a brilliant take (as he did with "Tendency To Lie", then disappear back into north London's complex scene of postpunk and retro soul groups). By the time we came to record the *We Know Nonsense* album in 1981 we were working in a proper studio, albeit a tiny 8-track off the Euston Road.

Steve and I took over the job of production, which meant that the group was more slick but also more consciously experimental and knowing in its appropriation of pop music genres. Most of the Promenaders took part, contributing their own songs and playing styles, along with other musicians who were drawn in through our network – such as Viv Albertine from The Slits and vocalist/music writer Vivien Goldman. It was as if we could all temporarily step away from our careers, our public faces, to follow a non-professional idealism. Collaboration was more important than technique, the most valued outcome being that the music should be charming, witty, relatively innocent, fun to play and full of genuine emotion.

Although The 49 Americans played live occasionally it was difficult to imagine performing a record like *We Know Nonsense* in a concert setting. I continued to work with Andrew Brenner, particularly in The Japanese American Toy Theatre of London (JATTOL), in which Andrew and Kazuko Hohki, from Frank Chickens, presented stories from famous films and novels – *Rebecca*, James Bond films and *Double Indemnity* – using a small wooden Victorian toy theatre. The characters of these stories were 'acted' by wind-up toys – clockwork Godzillas, plastic vegetables, ninja action dolls, a spinning clown, a walking telephone and walking shoes, a wind-up Buddhist monk and various soft toy animals – while Andrew and Kazuko changed the sets, manipulated the 'actors' and sang songs that linked the narrative. I would play a mix of live and recorded music, using recordings by the Love Unlimited Orchestra, Milt Jackson, Charlie Parker with strings, Martin Denny, Japanese enka and New York hip hop.

The principle was similar to Frank Chickens, Alterations, General Strike and The 49 Americans – a huge number of cultural references, some familiar, some obscure, with absurdity often masking a serious purpose. For a moment JATTOL hovered on the edge of bigger things. A film directed by video artist Akiko Hada – *James Bonk – Matt Blackfinger* – was shown on British television in 1987 and we played a strange mixture of gigs, ranging from cabaret shows to John Peel's birthday party but JATTOL suited the fashion for alternative cabaret, a phase like any other fashion, soon to pass.

In 2002, the 49 Americans records were issued on CD by Seigen Ono on his Saidera Records label, then issued again in 2013 by Staubgold in Europe. Markus Detmer of Staubgold was keen for us to perform live in order to launch the records and so on the 4th June, 2013 at Cafe Oto in London, we came together again, more than thirty years older, to play music that seemed to be from another age, or from our childhood years. New performers were invited in to replace some gaps in the line-up, with some songs performed by players who were not even born when we recorded *We Know Nonsense*. The audience was wildly enthusiastic and we were all happy but a second performance felt less successful. Better to leave it at that point before spontaneity became routine.

Performance with David Bloor and Rie Nakajima, Deptford X, 2017

# A DOUGHNUT IN MY HAND

A few music business people had noticed the productions for Frank Chickens and The 49 Americans. One of them was Geoff Travis from Rough Trade. He introduced Steve and I to a number of artists – David Thomas from Pere Ubu and Annette Peacock among them – in the hope that we could work together. Mostly they were suspicious of producers and not happy with the ideas that Steve and I put forward. The only one of these collaborations to take place was a record with Ivor Cutler, *Privilege*, released in 1983. The first time I saw Ivor Cutler play live was at Watford College of Art in 1969. Two students walked in late and Ivor stopped playing, glared at them and then resumed. Working with him was not unlike that first experience, often hysterically funny but he was also uncompromisingly resistant to most of what we suggested or any intervention to his songs.

Of course he was right to resist – his work was self-sufficient and perfect as it was – but we had been brought in to add some new ideas and both Steve and I could hear ways of making subtle additions to some pieces. One example was Ivor's "Jungle Tips", a series of short, witty narrations that I first heard on John Peel's radio show. I suggested making rainforest sounds with electronically treated flutes and small percussion instruments. Every time I played a sound, even the faintest low note on an alto flute, to demonstrate what I meant to Ivor he would wince and clutch his ears as if he had been attacked.

Awkward as he was it was a real pleasure to work with such a unique individual. Two tracks on that album had a strange afterlife: "Women of the World", originally sung by Linda Hirst with Ivor, myself and Steve on backing vocals, was covered as a hypnotically joyful psychedelic epic by Jim O'Rourke for his Eureka album in 1999. Then a more alarming cover version of "A Doughnut In My Hand" surfaced on YouTube in 2015, as an advertising campaign for Col. Sanders Kentucky Fried Chicken, the Colonel walking along accompanied by Ivor's original song now changed to "A Bucket In My Hand". Ivor and his bicycle could often be spotted at a health food shop called Bumblebee, near Camden Town. He hated all commercialism and anything synthetic. During our recording sessions he had thrown air fresheners out of the toilet window and was notorious for complaining about easy listening music in hotel lifts. How disturbing it was to see such a cantankerous, fiercely unorthodox artist hijacked by capitalism after his death.

Gigs Witnessed: 1981-85

Miles Davis, John Lee Hooker, Bobby Bland, BB King, Fela Anikulapo Kuti, Celia Cruz, Ray Barretto, King Sunny Ade, Alhaji Ayinde Barrister, Drummers Of Burundi, Jon Hassell, The Clark Sisters, Mighty Clouds Of Joy, Machito, Scritti Politti, Daf, Hector Lavoe, Tammy Wynette, Fearless Four, Afrika Bambaataa, Amadu Bansang Jobarteh, Grandmaster Flash, Sequence, Trouble Funk, Chuck Brown And The Soul Searchers, Albert King, Otis Rush, Ornette Coleman, Junior Walker, Gregory Isaacs, James Brown, Luther Vandross, Screamin' Jay Hawkins, Diamanda Galas, Lata Mangeshkar, Big Jay Mcneely, Chet Atkins, Etta James, Slim Gaillard, Sun Ra, Ebenezer Obey, The Last Poets, Tal Farlow, Herbie Hancock, Manu Dibango, Roscoe Mitchell, Run-D.M.C.


My Tastes 1980–85:

Japan, Ghosts
Grace Jones, Warm Leatherette
Afrika Bambaataa, Planet Rock
Grandmaster Flash, Adventures on the Wheels of Steel
Les Baxter, Jewels of the Sea
Jon Hassell Aka/Darbari/Java, Magic Realism
Brian Wilson, Smile Bootlegs
ESG, Moody
Nicolas Collins, Devil's Music
David Sylvian, Brilliant Trees

# *Bird*

A bird is in the loft.
It is morning and all is dark and still.
It taps with wooden feet.
Back
And
Forth.
Taptaptaptaptaptaptaptaptaptap
It is driving me insane.
I am sure it has a problem
And
I want to help the bloody thing.

    But:
It taps with wooden feet.
Back
And
Forth.
Taptaptaptaptaptaptaptaptaptap.
I won't wash tonight because my mother will wake.
That bird is definitely worried
Or trapped, perhaps.

    But:
It taps with wooden feet,
Back
And
Forth.
Taptaptaptaptaptaptaptaptap.
My toes are bare
And my action painting on the wall encircles them;
My sister smiles at me from a photograph
And I am alone except for a voice on the radio

And a bird I wish to hell I could help.

    But:
It taps with wooden feet,
Back
And
Forth.
Taptaptaptaptaptaptaptaptap.
Shut up you bleeder or I'll come up there and pull
    your wings off . . .

                                          D. TOOP

## VII. OCEAN OF SOUND

1966: With a poem called *Bird* I won joint third prize in a national poetry competition run by *Critical Quarterly*. Once divided up, the money amounted to just enough to buy one album. In the *Melody Maker*, a music paper I bought and consumed avidly each week, I had read some time before about a jazz saxophonist named Ornette Coleman. His name had come up in an interview with an older musician, who had described him disparagingly as a 'comic strip.' I liked the sound of that, so took my prize money to the local record store in Waltham Cross. The shop was run by one of the ex-members of The Hunters, a guitar instrumental group associated with Cliff Richard. His knowledge of free jazz being zero he ordered the only Ornette Coleman LP listed in the catalogue. When *This Is Our Music* arrived, it showed four men posed for the front cover, three of them black, one white, all dressed smartly in Italian suits, white shirts and slim ties. This was the Ornette Coleman Quartet: Don Cherry, Ed Blackwell, and Charlie Haden.

The record had been released on Atlantic in 1961. In 1961 I had been learning to play twangy electric guitar by listening to The Shadows. Somehow it seemed impossible that Ornette and his group had been playing their music during the same period of history. I couldn't quite understand the comic strip insult, partly because comic strips didn't seem a bad thing to me. After all, I'd grown up on them. Sure, the music was vivid, witty, and joyous, and sometimes seem to jump from one moment to the next without a smooth connection, like frames in a comic book, but the feeling was deep and serious. I felt my ideas about the nature of music were challenged at some profound level, at a moment in my life when I was asking for them to be challenged.

Partly this was because the music was jazz, sometimes blues, but there seemed no anchor to it. Everybody listened closely and interacted with great speed and skill, but if one of them had faltered for a second, there was nothing to support them, no layer of piano, or supportive wash of cymbal sound or warm bass. Drums, bass, trumpet, saxophone; all worked at the same level of intensity, happy to be exposed and free.

I was told that my achievement as a young poet would be acknowledged at school. The headmaster would mention my prize in morning assembly, before the whole school. I suggested that the record I had bought with my prize money could be played as the teachers walked off the stage to prepare for the morning's lessons. This was agreed. The headmaster spoke of my achievement, to my embarrassment, then began to walk from the hall, leading the rest of the teachers. The first track of *This Is Our Music* is called "Blues Connotation". I can sing it even now. With the sound of the first few notes, the headmaster stopped dead; all the teachers walking behind were forced to stop quickly to avoid bumping into him. This was one of my fondest memories of school.

One weekend I was playing the record at home. A neighbour came round to see my mother. There's a baby crying in the front room, she said. I had to admit that it was my new record. More recently, I read a statement by drummer Shelly Manne, who described Ornette's playing as "like a person crying . . . or a person laughing," so our neighbour was not so far wrong. This is what I learned from the record, the idea that music can go beyond style and fashion to be a genuine expression of human feelings, their sufferings and the necessity of giving form to life's radiance and struggle, even when very few people understand it.

THE MUSIC FILLS THE AIR

To be a musician who writes is fairly unusual. Many musicians are suspicious of writing; many writers start out as musicians but give it up, either too self-critical to continue or acutely aware of the dedication it takes to get anywhere in music. There has always been a struggle to bring these two very different activities together and yet writing and the practice of music both depend upon listening: listening to the 'voice' out of which ideas flow, listening to the sounds of instruments and the world, hearing music as a kind of writing as it emerges into time. What I noticed from early on was that I was analytical about music. Even when I felt overwhelmed by it I was still capable of clear thoughts through which I evaluated what I was hearing.

With some friends at school, probably in 1966, I produced a small magazine called *ONE*. Most of it was poetry and I included my *Bird* poem, but also contributed a review of a blues LP – *Dirty House Blues* by Lightnin' Hopkins (my first published review, uncomfortably dependent on the record's liner notes) and a sequence of two poems about my first experience of Dobell's, along with Collets one of the two main jazz and blues record shops in central London at that time. The poem on the verso page was written in a detached prose style, influenced by what I had read of Alain Robbe-Grillet and the Nouveau Roman trend of depersonalised style; the poem on the recto page interpreted the same subject matter as if written by one of the beat authors like Jack Kerouac:

In the midst of a sweating crowd on a summer's day

Is a hole

The stairs wind, one after another,

Twisting, turning,

And at the foot is a box,

Filled with people,

The Jamaicans,

The Beats,

The Sophisticates,

"Oh, man, it's Slam Stewart,"

"Yeah, baby,"

And the music fills the air,

So full, So very full.

This poem of two styles (to some degree Apollonian and Dionysian) encapsulated one of the dilemmas of my life: the desire to document and analyse, the pull towards writing, then the strong urge to be part of the action, making and doing rather than reflecting and observing. These contradictory impulses have been a source of conflict and unhappiness, yet I also recognise them as the engine that has driven me to map out a zone in which oppositional tactics can be fused together. Even though the seeds of this were sewn in my teenage years, it took many years of practice before I felt able to close the gap between the divided selves of my being – writer and musician – and feel capable of discarding such categories.

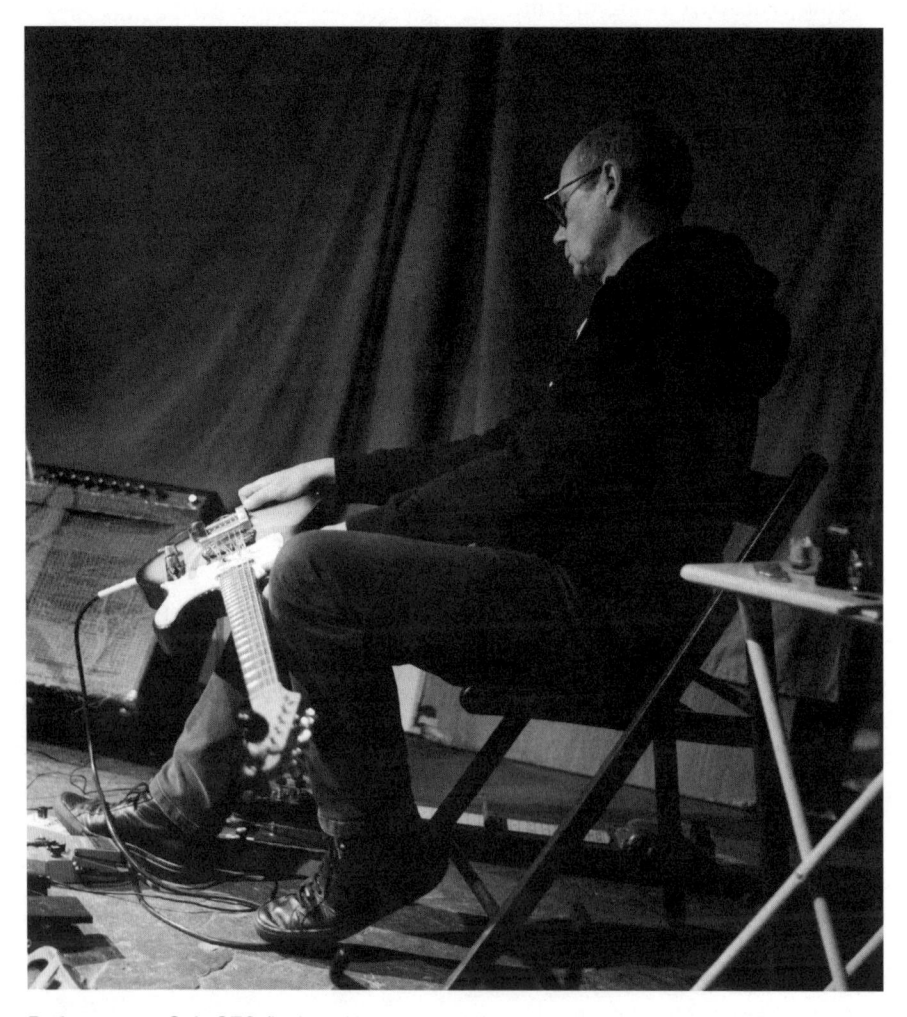

Performance at Cafe OTO (in duo with Ross Lambert)

## SWIMMING AFTER DEATH

Christmas Day 1978, swimming in the transparent waters of the Caribbean Sea off the coast of Venezuela. There is nobody else in sight. Not a strong swimmer at that point in my life I panic in the strange transparency of the water, get into difficulties, save myself from drowning only with a huge amount of thrashing about and an effort of will. Afterwards I feel so foolish that I keep quiet about the incident.

A few days later I was back in London, burnt from the sun but penniless, jobless and homeless. Everything was grey. It was the so-called 'winter of discontent,' a political crisis for the Labour Party that preceded the election of the Conservative Party the following May. Joseph Conrad, among others, implanted the trope of 'heart of darkness' as a spectre of primitivism haunting white Europeans but I felt I was returning to the real heart of darkness. Despite all these bad omens, extreme experiences in Venezuela and Amazonas had stripped away some of my inhibitions, giving me a totally new perspective on life.

The next five years was one of the most active periods of music making of my entire career yet I was growing increasingly unhappy with my financial situation. Now in my thirties, moving from one rented flat to another and never earning enough money to feel secure, I began to question the long-term viability of this life. With the decision to stop publishing *MUSICS* magazine in 1979 a void opened up. Steve Beresford, Sue Steward and I had already discussed possibilities for a new music magazine, one that was broader in its outlook and subject matter. *Collusion* was founded in 1981, with Peter Cusack as the fourth member of the team (though we decided that it wasn't working with Peter after the first issue, a decision that added some tension to Alterations). The central philosophy of the magazine was that no genre or style of music would be rejected. What we were looking for was an interesting approach to writing about music rather than factionalism, fashion or exclusions based on race, gender, ageism or cultural geography.

Many people dismiss this period of the early 1980s as a musical desert but there was a growing openness to the idea of a music scene less restricted by genre and all the old simplifications of binary oppositions: white and black, male and female, rock and soul, mainstream and avant garde. During the time we produced *Collusion* I was living in Tottenham, north London, in a flat above a record shop. The shop – Tiuna Records – had been started by my friend Nestor Figueras in response to the fashion for salsa, though he soon found out that there were not enough Latin music fans in that area. Tottenham had a well-established African-

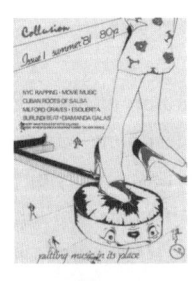

Caribbean community so most of the customers who came in wanted to buy reggae. Once the magazine was properly launched we found an office in central London but the first issue was produced in my flat. This was where Japanese music critic and editor Yuzuru Agi visited me for an interview for his *Rock Magazine*, probably in 1981. It was a strange situation. I had no furniture and no money to buy any so my parents had given me chairs that they were going to throw out. At one point in the interview, Yuzuru Agi asked me, "Do you live here?" Maybe he thought it was a kind of kitsch situation for somebody like me to be living with old people's furniture.

Issue 1 of *Collusion* contained articles about the history of salsa, hip hop in New York, Nigerian praise songs, Diamanda Galas, Simon Frith on Ennio Morricone, Robert Wyatt on listening to short-wave radio, Vivien Goldman with a feminist perspective on silence, Ragnar Johnson on recording sacred flutes in Papua New Guinea, an interview with Milford Graves by Paul Burwell and an essay on teaching music by Dutch pianist Misha Mengelberg. I contributed short pieces on the flamboyant rock 'n' roller, Esquerita, and the convoluted story of the Burundi drummers, whose sound had been appropriated by Bow Wow Wow and Adam and the Ants, among others.

Although I had written for magazines before, *Collusion* gave me an opening to write about subjects of my choice, in my

*Collusion* magazine issues 1 – 5

own style. The subjects of a few articles, in particular, presaged what was to come in my writing of the 1990s and after: *One Step Beyond*, a partly visual essay on the exotica of Martin Denny, Les Baxter, Arthur Lyman and Sun Ra; *Audiodrome* (the title inspired by the title of David Cronenberg's film *Videodrome*), a speculative, almost science fiction piece about hybridity, genre mixing and what we would now call mashups in music history; *Dawn of the Dead: The Mediumship of the Tape Recorder*, which explored the practice of embellishing or reworking tracks made by artists who had died, even to the extent of recording duets between a living artist – Elvis Presley, for example, with a living one such as Linda Ronstadt; *Surfin' (Death Valley) USA*, which traced links between Charles Manson, filmmaker Kenneth Anger and the Beach Boys.

For issue 2, in 1982, I interviewed film director Jeremy Marre about his films on reggae, salsa and the music of Nigeria, Brazil and South Africa. Not long after the interview was published I was approached by Jeremy to work with him on a series he was planning for Channel 4 television, a new channel that began transmission that year. His idea was to use broad themes for each programme – animals, work, love, crime, learning, sport, war, humour and ritual - as a way of understanding global music in more depth. To our disappointment, commissioning editor Andy Park insisted we make a series on music in England, the argument being that everybody looked abroad for inspiration, or focussed on British pop music, whereas amateur and traditional music making in England was ignored.

If we wanted to make the programmes we had no choice but to agree, so instead of travelling to Colombia, India and Jamaica we filmed working men's clubs in coalmining towns in the north of England, ageing comedians, ageing Neapolitan ballad singers competing with teenage beatboxers in Newcastle talent shows, violin playing shepherds in Northumberland, Christmas carol singers in Sheffield pubs, northern soul all-nighters, a Wild-West week at Pontins holiday camp, marching bands in West Bromwich, Hells Angels, reggae sound systems cutting dub plates in suburban London and young British-Asians at all-day Bhangra events. During the course of production I interviewed a motley crew of amateur musicians and semi-forgotten celebrities, including Bert Weedon, Joe Loss, Pete Murray, Tommy Trinder, Harry Secombe and the Nolan Sisters. We also went for a drink with legendary Music Hall comedian Max Wall, hoping that we could interest him in our film on music and comedy. After an hour in his company we both felt too depressed to take it any further. Risking another Beckettian encounter I also introduced Jeremy Marre to Derek Bailey. Derek's interview gave us valuable insights into post-war entertainment, particularly the shadowy milieu of dance halls and the undercurrents of sex and criminality that thrived at their edges.

Jeremy was intrigued by him and in 1992 went on to make a four-part Channel 4 series on improvisation, written and presented by Derek.

Although I quickly came to realise that working in television was not my future I had no cause for complaint. The stories people told were fascinating, the travel gave me insights into places in my own country that I would never normally visit. I was learning about making documentary film and finally earning a living wage. Working on this series – *Chasing Rainbows* – as a writer and interviewer for more than two years transformed my life. By 1984 my relationship with Sue Steward had ended. Living in a small room in short-life housing (houses in poor condition rented out cheaply on a short-term license) I shut myself away in order to write *Rap Attack*. Suddenly I was in a position to save enough money for a deposit on a flat, putting an end to more than fifteen years of moving from place to place. Andrew Brenner and his wife Cathy were also hoping to buy a place to live so we put our money together and bought a house in north London.

The effect of this unexpected relief from insecurity was profound. For one thing I no longer wanted to play music with other people – I was tired of the pressures, conflicts and compromises of playing in bands, tired of the travel and effort involved in playing live gigs. Publishing *Rap Attack* in 1984 didn't make me any money but it opened up other possibilities for a different sort of life. Contributing a monthly music column, essays and interview features for *The Face* was a direct consequence of that decision. In the 1980s, record companies wanted to place stories about their acts in *The Face* and were willing to pay for trips to America. I wrote stories on the Washington, D.C. go-go scene, garage house in New Jersey, Rick Rubin and Def Jam Records, Run DMC, LL Cool J, Kurtis Blow and De La Soul in New York, Nation of Islam hip hop in Chicago (where after a body search I was allowed through the doors of Mosque Maryam, the Nation of Islam headquarters, and elsewhere bumped into Farley Funkin' Keith, creator of the ultra-minimalist "Funkin' With the Drums," the first house record I ever bought). As if in a vivid dream I interviewed Bobby Brown in Florida, Luther Vandross in Atlanta, The Disposable Heroes of Hiphoprisy in San Francisco, Kool and the Gang in Lake Tahoe, the Beastie Boys and the Boo-Yah T.R.I.B.E. in Los Angeles. Often I would tag on extra interviews to the main story, squeezing in meetings with Don Cherry, the Watts Prophets or David Lynch while I was supposed to be doing something else.

Life was also transformed by meeting Kimberley Leston, who moved from a job as designer for *Smash Hits* magazine to being a section editor at *The Face* in 1985. By 1986 we were in a relationship, in 1987 we were married, by 1988 we had moved into a new house and in 1990 our daughter Juliette was born. I hadn't anticipated, let alone planned this turn in my career but suddenly I was a music critic, working for newspapers such as *The Sunday Times* and *The Times* and a bizarre variety of magazines, ranging from a monthly record review column in the women's magazine, *Elle*, to interviews and reviews in *The Wire*. Looking back I interpret this phase as an unconscious effort to change everything about myself. In the process I was creating an unsustainable divided self. I had withdrawn from playing live with Alterations and Whirled Music, cut myself off from many of my old friends and buried much of my personal and creative history. Of course it was doomed to failure, and worse.

After all the collective music making of the past sixteen years I wanted to work alone. The positive qualities that we value in music – its sociality and collaborative nature – had become anathema to me because of the perpetual conflicts and negotiations that came with them. It was a temporary condition but a necessary break if I were to grow. The last album I recorded during this period was *Deadly Weapons*, with Steve Beresford, John Zorn and Tonie Marshall, recorded for the French label, Nato, in 1986. Although the sessions were enjoyable I missed one of them, too tired from other work and too conflicted by my changing direction to fully participate or really know what I wanted to do.

In the dangerous way that comedians often hanker for legitimacy, I also felt a reaction against the comedy that was intrinsic to groups like The Promenaders, Alterations, Frank Chickens, JATTOL and the 49 Americans. Humour would always be a vital part of my music and writing but the balance seemed to have tipped too far away from seriousness. There was the memory of working on my record for Obscure in 1975, a brief period in which I had more control over the materials of the music. That was the atmosphere that was calling me back but with more contemporary tools that allowed self-sufficiency: electronic keyboards, drum machines and the computer.

Whenever I could find the time between journalistic assignments I composed music on the Atari computer, using a German sequencer program called Pro-24 and its successor, Steinberg's Cubase. Of course it was only possible to generate MIDI notes with the sequencer so most of what I did was influenced by acid house and techno. Manchester-based musicians like 808 State and A Guy Called Gerald were starting to release this kind of music in Britain. At one point I recorded two tracks – "Dizzy" and "Out Of Your Mind" – in the hope of getting them released but every offer fell through. Frustrating as this was, in the long run it was probably a good thing. I still have a letter from Rham Records offering a deal. This was the same company that had a big success with A Guy Called Gerald's "Voodoo Ray", then saw all the money disappear when their distributor collapsed.

The main benefit of this period was teaching myself to program techno. This turned out to be a quick route to understanding how to use the computer as a composing tool, a skill that would become increasingly important in the future.

*Ocean of Sound*

Meanwhile my career as a music critic was expanding. Ultimately, frustrations with journalism would lead me to the writing of my second book, *Ocean of Sound* in 1995 – but the materials and techniques that enabled the writing of that book were acquired during this period of intensive freelance work for commercial, mainstream publications. I was often conscious that the readership of newspapers and magazines with large circulation figures had little knowledge or interest in my subjects, so I was forced to find ways of making them more accessible. Though badly paid, music journalism was a job with many advantages – regular publication, free records, frequent travel and the privilege of meeting great musicians.

To be able to have lengthy conversations with Kate Bush, Sam Dees, Janet Jackson, Grandmaster Flash, Tupac Shakur, Robert Wyatt, Milt Jackson and Percy Heath, Björk, Bobby Womack, Lee Konitz, Scott Walker, Ryuichi Sakamoto, Ralf Hütter, Aphex Twin, Abbey Lincoln, La Monte Young, Lou Reed, Ali Akbar Khan, Giorgio Moroder, Sun Ra, Marshall Allen, Diamanda Galás, David Lynch, Derek Bailey, Lemmy, Isaac Hayes, Lee Scratch Perry, Lou Reed, John Barry, Burt Bacharach, Terry Riley, Youssou N'Dour, Gloria Estefan, Arthur Russell, Gilberto Gil, Nusrat Fateh Ali Khan, Arto Lindsay, David Sylvian, Pauline

Oliveros, Haruomi Hosono, Harold Budd, Brian Wilson, Sheila E, Ornette Coleman and Don Cherry gave me privileged insights into the motivations and histories of artists for whom I had either huge admiration or a sort of perverse curiosity. The prevailing interview technique of the time was to attack musicians before they put up their guard, either for their politics, general beliefs, lyrics or perceived musical shortcomings. Amusing as this could be, it rarely generated anything other than defensive counter-attacks so I tried to stay open-minded and listen to what people had to say, whether I was speaking to Professor Griff, Richard Carpenter, Enya, Billy Idol or Bros.

Sometimes these interviews were revelatory, as when I interviewed George Benson for *The Independent* newspaper in 1986. I knew the story of Benson's transition from jazz guitarist to globally successful singer but was unaware of his first career as child star 'Little' George Benson in 1954, managed and then coldly abandoned by Eugene Landy. Others were closer to a nightmare, such as my interview with Brian Wilson for *Arena* magazine. Ever since I first heard Beach Boys songs like "Don't Worry Baby", "The Warmth of the Sun" and "Don't Talk (Put Your Head On My Shoulder)" as a teenager I have been obsessed by Wilson's music, his composing and production skills and his history. To speak to him over the phone in the 1980s would have been easier if I'd known nothing of this legacy. As it was I struggled with his oblique, reluctant and sometimes bizarre answers to my questions, fully aware that the same Eugene Landy was in the background, by now an unscrupulous psychiatrist, manipulating Wilson's life and waiting to cut off our interview when the going got too tough. Human stories and the work of making music fascinated me. I felt compassion for the turbulent, damaged lives of those who had suffered at the hands of this often brutal business but whose achievements were transformative. The downside, however, was that I felt I was drowning in the music and lives of others, to the extent that I barely knew who I was as a musician any more.

The image of an ocean of sound was not a sudden revelation; it had to grow from somewhere. Partly it was seeded by the radio programmes I made for the BBC in the early 1970s and by the cassette mix-tapes I made from BBC sound archive recordings, music recorded from the radio, field recordings and improvisation rehearsals; partly it came from my record label, Quartz Records. Quartz (named after the quartz crystals once used by Aranda people of Central Australia when initiating a shaman) was intended as a statement about the divisions that are erected between different types of music: pop, classical, traditional, avant garde, world, amateur, professional and so on.

There is a closeness between certain types of experimental music and traditional global musics. My label was launched in 1979 as an affirmation of that closeness, so I released recordings of sacred flute music from Papua New Guinea, recorded by Ragnar Johnson, and my own recording of Yanomami shamanism from Amazonas, alongside records by Alterations, Whirled Music, Frank Perry and the duo of myself and Paul Burwell. As I had very little money when I started the label I was helped financially by Robert Wyatt and Evan Parker, both of whom believed in this more global, holistic view of music.

Quartz Records lasted only a short time – the financial and administrative pressures were too much for me at that time, particularly since I was hopeless as a businessman. Sales were barely sufficient to cover the production costs of the next record, let alone pay anybody. It was easy to launch an independent label if you could find enough money for pressings and cover printing but much more difficult to keep up the momentum. Independent labels had always been important to the record business but during the 1970s they became indispensable. This was either because they created outlets for music that had no possibility of mainstream support (hence, improvised music labels like Incus, FMP, ICP and Bead) or, like Rough Trade, because they offered an opening for musicians who wanted to bypass the big record companies with their A&R men, outdated attitudes and punitive economics.

My first record as an improviser – *Cholagogues* – was released on Bead Records. Bead was started in 1975 by Peter Cusack and the members of Chamberpot, a quartet of second generation improvisers. Peter, in particular, believed in collective action and do-it-yourself publishing so the label became open to any improviser who could afford production costs. The advantage of this arrangement was that musicians concentrated their efforts on their own release. As a result, the label released a sizeable catalogue of LPs, cassettes and CDs and was still active, through violinist Phil Wachsmann, in 2017.

By contrast, running a record label alone was a burden. Income from distributors was barely paying my rent, let alone building up funds to release new material, advertise, pay an assistant or even think about royalty payments. My dream of being able to release music according to my specialist vision had been fulfilled but the reality of keeping it going was too remote from what I actually wanted to do with my life. Nevertheless, I learned important lessons from the experience. One of these was the necessity of sketching out some sort of context in order for listeners to be able to engage with music that was unfamiliar and strange to them. From the beginning my writing was founded in making links (albeit often crudely) but from constant practice as a music critic I became more adept in this approach.

# AETHER TALK

One of my journalistic assignments for *The Face* was an ambient music festival at the Melkweg in Amsterdam, October 1993. The rise of ambient music gave me the idea that I could structure a book around its popularity. It was a relatively easy pitch to present to a publisher. The Orb's "Blue Room" had been a top-ten hit in the UK in 1993 (with Steve Hillage playing my Emmons pedal steel guitar on the track) so there was a general awareness of this new phase of ambient. I had also interviewed Aphex Twin twice, once when he was still a student and then a little later, when his notoriety as armoured scout car owner and lucid dreamer had begun to coalesce into myth. Suddenly it became clear that contemporary electronic ambient music of this kind could function as a gateway to other examples of immersive music from the twentieth century and earlier, with a symbolic starting point of Claude Debussy hearing Javanese gamelan at the Paris Exposition of 1889.

The problem was how to find time to write this book. My marriage was falling apart but I still had to find the money to support a family. The book advance I was offered by Serpent's Tail was too small to allow me to give up journalism. Ironically it was ambient music and journalism that supplied the answer. I had been commissioned to write hypertext material for a CD-i release (CD-i was a short-lived interactive multimedia system marketed by Philips in 1992) for a band called The Shamen. The digital media company commissioning the work went bankrupt before paying me but then Virgin bought them and paid my fee in one lump sum. This gave me enough money to ignore phone calls for three months and do very little other than write the book.

Serious problems were changing the course of my life. I had been trying to keep our family together for three years but in the spring of 1994, Kimberley decided to move out of our house, taking Juliette with her. The weight of failure was unbearably heavy, exacerbated by the anguish and loneliness I felt at being separated from my daughter. I started to write, driven by the will to survive, perhaps knowing that this could only be achieved by channelling any remaining trace of optimism about life and music into a book. On proof reading *Ocean of Sound* for its re-publication in 2018 I recognised a strong sense of melancholy in the writing, counterbalanced by the necessary optimism of being a father, an author and a musician.

*Aether Talk* was the working title I chose, reflecting the globalisation of music since the late nineteenth century and a recent growth in high-speed global

Performance drawing

communications. I wrote in almost total isolation, occasionally meeting a few friends, sometimes drinking heavily, looking after Juliette every Friday and Saturday, attending one of the new ambient clubs like the Big Chill or Robin 'Scanner' Rimbaud's Electronic Lounge, a regular fixture every week at the ICA in central London. At least at Robin's event I could maintain some sense of sociability, meet people involved in the ambient and electronica scene (that was where I met Ryoji Ikeda for the first time, as he walked around the club with a digital video camera asking people like me to speak about silence for one minute) and find some respite from my inner turmoil.

I wrote almost in a state of trance, often late into the night (sometimes drunk) and relentlessly, unable to bear the intrusion of other thoughts, particularly those in which I prophesied a bleak future for myself. Imagining the future of music was inspiring but my own prospects seemed headed for an outcome in which everybody would suffer irrevocably. As it transpired, what was to come would be far worse than anything I could envisage at the time. If I had known that then the book would have been impossible. Because of my vulnerable emotional state the style was more personal than anything I had produced before and the writing went quickly. I seemed to be in the grip of obsession, trying to obscure from myself a dread of having lost everything. In small gaps between working on the book I was producing a record (*Burn Baby Burn* by The Otherside, 1995) for singer Musa Kalamulah, a friend from Sierra Leone. He was confident that my marriage could be repaired but I felt an overpowering sense of unease at what I saw and what I surmised. Early in February we finished the album. I had also finished the book in that same week and delivered the manuscript to my publisher. On the Friday Kimberley asked me to look after Juliette for the coming week. She was painfully thin, suffering panic attacks and clearly in great distress. Friends were looking after her, she was seeing a doctor and a psychiatrist but I felt disturbed and anxious all weekend.

Then, late afternoon on Monday, February 6th, I answered the doorbell to find a policeman standing in front of me. He had been given an awful task: to break the news to me that Kimberley had taken her life the previous night. She was beautiful, funny, vivacious, an incredibly talented writer, editor and designer with a great future ahead of her; her loss to depression was shattering for a wide circle of family, friends, neighbours, colleagues and acquaintances. What followed was vivid, chaotic and unbearable to recall. More important than my own overwhelming grief was the urgency of what was ahead. Suddenly I was a single parent with a grieving child. Faced with supporting us both alone I could only cope by dealing with each task as it arose. Juliette's fifth birthday was seven days away so I had to organise her party and Kimberley's funeral simultaneously. Friends, neighbours and relations gathered round to help and so we survived, gradually establishing a new life in which Juliette's needs were cared for, the bills were paid and somehow I managed to work, write, record music, even travel a little.

The shock was traumatic but three months later my father died, then two months after that Juliette and I were burgled in the night. I felt my feet dragging through a violent, haunted landscape. Only when you become a suicide survivor do you realise how many others surround you: close friends and work colleagues who had never mentioned a brother, father, mother or grandfather taking their own life. These stories can be humbling. Often I felt I should just shut up and get on with it. Stubborn, slow and insistent, grieving's time span is totally opposed to the hype-and-discard pace that motors our lives. The news was full of Rwanda and Bosnia, the earthquake in Kobe; there would be child abductions, terror diseases, the Rosemary West trial, more carnage in Liberia and Burundi, IRA bombings, the Oklahoma City bombing, mass murder in Dunblane and Tasmania. Slowly, as I learned to turn my gaze to horrors in the outside world, my problems, along with Juliette's, began to fall into perspective.

Compounding the guilt and anger that follow a suicide is its unfathomable mystery. In the end we can only accept another person's right to choose to die. In Kore-eda Hirokazu's film, *Maborosi*, a young Japanese woman is haunted by the incomprehensibility of her first husband's suicide. Her new husband tells her about his father fishing and seeing a strange light at sea, the Maborosi, and feeling drawn to it. "The sea can be beguiling," he says. "Maybe we all experience the attraction of the Maborosi at some time in our lives."

I talked at length with my anthropologist friend, Ragnar Johnson, who told me of Australian Aboriginal rituals which sanctioned anger and aggression in bereavement: spirits haunting the resting place of the dead were attacked with spears. Our own bereavement rituals are models of self-control, bounded by taboos, silences and terrors disguised as respect, pursued by unspoken (sometimes spoken) expectations that life should return to normal as soon as possible. During this time I wrote texts which articulated those inchoate feelings that swirled within me and around me, envisaging them in musical settings. "Ceremony Viewed Through Iron Slit" was one of them, recorded in 1997 for my *Spirit World* album: "I saw six creatures in a circle, features barely visible. They passed a container round, refilling it and drinking more, groaning as the liquid spilled from the corners of their mouths, running like blood in the gloom, soaking their naked torsos, darkening the floor, spreading stains . . ." In Bern, Switzerland, I read an expanded version of this text during a solo performance for a live radio broadcast:

"We moved on, crossing rivers that looked like boiling liquid mud rather than water. Near-human creatures hung from the branches of trees, sometimes dropping to the ground in front of us. The holes driven into the earth by their death falls seemed bottomless, though we could hear the creatures calling, imploring us to follow them into the darkness.

"At the edge of a plain of white grass we stumbled into a deep pool of urine. A tortoise floated on the surface. My child picked the dead creature from the pool and peeled away the outer skin of its shell in a single piece. Underneath, the carapace had become spongy and was easily broken into segments. Inside was nothing but a bag.

"I was tired. I needed water. The sounds I heard were muffled: static electricity spiking through cotton wool; mist gathering on a mirror; a flutter of breath from beneath floorboards; the howling of ghosts. In recurring nightmares I saw corpses stuffed into cupboards, shadowed bodies hidden in corners, dismembered limbs buried by me, in sleep. In my easier dreams I saw blood spurting like fire, heads wrapped in cloth. My child dreamed of walking through a door with holes in it. Feeling half dead in the world of people, I came to life in the quiet of night."

"A bit morbid," the organiser commented afterwards.

# SOLO

The triviality of so much music journalism was unthinkable now but other possibilities opened up. After an evening of deep conversation and drinking at my house, Tony Herrington, editor of *The Wire*, offered me the opportunity to release a solo album on a new label the magazine was planning. This was an incredible opportunity to make my first real solo album after a gap of twenty years since recording one side solo for Obscure Records. How could I do it? How could I not do it? The challenges were immense. Somehow I had to find a way to write the material (mostly working on my Atari computer at night) yet at the same time raise my daughter and earn a living through freelance writing and whatever else came along. Then I had to find a way to record within the budget given to me. My answer to that was to book five days in a studio. Juliette stayed with her grandmother and every day I would go into the studio with a strict plan, work as hard as I could to stick to schedule, always recording overdubs in one take, and make sure that all the tracks were ready for mixing on the last day. This kind of urgency was typical of the way music used to be recorded, when artists like Fats Domino, James Brown or John Coltrane would record an album in a day. It was nerve-wracking to do it in this way but the pressure added to the emotional mood of the music.

I had a friend at Virgin Records, Simon Hopkins, and went to him to ask for advice about releasing a compilation CD to accompany my forthcoming book. What I was hoping was that he would suggest some small record companies that might be interested in such an unorthodox collection of music, everything from Aphex Twin, My Bloody Valentine and Miles Davis to howler monkeys, the World Soundscape Project, Music Improvisation Company and Pauline Oliveros. To my surprise he said that Virgin could release it. We worked quickly to make sure all of these three releases were coordinated and so the book, now titled *Ocean of Sound*, and the solo album, *Screen Ceremonies*, were released in November of that year with the double CD, *Ocean of Sound*, released in January 1996. So extreme was my state of mind at that time that I experienced this releasing of words and music into the world as an act of defiance against uncontrollable forces that threatened to crush me and my child.

## SUGAR AND POISON

The next few years had an extraordinary, contradictory character: sad, anxious, desperate and incredibly hard yet also joyful, expansive and intensely creative. It was moving to witness the bonds of community strengthen as a positive consequence of tragedy. My immediate energies were focussed on Juliette's school work, health and friendships, her happiness and her emotional recovery, along with maintaining daily work and projects that earned money. This had to be balanced with attending to my own grief and guilt. Making music was vital to my recovery, a form of catharsis and solace. I was fortunate to have supportive friends but it was also important to my self-confidence and hopefulness that *Ocean of Sound* and its companion CD turned out to be relatively successful after their publication.

Many things happened quickly. On March 11th Max Eastley and I were booked to perform in the Purcell Room, one of London's Southbank concert halls. The concert was to be recorded for broadcast on BBC Radio 3 and we had planned to perform most of the tracks of our *Buried Dreams* album using a huge range of equipment including Max's complex sound sculptures and my computer. Coming so soon after the shock of Kimberley's suicide this was a daunting proposition but I played in a dream state, too numb to be nervous.

In those first months of grieving I wrote articles about Arthur Russell, Terry Riley, John Barry, Chris Isaak, Goldie, Main, Jah Wobble, M-People, D'Angelo and the Master Musicians of Jajouka, drawing on experience, even habit, in order to be able to function. An interview with Chris Isaak turned into a near-comic two-hander out of Beckett or Pinter, him morose about the end of a love affair, me almost paralysed with grief, the pair of us lapsing into heavy silences that seemed mutually acceptable though not conducive to good copy. I was also writing a monthly column for *The Wire*, though with my life so bound up in parenthood it was difficult to know what I could say that would have relevance to a *Wire* reader. "*Wire* column from nothing, about not much," I wrote in my diary.

Simon Hopkins commissioned me to curate more compilation CDs for Virgin Records and so I began an *Ocean of Sound* series (with cover artwork on three of them by the same artist – Yoshihiro Furukawa – I commissioned for the *Screen Ceremonies* cover): *Crooning On Venus*, devoted to strange songs; *Booming On Pluto*, a collection of electro and electronic tracks; *Guitars On Mars*, which ranged from Holger Czukay and Spiritualized to John Lee Hooker and Captain Beefheart; *Sugar and Poison*, which was mainly soul ballads from the 1970s onwards, sung by artists ranging from O.V. Wright to Betty Everett. Of all of these compilations, it was *Sugar and Poison* that caused the most puzzlement. Intellectuals and experimental music fans rarely admit to liking soul ballads, assuming them to be escapist, excessively romantic and often sexist. For me, these were some of the most remarkable singers in any genre of music. The music was deeply moving, adventurous and beautifully performed. Then and now, soul ballads were at the heart of my musical tastes.

# EXOTICA

Fatigue, lethargy, anger, remorse, guilt, sadness. Often I had nightmares about dead people buried in our garden, fearful they might be discovered, either now or in the future (a dream that recurs to this day, though with less and less frequency). "Then my own tragedy fell out of the sky," I wrote in my third book, *Exotica*, "its mysteries as impossible to unravel as any other event of its kind." Yet like so many other suicide survivors, inner forces compelled me to attempt that unravelling. Then in my mid-forties I found it tough to maintain the double life of being a lone parent, feeling inadequate to the task and working long hours in many different jobs, none of them secure. What motivated me was unconditional love for my child and the almost unbearable compassion I felt for her emotional pain and loss.

One day I had to take Juliette to see a doctor. He enquired why it was me bringing her to the doctor's surgery and not her mother. I told him our history. "You're very brave," he said, then adding, "but I suppose you've got no choice." It was a typical reaction and not a particularly accurate reflection of my feelings yet it did make me think about the way we become committed to situations, often inadvertently, and then create images of escape to compensate.

Exotica fascinated me for this reason. Ever since I was given cassettes of exotic music by my friends in the Los Angeles Music Society I had been thinking about a book on the subject. I also wanted to extend the writing style of *Ocean of Sound* into an ambiguous area between fact and fiction. Exotica was a fiction in itself, a weird utopian synthesis of many global musics. It invited a hallucinatory approach in which the reader was perpetually unsure of what was real, what was invented.

The fragmented structure of *Exotica* was shaped by my state of mind and the demanding conditions of life at that time. Often I would write in the evening, Juliette on the floor in my work room, playing with her toys, drawing and reading books before bed time. The origins of the book lay in music by Les Baxter, Martin Denny, Arthur Lyman, Elisabeth Waldo and the other American composers of the 1950s-60s who invented this strange genre based on fantasy depictions of other cultures and non-existent lands. I wanted to propose a more inclusive view of exotica that could encompass Ornette Coleman, Haruomi Hosono, Josephine Baker, Burt Bacharach, Bill Laswell, Harry Smith, Sun Ra, Eden Ahbez and the Beach Boys, interspersing the music with references to fiction by Joseph Conrad. To be immersed in this curious, half-hidden world of musical eccentrics and visionaries was a welcome distraction, while the writing itself was cathartic, a way of articulating my anguish by speaking openly or through thinly veiled stories. The book ended with a quote from Conrad's novel, *An Outcast of the Islands*: "The discovery of new values in life is a very chaotic experience; there is a tremendous amount of jostling and confusion and a momentary feeling of darkness. I let my spirit float supine over that chaos." Conrad's words might have been describing the turbulence of my existence at the time, though I was still not capable of letting my spirit float over the chaos.

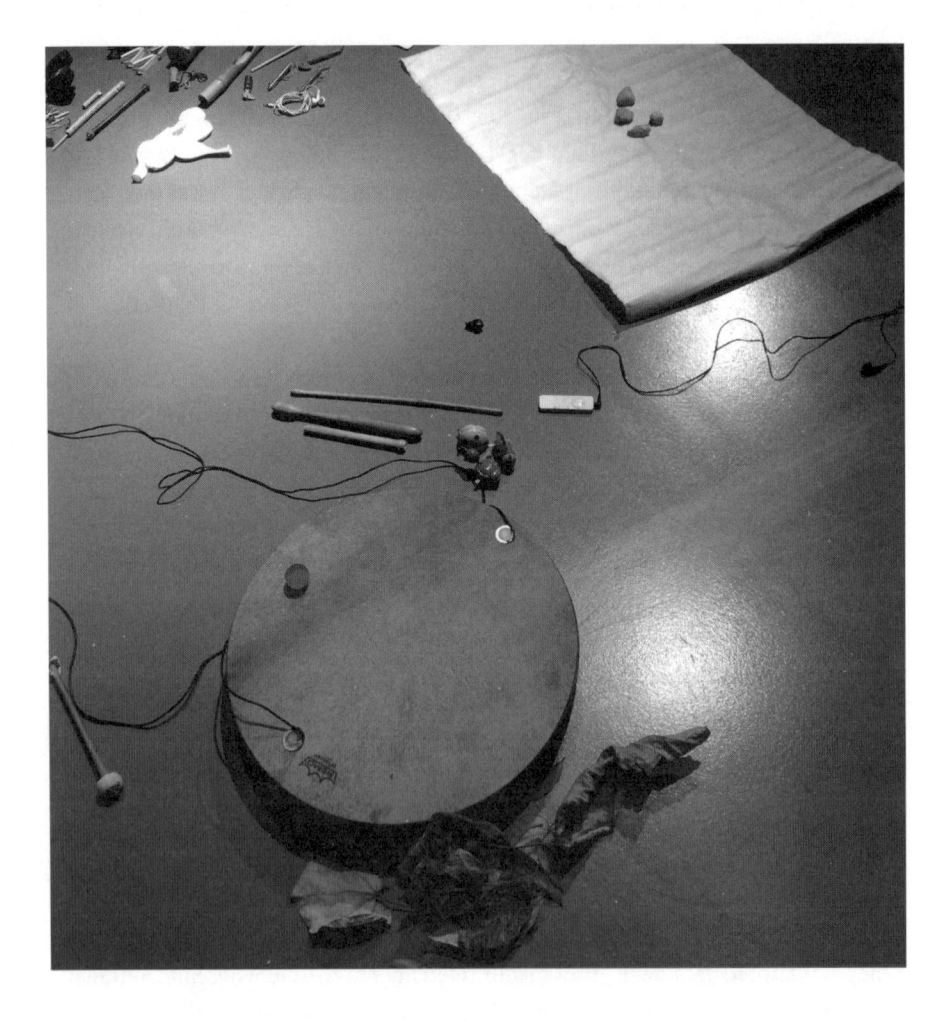

Contact microphones on drums, performance in Hong Kong

## ACQUA MATRIX

At the same time as writing *Exotica* I was composing music for *Acqua Matrix*. This was the name given to a spectacular outdoor show of sound, light, projections, inflatable and mechanical structures and fireworks that would end every night of Lisbon Expo '98 between May to September of that year. João Paulo Feliciano came from Portugal to explain the concept of the project, hoping to persuade me to take part. Given my restricted and difficult circumstances, the prospect of creating a soundtrack for such a huge event as part of a large multinational team was terrifying but I couldn't afford to be fainthearted about it. The planning meetings, often held in out-of-season Portuguese beach resorts, were entertaining. I particularly enjoyed observing Mark Fisher, stage set designer for Rolling Stones, U2 and Pink Floyd tours, sitting in silence through convoluted, unproductive arguments between the Portuguese creative group and the French production team. Mark would say nothing, sketching out a design in his notebook for one of his clients, Janet Jackson maybe, then finally speak up with a pithy comment that turned out to be the only useful statement anybody had voiced out loud for the entire afternoon. Finally I learned not to be afraid of scale. Simply create the music and the amplification would do the rest. It was a remarkable feeling to take Juliette to the opening night in Lisbon, to see tens of thousands of people gathered to hear music that months before at home I had composed on my computer as she watched television or played with her friends.

After *Screen Ceremonies* I was also recording new solo albums on a regular basis – *Pink Noir* in 1996, *Spirit World* in 1997, *Museum of Fruit* and *Hot Pants Idol* in 1999, then *Mondophrenetic* in 2000, *Black Chamber* in 2003 and *Sound Body* in 2006. A surge of creative energy offered some compensation for the desperate psychic lows to which I so often succumbed.

Previously there was a split between writing and music; now they were growing closer, both in my thoughts and in the technological means through which they were realised. Increasingly, everything happened in the computer. This was one reason why my first solo CD was called *Screen Ceremonies*. If writing was a projection of inner thought, then music was an externalisation of all those ineffable feelings, sensations and mental images that resist verbalisation. All of my life I wanted to live in a more magical universe – not the pragmatic life of compromise, emotional repression, financial prudence and conservatism of my parents (though some of those virtues I have come to admire in later life) – but a life more attuned to the strangeness of natural phenomena and the outer limits of being human. I had made my own compromises but now, at great cost to myself and others, I was appreciably closer to that state, partly through my heightened emotional condition and the ongoing consequences of grief but also because I now felt more free. The worst had happened; why hold back?

All of these albums were recorded quickly, usually within a week or so. Maybe once in a year it was possible to arrange for Juliette to stay with a friend or relative for a period of five days and so I would prepare meticulously, composing pieces in the computer, programming new sounds, planning each day of recording and organising guest players for specific days and times. Tracks came together through a convergence of the virtual with the physical: working, for example, with a pre-existing recording by Jon Hassell and bassist Dan Schwartz, adding live tablas played by Talvin Singh in one session, MIDI violin by Kaffe Matthews on another, finishing it off myself with percussion and a recording of night insects I made in Bali during a trip there with Kimberley, then naming it "Slow Loris Versus Poison Snails", partly in hommage to Chinese wuxia and Japanese chambara movies, partly as a reference to the way I had always taken inspiration from animal movement and sounds. My maxim for producing music followed the philosophy of Hong Kong film director Ringo Lam: "No money, no time; just do it."

By 1998 the strain of this was getting too much. Commissioned to make an album on the theme of architecture and music for New York label Caipirinha I decided to record at home and asked composer Paul Schutze to help me with the technical aspects of recording. After researching examples of contemporary architecture I decided to base my music on Itsuko Hasegawa's Museum of Fruit, a group of three glass and steel domes that squat in the landscape of Yamanashi like giant hi-tech pangolins, turtles, seed pods or sleeping snails. This was exactly what attracted me to Ms Hasegawa's work, a fusion of modernist computer design inspired by organic growth. I liked her statements: "Today, utopia can only be realised in fictional form," ". . . a new form of nature where devices enable one to hear the strange music of the universe," and her writing about the necessity of balancing digitisation with non-digital communication methods, ". . . because we feel it is necessary to bring in raw energy and the smell of human life . . ." She also spoke about "soft architecture", which could be a description of music.

These mirrored my own thoughts on making music in the encroaching digital age. Human beings were still noisy, sexual, messy, voracious beings, still part of the physical world, moving in space, making and destroying, eating and excreting, and yet doors were opening into a new virtual world, seemingly clean, pure, precise, without dimension or physical presence. How could I make music that reflected those two realities simultaneously? For that reason the album was recorded simply onto a digital format, using prepared bass guitar, flutes, prepared guitar and some electronic keyboards. As always, I tried to record everything in one take to retain spontaneity and a sense of risk. I also asked electronic music composer and ecologist Michael Prime for some of his recordings of fruit, made by transmuting variations of bioelectrical fields emitted by apples and bananas into electronic sound using oscillators, sounds that were indeed "the strange music of the universe."

In 2000, another friend, Neill MacColl, engineered part of the next album in his home studio, two houses away from mine. As part of an extensive musical dynasty that included his parents, Peggy Segger and Ewan MacColl, his grandparents, Ruth Porter Crawford and Charles Seeger, uncles Mike and Pete Seeger, siblings Kirsty and Calum and latterly his own sons, Neill had a lot to live up to. In part, he dealt with it by being open minded about music and working across a spectrum that ranged from contemporary folk to music for television. At the time he was married to writer Justine Picardie and our families were close. Even though our respective approaches and backgrounds could hardly have been more different, on the few occasions when we did work together it seemed to flow easily as a logical extension of all the other aspects of our lives. The album he engineered was *Needle In the Groove*, a collaboration with science fiction novelist Jeff Noon. My audio 'version' of his novel of the same title, with Noon reading and half-singing his own words, was released by Robin Rimbaud's Sulphur label on the same day as the book. This was another example of the convergence of words and sound, a search for intensities that could retain the physical and emotional impact of music yet at the same time evoke the complex imagery, characters and imaginative spaces of fiction. As with film, it presented the challenge of bringing a book to life, so that it existed not just in the silence of the reader's mind but as voices within a moving landscape of sound.

For most of my life I had been a night person. As a single parent this was no longer possible. Juliette suffered from acute insomnia after her mother's death. By the time she was asleep, often late in the evening for a child of her age, I was too exhausted to work, knowing that I had to be up early to get her ready for school. The nocturnal atmosphere of much of my music and writing had to be somehow conjured up in the light of daytime. This was why I liked recording studios with their lack of daylight, their sense of suspended time, but as my ideas became more complex I found it increasingly difficult to communicate what I wanted to recording engineers.

*Needle In the Groove* was a transitional record in this sense. In 2000 I bought a computer exclusively for music (5GB of memory!) and Emagic Logic software. For better or worse I would take over control of all aspects of the production of my music, working at home in my own time. Way back in 1971 when I first experimented with my cheap mono cassette recorder this was what I dreamed about. Then I overdubbed tracks of guitar, flutes, clarinet, a vacuum cleaner and other instruments by recording, then playing back on another machine, recording new overdubs each time and in the process accumulating tape hiss and noise. Music was a way of bringing into being a parallel world, as if there was another world that could be entered simply by listening. I could invite people in to the making of this world – guest musicians for my solo albums included Talvin Singh, Max Eastley, Jon Hassell, Amelia Kuni, Evan Parker, Robert Hampson, Scanner, Toshinori Kondo, Bill Laswell, Tom Recchion, John Oswald, Kaffe Matthews, Rhys Chatham, Sarah Peebles and Paul Burwell – but the world was formed primarily in my imagination.

The first record I made in my own studio (called The Bathosphere, in memory of my Obscure record) was *37$^{th}$ Floor At Sunset: Music For Mondophrenetic*, released by Sub Rosa in 2000. Mondophrenetic was a multimedia installation created in Brussels by producer Rony Vissers, artist/photographer Els Opsomer and writer/theorist Herman Asselbergs. The central focus of the work was the nature of globalisation at the beginning of the 21$^{st}$ century, represented by Els Opsomer's photographs of high rise buildings, shot in many locations around the world.

For me, the biggest challenge was to make music that could accommodate the interactive aspect of the work. A gallery visitor could control the sequence and timings of what they heard and saw by using a computer mouse. This meant that my music should have no clearly defined beginning or end. It should make sense even when accessed randomly.

The second challenge was to create a kind of background music that would also work in its own right, an ambient music that was worth listening to. I wanted to create atmospheres suggestive of buildings as living organisms (a continuation of the researches into Itsuko Hasegawa's practice) without reducing the soundtrack to a catalogue of sound effects. In his novel, *Highrise*, J.G. Ballard described the subtle relationship of an apartment block's nervous system to the disintegrating ecology of the mini-society of its inhabitants. Apartment blocks look much the same, whether in China or the suburbs of Paris, yet the lives within them may be radically different. The sounds of lift shafts, ventilation and heating systems, the murmurs of human activity, radio and television, have a universality to them which becomes distinct only in close up. Thinking of cargo cults and security procedures, empty malls and broken computer connections, I also wanted to create music that suggested globalism and the absorption of global cultures into an environment of signs, a kind of easy listening or aetherial mix that is detached from any recognisable source other than the perpetual movement of hybridised culture in the 21$^{st}$ century. Information is a kind of architecture, though like music, its walls are intangible, an ocean of sound. We barely knew it, but this was our future.

Gigs Witnessed 1987–95:

Madonna, Public Enemy, Eric B & Rakim, LL Cool J, Biosphere, Ice Cube, Don Cherry, The Orb, Barry White, Gilberto Gil, Ryuichi Sakamoto, Company, Chris And Cosey, Björk, Caetano Veloso, Tom Zé, Spiritualized, Beastie Boys, Horace Silver, David Sylvian, Beach Boys, Aphex Twin, Luther Vandross, Zapp, Cameo, Force MD's, O'Jays, Bobby Womack, 24-7 Spyz, Daniel Lanois, Djavan, John Zorn, Spandau Ballet, Chuck Brown, Guy, Salif Keita, Kraftwerk


My Tastes 1987–95:

Prince, Revolution/Parade
Phuture, Acid Tracks
Mr Fingers, Washing Machine
Beastie Boys, Paul's Boutique
Nitro Deluxe, Let's Get Brutal
LFO, LFO
Kate Bush, The Sensual World

## VIII. SONIC BOOM

The first exhibition I curated was rubbish, literally rubbish. It was probably 1966, with my friend Peter Sinclaire. We were given permission to create an exhibition for a small exhibition space in the Broxbourne Grammar School dining room. Heavily influenced at the time by textural artists like Jean Dubuffet, Antoni Tàpies, Alberto Burri, Robert Rauschenberg, John Latham and the Destruction In Art Symposium I suggested that we collect interesting objects from the streets, discarded rubbish such as a corrugated rubber tube, and then mount them in the display cabinets as if they were precious artefacts or sculptures.

Of course there was outrage – all the usual reactions like "Anybody could do that" and "That's not art". It was simple, both as a provocative exhibition and a concept of recycling. This was a formative moment for me but as my thinking moved into the field of sound and listening so the difficulties of showing work increased. Orthodoxies of presentation, whether in music, art or literature, were extremely limiting and so it became important to think about these formats of presentation. How could they be changed? If there was no change in the presentation format then could the work be considered truly experimental?

# MUSIC/CONTEXT

In the summer of 1979 I organised a festival of environmental music at the London Musicians Collective called Music/Context, a week of outdoor performances, concerts, discussions and an exhibition, proposing the idea that sound, silence, listening, music and the environment were all part of the same ecological system.

The inspiration for Music/Context came from a number of sources: a growing emphasis on the creative act of listening; the contact I had with R. Murray Schafer and the World Soundscape Project in the mid-1970s; the installation sculptures of friends like Max Eastley; John Latham's aphorism on contemporary art – "context is half the work"; the rise of the ecology movement (signalled in the UK by *The Ecologist* magazine's A Blueprint for Survival in 1972); the founding of Survival International following Norman Lewis's 1969 exposure of land theft and genocide of native people in the Brazilian rainforest, and a growing interest in music's historical connection to (or disconnection from) the natural, social and political environment. Could music be ecological, add to our understanding of entangled systems, break away from hierarchical structures and contribute to a growing discourse on environmentalism?

More specifically, in 1977 Paul Burwell and I participated in Albert Mayr's Suono Ambiente Festival in Milan. Both of us felt energized and validated by his approach of taking sound work out into the city and extending its parameters. So the festival invited many musicians, composers (and what we would now call sound artists and environmental sound recordists) to respond to this setting, with the final lineup including Trevor Wishart, the Feminist Improvising Group, Alvin Curran, Stuart Marshall, Jane Clark, Ian Breakwell and Bill Furlong, Peter Cusack and John Smith, solos by Steve Beresford, Frank Perry and Hugh Davies, guerilla (or gorilla) interventions by Lol Coxhill, street polemics on acoustic ecology by Albert Mayr, a canal project based on moving sounds organized by Michael Parsons and a seminar that included John Latham, anthropologists Ragnar Johnson and Jessica Mayer and many of the festival's participants.

One of the most ambitious projects for Music/Context was Evan Parker's proposal of a 24-hour concert called *Circadian Rhythm*. Evan is very generous about the direct impetus for his idea, claiming that it grew from a six hour performance given by myself and Paul Burwell at 2B, Butlers Wharf, on 10th December, 1976. "Extremely cold and dark and not what you would call audience friendly," is how Evan described that event in a conversation between us in February 2011, "but at the same time something very powerful. I thought I can't pretend I haven't been moved by that; I've got to give some thought to that approach."

The Butlers Wharf concert extended processes and techniques learned from earlier collaborations with artists such as Carlyle Reedy, Stephen Cripps and Annabel Nicolson; perhaps the biggest influence, however, came from our duo performances in two Marie Yates exhibitions in 1973, at Arnolfini, Bristol and Midland Group, Nottingham. She described these as Field Working Performances, and in their stasis and long durations, their resistance to the mechanisms, tensions and resolutions of music or any direct relationship to an audience, they opened up new concepts of performance-as-installation. As a performer it was possible to merge into the field of action, to become almost invisible, and so time became more malleable, shifting away from its determinant role as the locus of anxiety and propulsion.

Perhaps the mix of the group invited to take part in *Circadian Rhythm* seems unusual now – Evan Parker, myself, Paul Lytton, Paul Lovens, Paul Burwell, Hugh Davies, Annabel Nicolson and Max Eastley – but there were strong musical and personal relationships between us that stretched back to the early 1970s. Evan had played with Paul Lovens in the Schlippenbach Trio since *Pakistani Pomade* in 1972, with Paul Lytton in duo and other combinations

# MUSIC/ CONTEXT

since 1969 and with Hugh Davies in Music Improvisation Company between 1968 and 1971. He had also joined Paul Burwell and myself for a trio of high-pitched beat frequencies and heterodyning in February 1978 and performed with Max Eastley's mechanical sound sculptures at the Serpentine Gallery in 1976. Annabel had worked extensively with Paul Burwell and in February 1978, the Whirled Music quartet of Max Eastley, Paul Burwell, myself and Steve Beresford gave its first performance using whirling and spun instruments at the LMC building. The connections were labyrinthine, each of them shaping the resultant music in different ways but perhaps more to the point, influential on our collective desire to break through existing constraints on musical form.

Of course it was foolish on my part to programme *Circadian Rhythm* on the first evening of the festival. I was already tired from organising the festival, even before the concert started. After thirteen hours of playing it felt impossible to go on. Even so, the music (still unreleased in its entirety) sounds like nothing else from that period or any other. As for the festival, I made mistakes in its organisation but those mistakes turned out to be extremely useful years later when I curated bigger, more public exhibitions of sound work.

In the summer of 2017 I was jolted into another memory of the Music/Context festival. Sue Steward suffered a stroke in her garden in St Leonards and died the following week. When I was looking for somebody to help me out with the festival, Fred Frith suggested Sue. She was on the lookout for an activity that sparked her imagination and used her skills. It's possible she was between jobs, I don't recall exactly. Her contribution was invaluable: for example, I still have her rough outline of a complicated schedule for the week's events. On the final night there was a performance of Whirled Music on Primrose Hill. We all participated in that and went to our respective homes, happy but exhausted. Not long after I got back to my house the phone rang. It was Sue, asking me if I wanted to go back to her flat. I took a taxi to Camden and so we found ourselves in a different sort of relationship, one that lasted until 1984.

During those years a lot happened. Sue took part in LMC activities, often writing about free improvisation and instrument inventors for *City Limits*. In particular she got involved with *MUSICS* magazine, partly because issue 20 was devoted to the *Music/Context* festival that she had helped to create. It's revealing to note that on the first page of issue 21 there's a statement about sexist language in the magazine, a refusal to typeset any more articles that used sexist terms like 'girlfriend' or assumed that all musicians were male. Over the magazine's history its predominantly male perspective had shifted dramatically, partly because the editorial/production team now included feminist women such as Kazuko Hohki, Annabel Nicolson, Pamela Marre and Sue.

Looking back at the five issues of *Collusion* magazine we produced between 1981 and 1983, I'm struck by how much Sue's articles were ahead of their time: a piece on New York hip-hop in 1981, an interview with bass player Carol Kaye (now all over YouTube but then almost totally unknown except among those of us who did detective work on LA studio personnel), interviews with women DJs Sheila Tracey and Geetha Bala and Raks Sharki (belly dance) performer Suraya Hilal. These were women who held no interest for mainstream publication, fashionable magazines or the music press. *Collusion* was perceived as being avant garde yet through Sue's influence we were able to redefine what avant garde publishing might be.

Quite early in our relationship I travelled to Venezuela for the Yanomami recording trip. When I came back I was effectively homeless so lived for a while in spare rooms, courtesy of generous friends. My base camp was Sue's flat, where I took a small emergency stash of records. That included *Cachao Y Su Descarga 77*, a Sunny Ade LP released on his Sunny Alade label and Hector Lavoe's string-drenched epic, *Comedia* (produced by Willie Colón, who in 1999 wrote the foreword to Sue's book, *Salsa: Musical Heartbeat of Latin America*). For me these records were aspects of my tastes at the time, they still are, but Sue became entranced by them and set out to learn all she could. In a short time she established herself as one of the leading UK writers on African and Latin music, eventually becoming an authority on many different forms of Latin music, visiting Brazil and Cuba and being well-loved by many Latin music stars. In 1993 I interviewed Gloria Estefan for *The Times* about her *Mi Tierra* album. At one point she asked me if I knew Sue. During my negotiation of that awkward question she raised her eyebrows and said, "Were you two an item?". After that she spoke so warmly of Sue, how much she had helped to spread the word about Latin music.

In September 2016 I visited Sue in her new house by the sea in St Leonards. During that day we spoke frankly about strands of life that were troubling us both, as if we had both reached a point that was mutually recognisable despite its vast differences. Most of that centred on age and isolation, which may sound incomprehensible, bearing in mind the wealth of friends, acquaintances and colleagues in both our lives, not to mention outward appearances of being settled and content, accomplishments in the ledger should anybody ask if we had wasted our lives. Things are not always what they seem, are they? Certain subjects otherwise shrouded in secrecy can be exposed to the light, given a propitious moment in a friendship that remains deep and sympathetic, no matter how much turmoil it has weathered.

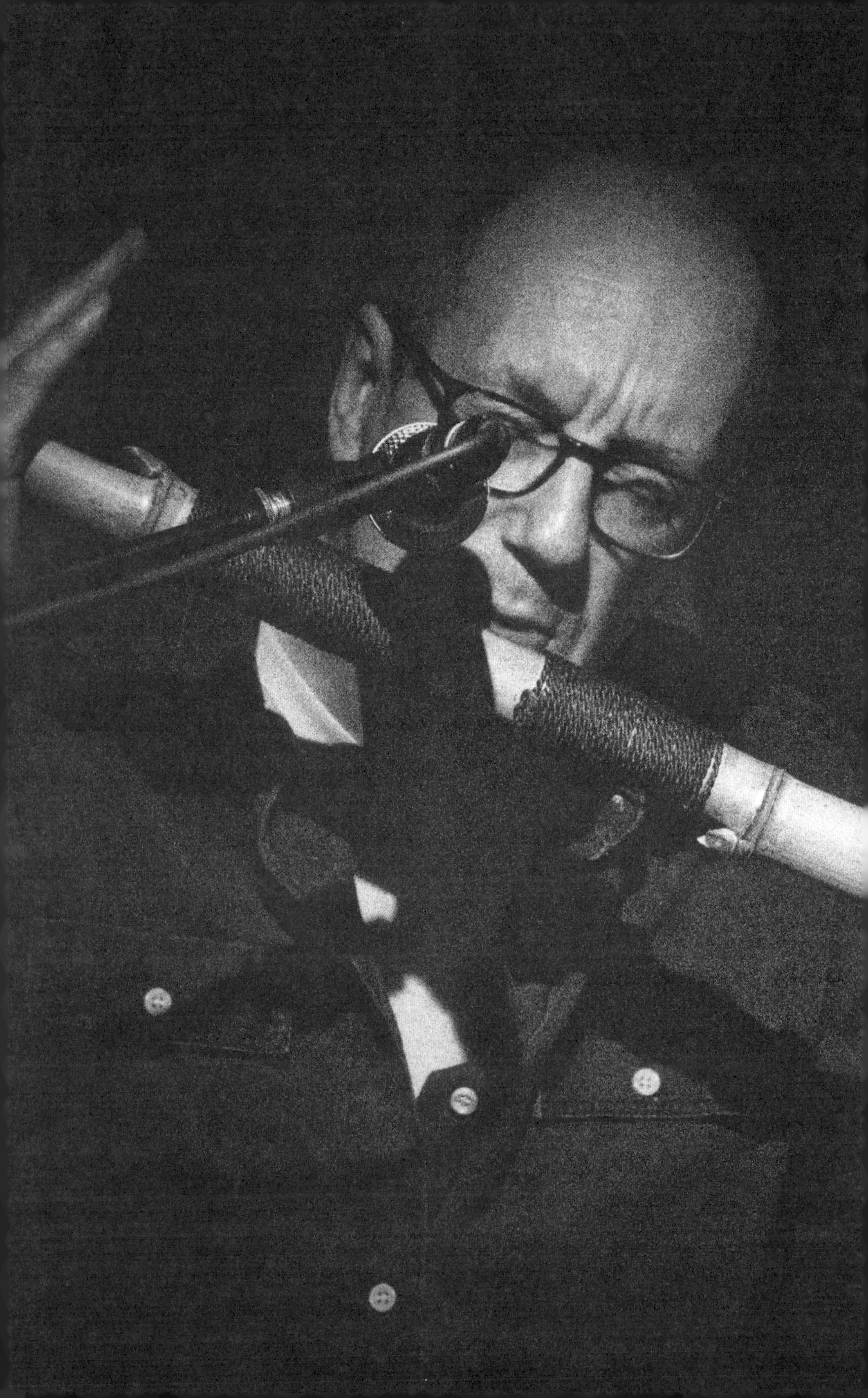

When I got back home that night I wrote what I suppose was a letter, though for reasons which are still not entirely clear to me it was never sent. These are some extracts: "When I said age is a devastation I meant not in itself but in the way we become victims to it through self-loathing, a collapse in confidence, the feeling of entering into a kind of shadowland. But more and more I've been thinking of time going in circles, back on itself to beginnings, each time refreshed or seasoned, almost broken, a skin that is thinner but toughened or sometimes stripped away completely to reveal the rawness underneath, rawness always there from the beginning.

"This afternoon I was looking at an old tree in Alexandra Park, maybe not so old in tree years but substantial and twisted, beautiful in the flow of subtle colours encircling its bark. I was waiting for the bus but something came from the tree into me, I don't know what, not in a mystical sense but in understanding, the way a silent thing can speak to you. I read recently that trees communicate with each other in various ways, particularly through their root systems. Whether that means trees have self-awareness and so become conscious of their longevity and decline I don't know, but their stillness is sometimes impressive, when we stop to engage with it . . . Age is lined and imperfect but also elegant, potentially, like slow ancient music, and full of knowledge, wicked in its awareness of how much depth of feeling and sensation and imaginative power there can be in the world."

Part of these thoughts came from our long history together, the raw experience of losses and the fact that though neither of us was exactly *old*, we were getting there and coming to some understanding of the process and its consequences, good and bad. When we were in a romantic relationship, nearly forty years ago, love was a word we never used. In the maelstrom of urgent debates about feminism, gender stereotypes and relationship dependencies it was too problematic. Now I can use it. One of the peculiarities of this type of trajectory, moving from romantic love to a deep but intermittently acknowledged friendship is that the relationship retains intimate mutual knowledge and yet you are aware that you have become unknown to each other. So many things have happened, so many changes have taken place. In a sense you are strangers who know too much.

Bamboo flute performance at Alterations Festival, 2017

SONIC BOOM

By 1999 I was in a new relationship. Eileen Peters and I first met when she was publicising the Philips CD-i player in 1994. We met again by chance at a 21st birthday party for Daniel Pemberton (now a film and television composer) and quickly fell in love.

After a long dark period in my life my spirits were lifting. Suddenly it seemed that my knowledge and experience had a place in the emerging world of sound art. A few years before I had been approached by Greg Hilty, then a curator at the Hayward Gallery, one of London's largest public contemporary art galleries. The Hayward had been showing themed exhibitions – art and cinema, art and politics, art and fashion – and now wanted to do art and sound. The ideas I put forward were close to those in *Ocean of Sound*, the development of sound art from various strands of 20th century experimental music, electronica, hip-hop and techno, sound installations, conceptual and performance art, art using sound (including sound sculpture) and field recordings of both natural and urban environments. Greg Hilty liked my idea and so I began work on curating the show.

As with Acqua Matrix in Lisbon, the scale of the project was intimidating but I had some clear ideas about what I wanted. For one thing I imagined the exhibition as an immersive experience. What I wanted to avoid was the didactic feeling of previous sound shows, full about educational information about what happened when and who did what. Instead, I felt that the work should have a relatively unmediated effect. There was also pressure to choose work that had a strong visual component and clearly, in a mixed exhibition of this size, it would be impossible to present work that demanded complete silence for proper appreciation.

Trying to bear all of these competing factors in mind I invited some artists from an earlier generation of sound art – Christina Kubisch, Max Eastley, Paul Burwell, Stephan von Huene and Brian Eno – and some from the generation who had come to installation work through other routes – Ryoji Ikeda, Christian Marclay, Scanner, Mariko Mori/Ken Ikeda, Disinformation, Philip Jeck, Angela Bulloch and Pan Sonic. The main problem was the gallery itself, a huge space with open areas running from the bottom of the building to the top. Architecturally, it was effectively a giant enclosed loudspeaker. I soon realised that I would have to accept the fact that each piece (certainly the louder ones) would impinge on all the others and 'tune' them by adjusting volume levels so that the exhibition worked as one single 'instrument'. There were many difficulties in dealing with acoustic space and the unavoidable realities of sound, the consequences of which became increasingly evident with this move of sound into art galleries. Fortunately I was supported throughout the entire process by Hayward curator Fiona Bradley (now director of the Fruitmarket Gallery in Edinburgh), who deftly and generously guided me through the convoluted process. The opening date for the exhibition was brought forward to coincide with the opening of Tate Modern, based on the reasoning that London would be full of art aficionados in May 2000 and a good proportion of them would also walk along the Thames to the Hayward. Being forced to speed up was no bad thing. For all its faults, the show had an urgent energy about it. Though I would do many things differently now, I felt it made a strong statement about sound, that sound had a place in the gallery, that our faculties as listeners were undervalued and neglected and that the future would demand a more complete sensory engagement with the world.

Curating Sonic Boom opened up many new possibilities for me. While the show was running I was offered the post of Visiting Research Fellow at London College of Communication. I had no idea what a Visiting Research Fellow was but accepted, thinking it would last for a year or two. Because of my troubled history as a student and an innate hostility to academia I found it difficult to feel at ease within a higher education institution. My way of coping was to teach. I discovered that I enjoyed working with students and in 2005, at the beginning of a three-year research project to study digital improvisation, I started an annual class in improvisation for second-year undergraduates studying sound art and design. At the time of writing in 2018, this class continues, as does my association with the college. I was made a Senior Research Fellow, a Visiting Professor, a full professor of University of the Arts London, the university of which London College of Communication is a part, then a University Chair of Audio Culture and Improvisation, with the freedom to organise events and give seminars in my own way.

Other exhibitions followed Sonic Boom. Almost immediately afterwards I curated sound for Radical Fashion at the Victoria & Albert Museum, a show featuring the work of Issey Miyake, Alexander McQueen, Vivienne Westwood, Junya Watanabe and other radical designers. The curator, Claire Wilcox, liked *Sonic Boom*'s immersive sound so I invited a small group of composers – Björk, Ryuichi Sakamoto, Ken Ikeda, Christophe Charles among them – to create a similar web of continuous sound throughout the exhibition.

Another mixed show of sound art - Playing John Cage - followed at the Arnolfini Gallery in Bristol in 2005. I was happy to be able to include two of my favourite artists – Akio Suzuki and Rolf Julius. Both of them were brilliantly inventive pioneers of this way of thinking about sound and listening, a deliberate shift from sound-as-music. This had been a preoccupation since the 1970s but in 2000 it gathered momentum as a movement. In January 2000, for example, Max Eastley and I exhibited an installation and performed in Sound As Art Sound As Media, curated by Minoru Hatanaka at ICC in Tokyo.

One experience during this visit to Tokyo really struck me with tremendous force, a performance in which some players used only laptops, others used more traditional means, such as violin and voice. In the problematic contrast between them there were intimations of an unprecedented musical future, in which digital technology would change the way we think about creating and listening to music. This became the starting point and theme for my next book, *Haunted Weather*, published in 2004. It was about a shift from conventional concepts of music-making towards virtuality, disembodiment, long durations and the discarding of all musical frameworks.

Over forty years of working in the field of music, sound and listening I had experienced many changes but the changes which were about to happen, whether in the distribution of music, its production, its availability and its sonic potential would be as dramatic as the introduction of recording technology in the late nineteenth century. In 2001 I was invited by Nicolas Collins, editor of *Leonardo Music Journal*, to curate a compilation CD for an issue he was planning, called *Not Necessarily English Music*. This was a timely project, allowing me to go back to the first signs of British experimental music in the 1960s and range across different factions, styles and strategies, from Cornelius Cardew's Maoist period to Daphne Oram's electronic music, improvisation from Evan Parker and Paul Lytton, a performance by the John Stevens workshop group, eccentric pieces by Ron Geesin, important groups like Gentle Fire, Intermodulation and the Scratch Orchestra and an early performance by Rain In the Face. So much had changed yet the basic principles remained the same: artists came together without money, found ways to put on their concerts, record and sometimes release their music, use whatever means they could to survive in an environment in which their music was invariably treated with indifference and hostility.

My Tastes 1998–2015:

Fennesz, Endless Summer
Otomo Yoshihide And Sachiko M, Filament 1
Taku Sugimoto, Opposite
David Sylvian, Blemish
Akiyama / Nakamura / Sugimoto / Wastell, Foldings
Keith Rowe / John Tilbury, Duos for Doris
Ami Yoshida, Tiger Thrush
Alva Noto + Ryuichi Sakamoto, Vrioon
Haruomi Hosono, Hosono Box 1969–2000

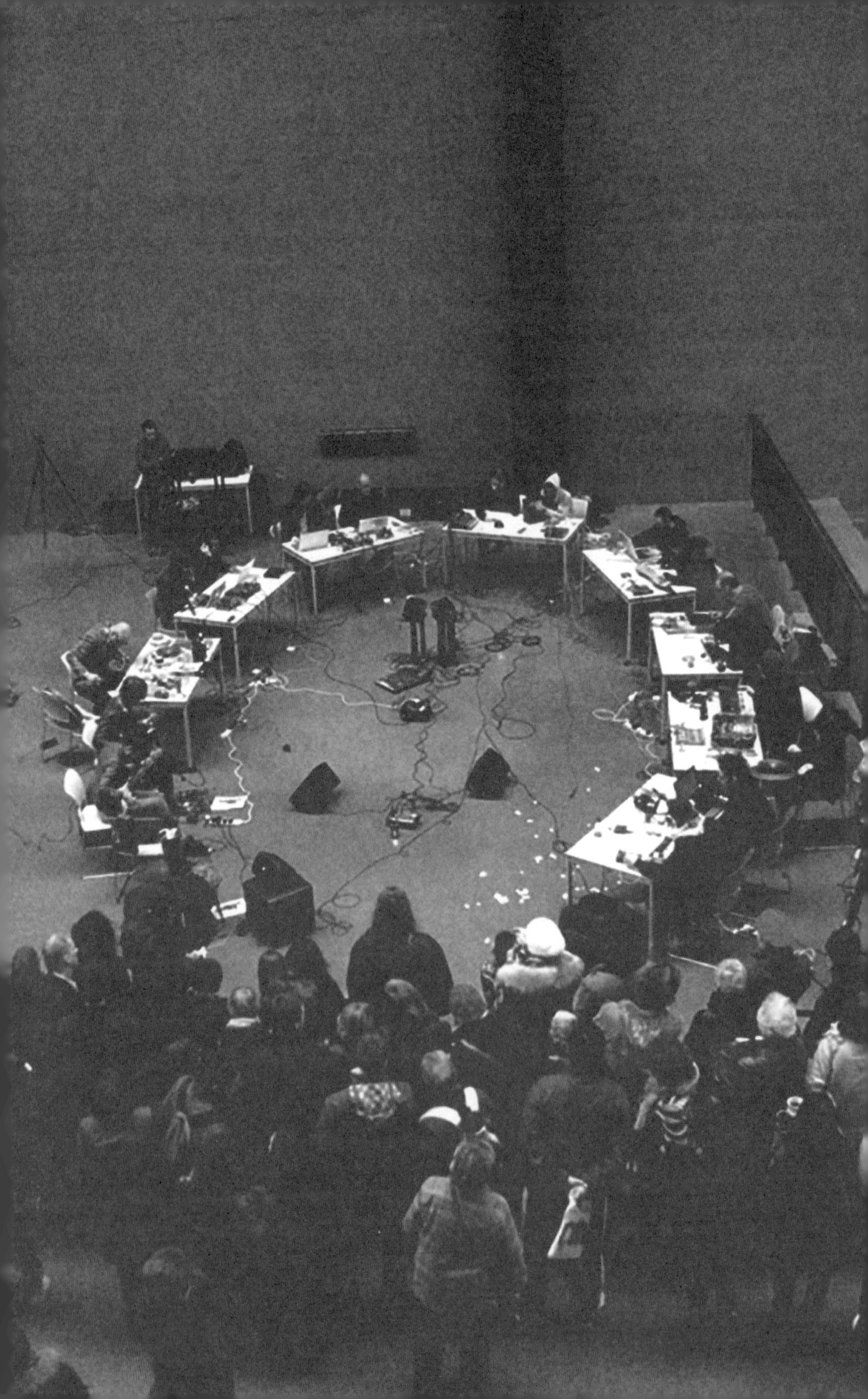

## 9. SINISTER RESONANCE

Late in 2006 I was phoned at home by Anne Bean. Between 1983 and 1990 Anne had been a member of Bow Gamelan Ensemble with sculptor Richard Wilson and Paul Burwell. Now she was calling to tell me that Paul was in a desperate stage of alcoholism. Perhaps if I were to put together a compilation CD of his past recordings, it might help him to regain confidence in his own talents. That was her hope. I felt overwhelming despair that an old friend, the first person with whom I found a real musical bond, should be so close to destroying himself. I agreed to do it and started to collect recordings together immediately. There wasn't enough time to complete the job, however, because of a commitment to fly to Australia and New Zealand for performances and lectures, my return date set for a few days before Christmas. The project was put on hold, my intention being to return to it in the new year. Then in January she phoned me again. Paul had been found in a coma, lying on the freezing ground in the park within which he lived in Hull. The circumstances were mysterious and desperately sad, leaving questions that were never fully answered and a feeling that a dear friend had managed to slowly kill himself with alcohol without any us being able to stop him. Early in February he died, never having regained consciousness. He and I were born days apart from each other. We were both 57 years old.

SOUND BODY

My solo album, *Black Chamber*, released on Sub Rosa in 2003, included recordings made of Paul Burwell's drumming during the 1996 sessions for *Pink Noir*. Regrettably, his name was misspelled on the cover artwork but when he received the copy I sent him he was intrigued by these transformations of acoustic sounds in the computer. Both of us felt that more of these experiments were possible in the future. In partnership with another artist he had bought a boathouse, the Kingston Rowing Club, in Hull. At first, living there seemed to be very productive, for him and for all the artists who came into his orbit, but as they will, things gradually fell apart. Our old friendship was hard to maintain, easy to neglect, partly because we were living such different lives in different cities, partly because it became increasingly problematic to contact him. Gradually communications between us fell silent; too late I learned of his decline and death. "Radiating out from the caravan to which Paul retreated during his last days," I wrote in 2010, after a wintry visit to the abandoned boathouse, "are the remaining signs of a singular energy: spaces filled with more playful devices, an informal cluster of buildings, containers, plantings and shelters, indecipherable constructions, the echoes and shadows of monstrous sounds, firelight and other anomalies. In particular I remember a rain seat, a frame within which a listener could sit and listen to rain falling on the drum fixed above her head . . . Here is an artist who found it neither possible nor morally correct to separate work from life or life from work. The name of the artist is less important than the examination of this strategy, an approach to life which many would find wasteful and self-destructive, but others would treat as a selfless call to arms in its relentless drive."

Paul Burwell's presence on *Black Chamber* was to some degree an honouring of our past work together, no longer feasible in physical space yet still bound closely in the digital domain. I felt that the collaborations of this album and its follow-up, *Sound Body*, were even more important in an era when it was possible for me to record and play everything by myself, isolated in a home studio. Other musicians brought life and air into that closed, rather solipsistic process, adding material that was their choice rather than mine, often with greater virtuosity than my limited technique would allow. Lol Coxhill, Terry Day, Tom Recchion and Yurihito Watanabe all made important contributions to the Sub Rosa album, giving it a richly dark and torrid atmosphere that suited the implications of the title.

Lol Coxhill, in particular, played soprano saxophone beautifully on three tracks, all with titles taken from Henri Michaux's writings – with a floating, fractured lyricism on "Soft Cavities", convoluted and harsh on "The Slapping Gun" and with exquisite tenderness on "Plume, preceded by far off inside." I had known him and worked with him since 1971 and felt privileged to be able to play with somebody who was both virtuoso musician and uniquely funny, original and generous as a person. When he died in 2012 I felt the sadness of losing contact with a truly remarkable man. In my blog I wrote: "He actively sought out tricky situations. To me, this is the measure of an improviser: a player who moves beyond their comfort zone, chips away at their own aesthetic and tics, risks foolishness and failure and yet builds operational spaces in every situation, no matter how rote or ridiculous. The rest are just stylists. I say this knowing that Lol was never graced with the status of true improviser by the commissars of the game; his sidelines were his centre, his rambling ways the shadowing of his bald soprano, its convolutions and folds, its serpentine unfoldings in the inaudible dark. He was dogged by eccentricity, busking, the look of him, his clothes, his baldness, his comedic turn yet never shied away from the heavy responsibility of lightening proceedings."

Collaborations are usually taken for granted when they are happening. Only later do you realise how fortunate it is to be able to work with so many great musicians. *Sound Body*, released on David Sylvian's samadhisound label in 2006, extended this collaborative principle, with contributions from eleven musicians, including Rhodri and Angharad Davies, Haco, Miya Masaoka, Emi Watanabe, Lee Patterson and Rafael Toral. With this record I was beginning to feel in control of the plasticity of digital composing, its potential for combining improvised performance, recordings from disparate spaces and times and the finest calibration of sonic proportion and relationships. The computer and its screen acted as a dish, an alchemical vessel, a screen ceremony in which all of the materials could be mixed into a single body.

I first met David Sylvian in 1988, when I was asked to write a short essay for his *In Praise of Shamans* tour book. We met occasionally after that first encounter. At a back stage party during the *Blemish* tour of 2003 he suggested I visit him at home in America, to use the recording facility there. I was unable to find the time or right circumstances for that so as an alternative he invited me to release an album on his label. Having followed the convoluted path of his work for so long I felt privileged to be associated with it through his label, also happy to introduce him to the paintings of my friend Mariko Sugano, who contributed works to the cover. His story is inspirational – he is one of the few artists who have made the difficult transition from pop star to genuinely experimental musician. During our first conversation we spoke about the attractions both of us felt for melancholic music. "I enjoy that in music," he said, "and it always seems to be a sign that somebody is searching within themselves. They're always introspective people. I spend a lot of time alone and I spend a lot of time thinking about the spiritual nature of things which is essential to creating the kind of music I work on . . . music has to enable the listener to reflect upon themselves. It puts you in contact with parts you're not normally in contact with."

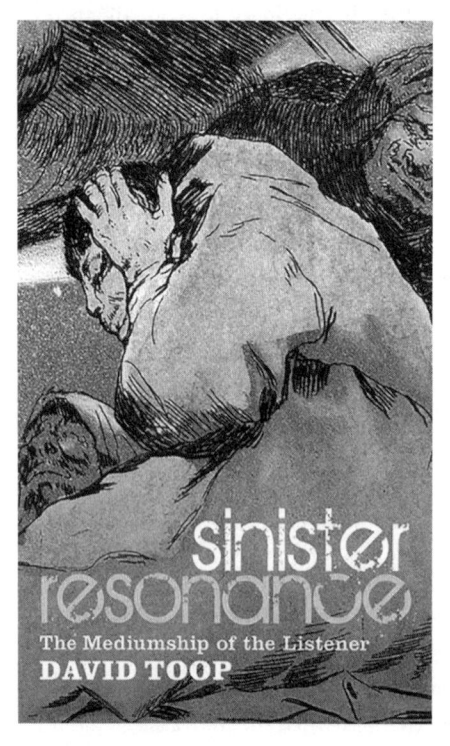

Sinister Resonance, 2010

## STAR-SHAPED BISCUIT

In 2010 I wrote the music and libretto for a semi-improvised opera called *Star-shaped Biscuit*, a title derived from the biscuit encased in a small star-shaped casket by writer Raymond Roussel, then found in the mid-1930s by photographer Dora Maar in a Parisian flea market. The story, such as it was, was loosely based on Dora Maar's life: her photography and poetry, Picasso's abandonment of her, the ECT administered to her after a breakdown, psychoanalysis with Jacques Lacan and then her final retreat into painting, isolation and silence. This was the direct consequence of signing up for an Opera Writing programme in Aldeburgh in 2008. For some reason, not entirely clear to me either then or now, I wanted to take this course in order to learn more about the dynamic potential of three interrelated subjects: voice/sound/staging. There were twenty of us – composers, writers and directors, all different ages and backgrounds working together for three weeks in a hothouse atmosphere with tutelage from composers such as Harrison Birtwistle and Giorgio Battistelli.

My reaction to the situation was a mix of excitement and extreme discomfort. At the age of 59 I was teaching Sound Arts and Design students at London College of Communication, at that time a Senior Research Fellow and Visiting Professor, yet suddenly I had to become a pupil. All the bad memories of my education – my failures at grammar school and dropping out of art school twice – came back to me. Sometimes I felt as vulnerable as I was in my first years at primary school, like a child who didn't know what to do, who feels so intensely self-conscious in the gaze of all the other students that normal functioning is disrupted. Yet most people were kind and I made friendships that lasted beyond the course. Also, I learned a lot. For example, we would be asked to write a very short opera to be performed by small ensembles of singers and instrumentalists. Not being able to write music using conventional notation I had to quickly devise methods for communicating ideas for improvisation (not easy because some of the singers were hostile to this method) and at the same time compose an electronic music piece on my laptop. The pressure of doing this was intense but also very instructive.

In the first week of the course we all gave a short presentation about ourselves and our current work. I talked about the book I was writing at the time – *Sinister Resonance* – and its core idea of sound as a ghostly example of the Freudian uncanny. The roots of this were my experiences of being frightened by sounds as a child but I was also fascinated by the idea of sound in silent media. So the book was an exploration of sound as something unstable and unreliable, a intangible phenomenon that resisted description or explanation. I started to look at paintings that represented sound in some way, particularly a series of six 17th century paintings, all variations on a theme of eavesdropping, by a pupil of Rembrandt, Nicolaes Maes. What impressed me in these paintings was the way Maes conveyed the act of listening, as if it were possible to hear a sound across the centuries that separated events in Maes's time from the 21st century.

By 'listening' to paintings as part of the research for *Sinister Resonance* I was unconsciously establishing a *mise en scène* for an opera. Without wishing to sound too mysterious I would describe it as a form of magic, a way of forming an intangible environment of ideas and feelings through which forms begin to emerge. Creating a world for entities is close to dream or hypnagogic images, fed by literature, cinema, theory, music and other art forms, built up from notes, dozing, gazing, listening, travel, taking photographs, lecturing and engaging in conversation. If I can form a mental image and feel its atmosphere then I can compose a piece of music that reproduces both.

The location of the first performance of *Star-shaped Biscuit* was decided much later but it was always at the back of my mind. The opera itself was strongly affected by being in Suffolk, absorbing the Benjamin Britten/Peter Pears presence that suffused Aldeburgh and Snape Maltings, learning about their history (particularly Britten's discovery of Noh theatre during a tour of Japan) and feeling the ghostliness of Suffolk's seascapes and the reed beds around Snape. My thoughts turned to Kenji Mizoguchi's films, particularly *Ugetsu Monogatari* and *Sansho Dayu*, but then Mizoguchi was also strongly influenced by the Noh. I was also reminded of *Ask the Fellows Who Cut the Hay*, George Ewart Evans's social history of Suffolk agriculture in the 1950s. I had studied the book for English Literature A-level at school and one passage in particular stood out: "But if a company of men was threshing, the work was much easier, simply because they were together at a shared task. They also had certain devices for relieving the monotony. If the company was all bell-ringers they stood round the threshing floor, which was usually made of elm, and they rang the changes with the flail, in exactly the same rhythm as they did in the steeple with the bells, all coming in their proper turn, and changing and changing about at a signal from a leader. From a distance this rhythmic beating of the elm floor made an attractive simulation of the bells."

At a certain moment I spotted the old factory buildings, wondered what they were and asked Jonathan Reekie, then director of Aldeburgh Music, if they could be used for performance. He told me they were too dangerous but then they started to use two of them for exhibitions, made them a bit safer and realised that one of them, at least, was usable for public performance.

I was in a difficult situation, having composed and written an opera, developed it through improvisation with singers and instrumentalists, recorded it but then found I couldn't get it staged anywhere. I had always imagined the opera in a ruined landscape and when I took photographs of what was once one of the complex of buildings used for the malting of barley for beer it seemed exactly my vision of the space within which the characters existed. It was full of strange machines, rubble, old cars, burnt wood and other detritus, even the remnants of a horse-drawn wagon. There was a powerful sense of history washed up in a flood, remnants of an incomprehensible civilisation, all of which fitted the theme of my opera – drowning, ghosts and memory.

The performance setting was beautiful with the audience sitting outdoors on a cool September evening, bats flitting about in the night sky and weird machinery shapes looming in the darkness. The singers – Lore Lixenberg, Jamie McDermott and Elaine Mitchener — were extraordinary, as were the musicians, all of them embracing the atmospheric mood. Unfortunately those circumstances are almost certainly unrepeatable. Subsequently I came to realise that opera is hemmed in by the kind of practical considerations that need energetic ambition and full, rather than part-time attention. I really don't have much interest in adapting it for a concert hall, nor do I have the time to devote that attention to developing any kind of career in opera. Instead I made less ambitious pieces – notably an audio-video work performed live by Elaine Mitchener, called *Of Leonardo da Vinci* — which have had a more active life. It was a matter of asking the question, what is opera? Was it a narrow historical tradition, a bureaucratic category, a set of rules and clichés or something deeper, more primeval that connects us to the physicality and drama of the human voice? As a question, it proved to have a bearing on connections between all aspects of my practice.

Yet the attractions of this type of production remain, a bringing together of voices and sound within a theatrical or cinematic sensibility, and the possibility of dealing with big ideas. In 2013 I had discussions with Ryuichi Sakamoto about presenting *Star-shaped Biscuit* at the Sapporo arts festival. He was very supportive but unfortunately it proved impossible for a variety of reasons. Even though this was disappointing, the suggestions that arose during the conversation – to perform it with British singers and Japanese musicians or even to perform it with a benshi narrator – were very alluring. They suggested to me that I may return to this work and in a more general sense to the creation of opera.

NO EARTHLY MAN

In 2005 I was browsing in the basement of HMV Records in Oxford Street. Suddenly, music came over the PA system, chilling me to the bone. I rushed to the information desk to ask who it was. Alasdair Roberts, I was told, a name which meant nothing to me. The album was *No Earthly Man*. I bought it, took it home and played it. The family reaction was that I should never play it again except when alone in the house.

Undeterred, I secretly decided that one day I would collaborate in some way with the singer of these patiently unfolding, exquisitely sombre murder ballads, "Lord Ronald" and "The Two Brothers." A commission from Jan Bang to produce a sound installation for a lighthouse in Norway gave me the courage to approach Alasdair for a vocal track. Immediately after the performance of *Star-shaped Biscuit* in 2012 I talked to Graham McKenzie, artistic director of the Huddersfield Contemporary Music Festival. His opinions about opera composing were caustic. Everybody wanted to write one but the results rarely warranted the effort. You should be able to perform an opera in a pub, he said. I reflected on this, eventually realising that I agreed, more or less. Never a lover of grandiosity, over time I have come to increasingly dislike the orthodoxies of music presentation and have no tolerance for hugely expensive

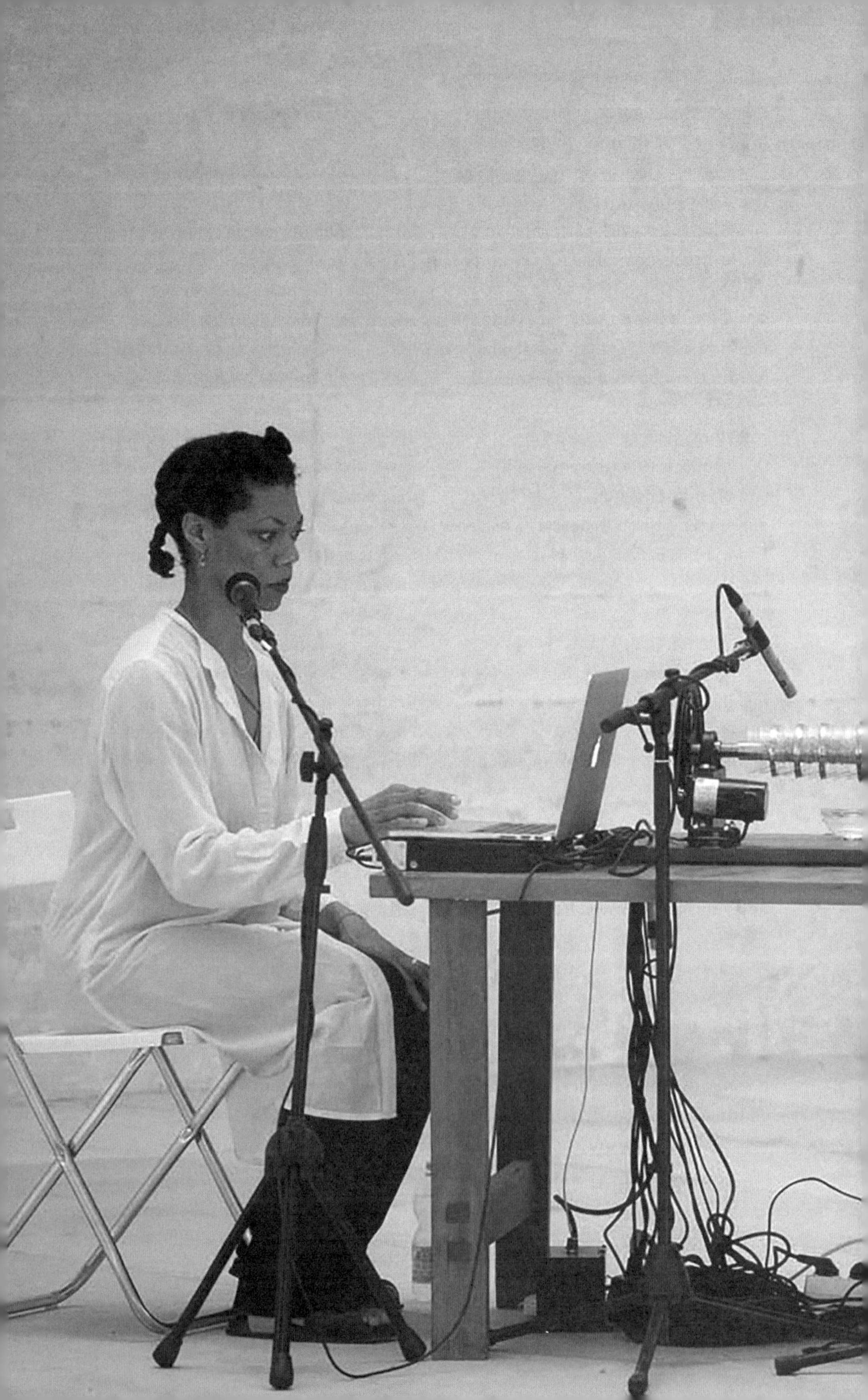

Camille Norment & David Toop
at Venice Biennale. 2015

productions. I was also drawn to the idea of an opera performed by a non-classical voice: an R&B voice or a folk voice, perhaps. Korean pansori, grounded in shamanism and street entertainment, sung by remarkable female vocalists like Kim So-hee and An Sook Sun, was a better example to follow than *Parsifal*.

I proposed a small-scale piece to Graham, who agreed to programme it in the festival in 2013. The title was *Who Will Go Mad With Me* and it was performed by Alasdair Roberts on voice and guitar, Sylvia Hallett playing strings and hurdy gurdy, Luke Fowler, showing 16mm film and playing analogue electronics and myself on pedal steel guitar, laptop, guitar and flutes. "Not in any sense an opera, nor song," I wrote at the time, "but out of both, *Who Will Go Mad With Me* is a collaborative performance evolving, a discussion or confluence of ideas scraping together, not grafted so much as asking what might happen if a portative opera were constructed according to the symbolic struggles of Pieter Brueghel's Fight Between Carnival and Lent, or the gathering of disparate fragments of Ed Ruscha's exhibition, The Ancients Stole All Our Great Ideas: a book of writing patterns, a collection of ladybirds, bezoars, The Head of Medusa by Rubens, or, in this case, the elevated and the abject, cheap talismans and good-luck charms, magical instruments, markers and entanglements out of which a path may be fiddled."

The seed had been planted in 1972, when I was delving into the BBC sound archive and heard a recording of "Hi Hoireann o co mire rium" ("Who will go mad with me") by Mary Morrison of Barra, a whirling, flirting, teasing clapping song on the brink of collapse, breathlessly ecstatic. I also had in mind the walking journeys I made with Marie Yates in the same year, the discoveries of listening and making that came about on Dartmoor's black hills and the wild cliff top land of the Cornish Penwith Peninsula, both scattered with irregular groupings of standing stones. There were unclear connections between these originary points and the clustered motifs and threads that followed some 40 years later. These included "The Ruby In the Hawthorn", a song-in-progress by Alasdair Roberts based loosely on Theodor Adorno's essay of 1952-3, *The Stars Down to Earth*, not to mention Jung's writings on alchemy, the magic fiddlers of folk tales and ballads such as "The Jew Among Thorns" and "Jack Orion". How can this be summed up, other than as four bodies within a moonlit henge, asking thorny questions (as did Adorno, Jung and Mary Morrison) of the irrational and its post-alchemical objects.

INTO THE MAELSTROM

SCULPTURE

August 23, 2012: I was playing at Cafe Oto in a trio with drummer Steve Noble and saxophonist Seymour Wright for Festival Fukushima, a concert to raise money for victims of the Tohoko earthquake and tsunami. Rie Nakajima was also performing. I had never met her before but before the concert began we talked about the large koto owned by her grandmother, the beauties of the ichigenkin one-string koto and some other subjects. Later she performed, using many battery powered and mechanical sound makers. I was so excited that when I got home that night I wrote an enthusiastic blog post about her. "Sometimes children lay out old and unwanted toys on the pavement, sit together and hope to sell a few things," I wrote. "This is what it looks like: plastic pails, cups, wires sprouting here and there, electrical scraps, unknown devices. Rie Nakajima sits with the quiet authority of a proprietor supervising her market stall. She activates without performance. We are rapt."

Rie Nakajima & David Toop
In Conversation booklet

Not long after this incident Rie and I were invited to record a conversation together for Cafe Oto's radio show on Resonance FM, then given the opportunity to curate a night at Cafe Oto. What emerged from our radio conversation was a shared desire to question the norms of performance. "After the production or performance there is always something to resolve," she said, "some question for my practice, that I have to think of for the next one. That's why I continue to perform otherwise I would stop."

We decided on a format defined by duration rather than style, genre or practice. We can invite anybody – musician, poet, video artist, dancer, artist – but they must choose a duration, maybe five or ten minutes, for their performance. There will be no gaps for applause or set-up in the event. If one person performs for longer than their stated duration then the next person begins without waiting for them to stop. We decided to call this event Sculpture. Since the first Sculpture at Cafe Oto, March 26, 2013, we have organised seven Sculpture events in different venues, each of them with different participants.

I am convinced of the importance of discovering new formats through which we can exchange ideas. From 2013 I presented formats such as Offering Rites and Table Manners as part of my role as a University of the Arts London Chair of Audio Culture and Improvisation. For Offering Rites, a group of participants present some aspect of their practice without introducing it; then the audience is free to ask questions before we move on to the next person. For Table Manners, two performers sit opposite each other at a table. They begin a conversation which then slides imperceptibly into music performance, floating back and forth between talking, playing, singing. I have performed Table Manners three times now – with Elaine Mitchener, Haco and Rie Nakajima. Each time feels awkward, strange, risky, a collision of contradictory performance modes, different states of mind and body, uncertainties for both performers and audience about what is happening at any given moment.

DRAWING

Working with Rie Nakajima has helped me to free myself from the constraints of practice. For many years I wanted to draw just as I did when I was a teenager. I would buy drawing equipment – paper in Korea, bamboo pens in Japan, pencils and inks in London – but every mark I made left me dissatisfied. Then Rie began to talk about drawing. She bought carbon paper and we made drawings together, first of all using her battery operated vibration motors and my handwriting to make marks on white paper through the carbon paper. Finally we made action drawings during performances, using any action or device that would leave a mark on paper. Inspired by this breakthrough I found other ways to 'draw' with sound, smashing charcoal with a hammer, scraping powder with plants or blowing pigment through whistles.

This sparked a reminder of performances in 1976, some of them with dancers Miranda Tufnell and Martha Grogan, then a solo at Action Space in London. I was using sand, dropping it like fine rain onto a metal plate amplified by a contact microphone. Many years later I used dry leaves, twigs, seeds and dried lengths of equisetum hyemale (horsetail) dropped or handled close to specially commissioned microphones. Then I began to use paper, fascinated by a strangeness that we take for granted, either treating it as a drum or crumpling and tightly compressing tissue paper close to microphones, allowing it to unfold slowly as if giving up a contained secret, its faint crackle fading with the gradual loss of elasticity. There was a world in there, close to what we hear when we are alone, nothing stirring, without movement, minds drifting and open. I photographed the compressed paper or scanned it, finding I had made drawings without the need for pencils, brushes or pens.

I asked myself, is it possible to share this micro-world, as listeners collective yet separate? At the launch of a book by Daniela Cascella I experimented with a performance called *Many Private Concerts*, scrunching up large sheets of tissue paper, holding them to my ear, then inviting members of the audience to do the same. Showing them by example, without speaking, I ran into failure. I tried again; it failed. Then I tried with a group of my students. Finally it began to work, an incredible sense of intimacy and sharing emerging with no central focus, no notion of division between performer and audience.

Some Books I Treasure, Moments Of My History:

Mircea Eliade's *Shamanism: Archaic Techniques of Ecstacy*; Vilmos Diószegi's *Popular Beliefs and Folklore Tradition in Siberia*; *The Photographs of Daido Moriyama*; *Darkness Moves* and *Untitled Passages* by Henri Michaux; *The Gibbon in China* by Robert Hans Van Gulik; *In Praise of Blandness* by François Jullien; A Translation of *The Sakuteiki, The Eleventh Century Manual of Japanese Gardening*.


Certain Vinyl Records I Return To, Over And Over:

The Mysterious Sounds of the Japanese Bamboo Flute by Watazumido-Shuso; John Levy's Recordings of Music from Bhutan, Chinese Ch'in, Korean Court Music, Vedic and Buddhist Chant; Jacques Brunet's Recordings of Music from Java, Cambodia and Laos; Flutes from Rajasthan; Ragnar Johnson's Recordings of Sacred Flute Music from Papua New Guinea; NHK Recordings from 1962 of the Gagaku Piece Ryoo; Okinawan singer Kochi Kamechiyo; Recording from Chad and the Senufo People of Upper Volta and Ivory Coast; The Omizutori Ceremony from Nigatsu-Do, Nara; Recordings of Ainu Singing; Songs from Arnhem Land in Australia, particularly the Djanggawon Ceremony recorded between 1958–60, Song accompanied by the profound drone of a "Didjeridu Some Twelve Feet Long, Painted with Several Representations of Water Goanna," according to the notes by Recordist L. R. Hiatt

## ARCHIVES

In the present, time is still scattered in fragments; too close for me to discern any patterns without the perspective of deep time.

During the twentieth century many forms of music fell victim to a great extinction. Others are preserved as antiquities, beautiful anachronisms in the 21$^{st}$ century. These unique forms, each one of them exemplifying music's capacity to embody the complexity of human thought, body expression and social structuring, were eradicated by missionary zealots, purgative authoritarian regimes, wars, persecution, tourism, modernity and the spread of capitalism. As with flora, fauna and ways of life their vanishing was rapid but the difference was that few people noticed or cared. A panda is loveable, at least it looks that way from a distance; a funerary chant from the Cardamom mountains in Cambodia maybe less so.

Since May 2014, Evan Parker and I have been presenting a public event called Sharpen Your Needles, in which we play recordings such as this, on vinyl from our personal collections. This is not an academic exercise. We may talk a little between tracks (usually with a great deal of laughter) but the aim is to make a listening space for revenants from a lost world of music and for those who wish to hear their ghostly sound in the company of strangers.

Time circles. New Year's Day 2012, alone and silent. I make a bamboo flute; write an essay for a new release of my recordings of Yanomami shamanism, songs and rituals from 1978. This is work I have been attempting, without success, for some years. Now in desolation, stillness in the world outside my window, the words begin to flow. I call it *Lost Shadows: In Defence of the Soul*. The rich and shadowy culture of the Yanomami is part of it, but also the soul itself (consciousness and fluctuating identity in all their complexity) threatened by time and the vicissitudes of life.

## LATE AUTUMN

In 2013 I am living alone again, my marriage to Eileen ended. This is life alone for the first time in thirty years. Aged 64, chastened and battered by life, I withdraw, write, listen, contemplate the realities of beginning again, feeling strangely *rescued* for myself, slowly more optimistic. In 2009 I gave up drinking for the second time in my life. The first period without alcohol lasted ten years; this time is permanent.

The world is experienced through that appalling, vibrant lucidity spoken of by others who have renounced drinking. I can celebrate its liberating effects on me, back when I was inhibited and afraid. I can acknowledge, though not regret, its poisoning action on my system. Many other objects and states now exist only in the archive of memory. My house and its Japanese garden has been left behind, both in a good state. Now I must make a new garden. I begin with a pond. Frogs soon appear. Then Damselflies. Then Dragonflies.

Every few years I watch all of the films I have by Yasujiro Ozu. Who else expresses with such profundity the depths of human feelings, the flutter echo of the heart?

August 2013, Queensland rain forest with Akio Suzuki and Lawrence English. Impenetrable night, so dark that there is no difference between eyes open and eyes closed. Small insects make sounds like needle points of thin time and from every direction there is a perpetual dropping, falling and settling of organic matter from the trees. Two trees rub together in the distance and I hear hallucinations of voices, a fairground, strange distant cries. We are all making sounds. Later, Akio-san mentions the flute sounds I was making. That was the trees rubbing together, I said. There is a lump just under my earlobe, a tick from the forest. Lawrence extracts it neatly with tweezers, still alive.

New Year's Day 2014, I made the first faltering steps to begin the book I have been contemplating for some years, an account of free improvisation called *Into the Maelstrom*. Dispirited, I abandon this attempt after only a few days. In June I return to the work, writing in the studio at the end of my garden, no internet or phone signal, only the frogs for company. After four months of writing I stop, leave for Hong Kong, Naha, Taipei, Nara, Osaka, Ogaki, Tokyo. On New Year's Day 2015 I resume the writing and by June the book is finished and delivered to the publisher, yet not finished. Overwhelmed by the amount of material I decided to write two volumes. Free improvisation continues to shape my life.

October 2014: Hong Kong, where I perform a long and beautiful trio concert with Akio Suzuki and Aki Onda. I travel from Hong Kong to Okinawa, flying into the path of an incoming typhoon. As the aircraft is tossed about in the sky over a boiling slate-grey sea I am convinced I will die. The plane is unable to land in violent winds, returns to Hong Kong. Two days later I arrive in Okinawa. With Syo Yoshihama and two of his friends we travel to Kudaka Island. In the heat we walk slowly around the island. I hold out my hand - a butterfly lands, settles on my skin for a moment. We come close to the entrance where only women can go, the sacred grove for noro ceremonies. In a strange, near empty building we look at Higa Yasuo photographs of these noro ceremonies from the 1970s, like peering into another world, now lost to modernity.

From Taipei I travel to Nara, quiet on my own after so much talking and performing. I visit the hall of Nigatsu-do, where the shuni-e service takes place, the Omizutori, fire and water. This week-long ceremony has been held every year for at least 1,266 years. New water from a spring is added to a pot in which water has been collected since the origins of the ritual, thereby implying the dizzying prospect of water that is, in some infinitesimal part, older than a millennium. My first encounter with the ceremony came from a JVC six-LP box set, acquired for Dillons record department when I was manager in 1976. Then in Kobe, 1993, I heard Yoshihiro Kawasaki's dramatic recordings of the chants, the conch shell horns, the clattering wooden sandals and the crackle of fire. During my visit I walk around the back of the hall, where almost nobody goes. A solitary monk is performing a complex ritual with fire: the clinking of metal objects, a sudden sharp snap as he adds to the fire, the friction of rosary beads rubbed together, hands clap, then chanting from the sutras. He follows the book undisturbed, unaware of my presence.

After this I drink matcha, eat warabimochi, then walk to the great bell close to Shunjo-do, stand under the bell, look up, see a far planet encircled by the swirling of cosmic forces.

Then in Tokyo I returned to ICC for a public interview with my friend Minoru Hatanaka, followed by a solo performance. We spoke about many aspects of my life and career, trying to encapsulate much of what I have written in this book within one conversation in front of an audience. I found myself speaking about a way of living that is not human-centred. How can we listen as a moth listens, a stone listens, a building listens, darkness listens? Is it possible to play music as if the sound is gathering in rather than sending out? Is it possible to be the instrument or the floor rather than being the performer? Is it possible to think of a piece of paper, even the marks on a piece of paper, as a musical instrument? To voice such speculations in front of an audience is a good test of conviction – do they sound ridiculous or silly, or are they serious propositions for a future way of living (as Takuma Nakahira said about his photography: for a language to come)? My conclusion was that these ideas that preoccupy me can be hard to explain or understand. This is something I have to pursue through my lifetime.

People talk blithely about influence as if the simplicity of direct causation can be picked out from among the convolutions and improvisations of what we find

David Toop & Tom Recchion, Ghent, 2016

ourselves doing. In contradiction of this simplification, certain incidents stand out in my mind: a duo concert with saxophonist John Butcher, September 2011, at a Friends Meeting House in Walthamstow. I had been thinking about very small sounds, resonators and amplified surfaces, small cardboard boxes and earbuds as loudspeakers. Dave Hunt had made me small microphones of various types and I was combining these with contact microphones to amplify specific surfaces of instruments. After I wrote liner notes for one of his solo records — *Invisible Ear* — John and I discussed the way he used feedback and circular breathing and speculated on this unorthodox, problematic method of recording all the surfaces and chambers of an instrument simultaneously. "It's difficult," he said. The gig in Walthamstow was small, intimate, enjoyable. At the time it seemed no more than just one fragment in an endless flow of musicking (to borrow Christopher Small's neologism). Retrospectively, however, I can deduce its significance as a tiny explosion that set off a chain reaction. For one thing it existed within a network of players and playing, a resilient community of practice stretching in all directions and back through time. I had been performing with John and Phil Durrant; they had been playing together for many years, in the past as a trio with guitarist John Russell. In 2010 we played as a quartet at the Whitechapel Gallery with Aleks Kolkowski, performing my composition — *Flat Time/sounding* — based on John Latham's theories of flat time. These small sounds and experiments with resonance peered back into the rehearsals and live laboratories of the 1970s; they reflected on technologies and physicality in an increasingly disembodied present; they anticipated the future, in which acts of playing would demand a dismemberment of the instrument into many parts.

2015: I find myself playing small concerts of improvised music again, sometimes in tiny venues to audiences of five or ten people. In these intimate, almost private settings the music is at its most inspiring, intricate and free, and I feel fortunate to be able to treat these situations as laboratory sessions, without needing to entertain or satisfy anybody's expectations. Over the past few years I have played again with old friends – Max Eastley, Steve Beresford, Terry Day, Alterations, Mike Cooper, Akio Suzuki – and many more recent collaborators – Camille Norment, Haco, Elaine Mitchener, Rie Nakajima, John Butcher, Aki Onda, Yannick Dauby, Phil Minton, Adam Bohman, Jennifer Allum, Daiichi Yoshikawa, Sharon Gal, Emi Watanabe, Sylvia Hallett, Mark Wastell, Ryoko Akama, Orphy Robinson, Pia Palme, Tomoko Hojo and Rahel Kraft. Finally I feel I can play this music.

ENTITIES INERTIAS FAINT BEINGS

January 31$^{st}$, 2015, I am one of a number of musicians who perform in the context of Christian Marclay's solo exhibition at White Cube. Christian has collected many glasses from the streets, the debris of London's love affair with alcohol. He invites us to use them, or the space, as we wish, the only proviso being that the glasses should remain intact. For my solo I fill some of the glasses with water, activating them with aquarium pumps. All of these concerts were recorded by The Vinyl Factory, pressed onto vinyl in the same week and put on sale in the gallery. I title my record: *The Myriad Creatures will be Transformed of Their Own Accord*, for strings, autonomous devices, water and air, digital electronics, Korean paper, glass vessels. This Taoist title connects the work to my past but it lingers also as a focus of reflection. As winter moves to summer it stays on my mind.

Summer 2015, St Ives, Cornwall. Alone for a week, I barely speak aloud except in shops, hello, thank you, goodbye. Time moves in eddies; I drift with its rotations, gazing at light and the ocean, sleeping on rocks, photographing dusty objects in the quiet of the Leach Pottery, buying ceramics, regarding holidaymakers as shadow people, watching DVDs of Otto Preminger's *Fallen Angel*, Béla Tarr's *Werckmeister Harmonies*, Kenji Mizoguchi's *Ugetsu Monogatari*, reading Timothy Morton's

*Hyperobjects: Philosophy and Ecology after the End of the World*. All of these stimulations seem to have a message for me. Morton writes about intimacy, music coming from some place of archetypes or from the trauma of unspeakable secrets, the prospect of forging new alliances between humans and non-humans. It was as if my private thoughts of the past forty five years were speaking back to me.

My intention in Cornwall was to write and draw. Instead, using just my laptop and headphones, I take the first steps in making a new album, inspired by many disparate sources: the photography of Takuma Nakahira, Tomatsu Shomei, Kawada Kikuji and Masahisa Fukase; the Noh play *Aoi no Ue* and Carmen Blacker's book on Japanese female shamans, *The Catalpa Bow*; the boxing essays of A. J. Liebling, Clarice Lispector's *Agua Viva* and James Agee's *Let Us Now Praise Famous Men* (first read when I was a Foundation students at Hornsey College of Art); the principles of stone setting in the *Sakuteiki*; Mukai Kyorai's *Sea Slug*. I want to make a record that is unbalanced, a growth of organic creatures and their silent world. The name of the record is *Entities Inertias Faint Beings*. I wanted it to speak for the unspeakable within me. In this ambition I was inspired by Clarice Lispector, a writer whose work was introduced to me by my friend Daniela Cascella, herself a brilliant writer. Many of Lispector's sentences in *Agua Viva* spoke for this unspeakability: "To tell you of my substratum I make a sentence of words made only from instants-now. Read, therefore, my invention as pure vibration with no meaning beyond each whistling syllable . . . What I wrote you here is an electronic drawing without past or future: it is simply now."

The gap between this record and its predecessor (*Sound Body*, released in 2007) was very long. Being alone and away from London gave me some perspective on the musical pieces, fragments and experiments I had accumulated during those intervening years, all of them collecting like cobwebs in a folder on my computer. Some of them had been performed or broadcast, some were part of live sets in which I used a laptop, some were sounds created for bigger projects and others were discarded digital scraps or ideas for compositions that had never been completed. Listening to these files in between staring at the sea or walking on the beaches and cliffs, I felt there was potential for a record that reflected all the dramatic changes in my life, the rethinking of live performance, the thoughts on how my music might continue to evolve in the 21$^{st}$ century.

One piece – "For a Language To Come" (its title taken from Takuma Nakahira's famous photobook from 1970) combined two separate experiments with recording techniques. For one of these I had attached a number of contact microphones and tiny air mics to a steel guitar, using one of these to 'play' the strings (by scraping and plucking the strings with the head of the mic); for the other I recorded Rie Nakajima's battery powered objects, changing their sound by moving them on paper and using a different type of small microphone to audibly 'draw' on the paper as it closely followed the objects. As with the other tracks, this was an exercise in contrasting speeds and texture. I was also thinking about melody. In the absence of conventional harmony, what is a 21$^{st}$ century conception of melody at this level of microsound? Melodies can exist at varying levels: as sequences of pitches within twelve-tone equal temperament and other tuning systems, as tuned percussion or as the fluctuations of tones within an ambiguously pitched flow of sound. If I listen to Steve Beresford play piano in a duo, for example, I can hear him identify pitch and melodic information instantly from any sound that the other person plays, whether it comes from a conventional instrument or any other audible event.

All of the tracks on *Entities Inertias Faint Beings* explore these variations on melody. At the same time they are structured according to very irregular rhythms (many of these constructed by recording individual drum hits by percussionist Roger Turner, then organising them into rhythms in the computer). Every track is saturated with some personal significance. "Stone Setting", for example, is a collaboration with two friends – painter Mariko Sugano and flute player Emi Watanabe. Some of the sounds in the piece are underwater hydrophone recordings of creatures in my garden pond but the main inspiration came from studying and visiting Kyoto gardens, creating my own Japanese-style garden, and reading the Sakuteiki, the nearly 1000 years old manual of Heian-era gardening.

The germination of the album began during three periods of solitude. The first (organised for me by Lawrence English, who later came to release the record on his ROOM40 label), was in Queensland, on Tamborine Mountain (an aboriginal name), so silent at night that I listened to recorded music – Japanese gagaku, Buddhist ritual from Bhutan, Korean Confucian music, slow Javanese gamelan, Australian Aboriginal ceremonies – as if drifting into cavernous black space. Stepping into sleep I saw a hypnagogic image - a transparent swimming pool suspended over the mouth of a volcano. I read Stephen Mansfield's book - *Japanese Stone Gardens: Origins, Meaning, Form*. "Successful stone arrangements seem almost alive," he wrote, "the elements conversing among themselves with an occult vitality, the call and response that has been noted between well-placed rocks resembling the chanting of Buddhist sutras." In daylight, listening in chill air, I heard extraordinary bird song — whip birds, butcher birds, noisy mynahs, kookaburra chatter, rainbow lorikeets – and attempted to write descriptions of their sounds: catapult elastic, ghost flutes, radio waves in a kettle, electric buzzers. In Mansfield's book, the importance of chance and spontaneity in Japanese gardens is underlined, the incorporation of weathering as stone surfaces darken, the growth of lichen and moss spreads, plants expand and retreat with the seasons. I felt the same about my sounds, that they were in perpetual flux, their surfaces transformed through weathering, the tactile sense of them vacillating between hard and soft, their occupation of space both uncomfortably close and so distant as to be barely present. Memories of poems read many years before came back to me, particularly Tu Fu, writing of the Temple of the Hsiang Consort:

> Insects trace characters in the moss on her jade girdle.
> Swallows dance in the dust on her halcyon canopy.

The second of these periods of solitude was on Queensland's Gold Coast, where I gazed at a distant humpback whale breaching out to sea, watched Yasujiro Ozu's 1934 silent version of *A Story of Floating Weeds*, walked on the singing sands of Echo Beach. This was solitude, not silence, because the roar of tyres on the Gold Coast highway was perpetual and music rose up from nowhere, birds screaming at the going down of light at dusk and cicadas unleashing their friction song into the atmosphere with every passing helicopter as if to contest these small efforts of collective sounding against the monstrous wings of a behemoth. Not silence, because inner voices are always present, murmuring like formless creatures in the dark. Not really solitude either. Looking out at the night I see flat screen TVs in all directions. blasting image holes into the universe. Their lurid colour, their dominance of space, forms a second reality. Staring down through glass at sunbathers around the pool, my ears hiss.

The third period of solitude, of course, was in St Ives, Cornwall, where the record began to come into being. Through cycles of time we return to where we began. I ask myself, what is the point of music? Music describes space we have never entered, substances we have never touched, air we will never breathe, beings without shape, time we can never measure, parts of ourselves we will never truly know. By entering time we move outside time.

UNFINISHED

December 2015. At home in silence I listen to koto music from a box set of four red vinyl records released on Toshiba – Sokyoku Kotenmeikyoku no Hikakukenkyu — composed by Kengyo Yatsuhashi in the 17th century, played by Mina Inoue and Shin Sanada, recordings that have sustained me since 1976. Notes cut into the surrounding silence as a heron's beak pierces the placid surface of a pond. Is the music slow or simply the tempo of another age?

March 2016. My daughter Juliette gives birth to a baby girl. Life shifts and stirs once again. The philosopher and sinologist François Jullien writes about life as respiration, never as end points, only transitions. The first two sentences of his book – *The Great Image Has No Form, or On the Nonobject through Painting* – are these: "This book is only a chapter and has no conclusion. It forms a nodal point in the body of my work." For more than a year now I have been reading the almost forgotten English writer Dorothy Richardson, her long autobiographical novel written in book length parts over many years. She began its writing in St Ives, working alone in a supposedly haunted chapel in 1912. "Suddenly the world had dropped away," she wrote of this solitary time in Cornwall. "But never had humanity been so close. Everything took on a terrific intensity." The concluding novel was found after her death in 1957. Each section had a separate title yet for Richardson, the whole had only one title: *Pilgrimage*.

March 2018. Last year there were concerts that filled me with optimism. At Punkt Festival in Norway, a duo with singer Sidsel Endresen that felt wild and shamanistic, peppered with silences and unknown languages; a solo in Buenos Aires, in a building so vast that its edges seemed to melt into the night, where I began by rustling garlic skins so quietly that even I could barely hear them; a trio with Rie Nakajima and Lucie Stepankova at Flat-Time House, where the walls, the bookshelves, the floor and the garden of the house where John Latham once lived came alive with sound; a solo at Ftarri in Tokyo, during which feedback through my flute and in the air of the room played thin, eerie melodies as I moved. Carl Stone sat in the front row, a few feet away from me. You're really interested in resonance, he said. I could have hugged him.

Over the past few years I have been using bone conduction speakers, experimenting with attaching the tiny speakers to various objects such as a giant buffalo bell bought in Beijing, a small iron pestle and mortar, tins for storing gramophone needles or tea, books of relevance (a Phil Spector reader; Victor Segalen's *Voix Mortes*; Gladys Reichard's *Prayer: The Compulsive Word*, a study of the Navajo prayer known as First Night Male Shooting Chant Evil; A Lute of Jade, a collection of Chinese poetry seen in Bernard Leach's bookcase), paper and snare drum wire – twenty strands of quivering silver steel, like curling hair - resonating the latter set up with a drum bought in Chiang Mai and a bell bought in a Tokyo shrine, the reason for the bell being its iron clapper, useful for magnetically attaching the tiny speaker within the bell's inner cavity.

I tried playing old cassettes through this instrument-without-a-body: spirit medium séances of Malay indigenous people, a herd of wildebeests, trance dances of Laos hill tribes imitating the sounds of dog, monkey, goat, sheep and cat, and finally an interview I recorded with my grandfather and uncle in 1979. That gravitation toward a kind of spectral oral history of distorted voices – human/animal/spirit — makes sense to me. The bone conduction elements of this configuration were developed for me last year by David Bloor for an installation at Flat-Time House, The Body Event II, that played back my conversation with John Latham through objects, as in a Vanitas painting, into the space where I recorded it shortly before his death. To hear the dead speak through objects, living on borrowed resonance, their voices thinned, abraded and disrupted by host materials and the lack of a tangible body is uncanny, the radio of things.

I describe this as a distributed conglomerate instrument, there but not there, material but without body, all its parts linked by a web of time, as close to food or jellyfish as to music. While eating shojin ryori cuisine at Izusen, Daitokuji temple, Kyoto, in April 2017 I reflected on François Jullien's In Praise of Blandness, the appreciation of blandness or insipidity in ancient Chinese aesthetics and ritual practices. Commenting on a text describing the use of muted music during ritual offerings to the ancestors he says this: "For the most beautiful music – the music that affects us most profoundly – does not . . . consist of the fullest possible exploitation of all the different tones. The most intensive sound is not the most intense: by overwhelming our senses, by manifesting itself exclusively and fully as a sensual phenomenon, sound delivered to its fullest extent leaves us nothing to look forward to. Our very being thus finds itself filled to the brim. In contrast, the least fully rendered sounds are the most promising, in that they have not been fully expressed, externalized, by the instrument in question, whether zither string or voice."

The seemingly endless succession of small dishes that form the experience of shojin ryori are not bland in the sense of being indistinguishable or boring. Each one has a particular character and subtlety of taste and texture but the cumulative effect is to balance rather than overwhelm the others. The look of them as diminutive sculpture is so striking and their taste so delicate that they leave what Jullien calls "the leftover tone, the 'lingering' or 'leftover flavour' (yiwei) [evoking] a potential, inexhaustible value . . ."

Another important aspect of shojin ryori is its relationship to time. Green tea mochi, yuba, fried plum, cherry blossom rice cake, sesame tofu, tofu skin, bamboo shoot, tempura, soup with kombu, edible flowers, bamboo and perilla leaf all follow each other at a steady pace without overlapping. They are specific to a moment yet they constitute a meal. This is consistent with many of the gardens of Kyoto temples – Zuiho-in, Kohrin-in, Oubai-in, Daisen-in, Tofukuji temple, Ryogen-in and Taizo-in. Many of them reveal themselves gradually. A corner is turned; a path is taken; a threshold is crossed. At Ryōgen-in, a small enclosed stone garden called Kodetei lies under the eaves of the study. It has another name – A-un – which represents the inhalation and exhalation of breath, indivisible pairs, positive and negative current. The dimensions of the garden are tiny, its stones visibly linked yet separated (symbolically, at least, and within deep understanding the longer it is contemplated) by a vast body of water.

In my early twenties I was drawn to a book called Animals Without Backbones, thinking that by studying invertebrates I could gain a greater understanding of the so-called formlessness of free improvisation. I was reminded of it, reading an account of "an unprecedented number of Atlantic portuguese man o'war" washing up on the Cornish coastline. Customarily thought of as jellyfish, portuguese men o'war are a species of siphonophore, a colony of clone individuals with four specialised parts, all working together as a single organism. They go where the wind and ocean currents take them, often travelling in vast flotillas, which is why such sudden, mysterious 'invasions' become news. In the past I have been asked about my 'lineage', usually an invitation to reel off lists of so-called great men. If I have to talk about influences, I am more inclined to speak about siphonophores, dry gardens or shojin ryori.

Concerts have been and gone already this year, any one of them far more satisfying than much of the work I produced between my teens and early sixties: a solo in Naples, a duo with Miya Masaoka, a duo with violinist Jennifer Allum, a quartet with Tania Chen, Thurston Moore and Jon Leidecker. "You always break things when we play together," says Tania, laughing. True. Music allows actions that are unacceptable outside music; also it allows the plurality and contradictions of character to be embodied. What did I learn from John Latham and Gustav Metzger all those years ago? That destruction was a mirror of creation.

In February I was invited to play field recordings at a London venue called Hundred Years Gallery, a small Hoxton café with a basement of exquisite acoustics. What are field recordings to me, I asked myself, then chose a selection of cassettes and minidisks, recorded over a fifty year span: the conversation with my granddad Syd and uncle Bob, both speaking about smog in London; a wasp recorded in 1971; interviews with Don Cherry, Ornette Coleman, Björk; a lo-fi tape of my duo with Paul Burwell, me singing "Do the Bathosphere," Paul playing bamboo trumpets; The Promenaders on Brighton Beach, featuring Phil Minton singing his own composition — "For You I Have the Time" — in the club style (as Vic Reeves might say); moving slowly around a Beijing department store, cheap jewellery in display cases, strip lighting audibly on the blink and a climactic piano rendition of Andrew Lloyd Webber's "Memory" on the PA; my daughter Juliette and her mother, Kimberley, in the bath, happy, laughing and playing; then Juliette at the age of five or six, singing her self-composed song, "I known that you and I, I know that you and I, I know that you and I, will be my family for the whole wide world." Also tape noise and silences, the handling noises of the machinery.

Field recordings, in my personal definition, constitute an archive of auditory memory: scattered, incomplete, patinated, jumbled, empty but for the low hiss and hum of consciousness, funny, mysterious, sensuous, painful, intensely personal yet hidden in plain sight. Beforehand, I recalled buying This Is Our Music by the Ornette Coleman Quartet, back in 1966 when I was 17 years old, then half a century later bringing together the voices of two of its members after their deaths, both speaking to me in places separated by both geography and time. Afterwards, I thought about the indiscretions and open wounds of memoir.

April 2018. I write, now on the brink of my 69th birthday, conscious that time grows shorter, just as the days grow shorter in autumn. One morning in 2013, driving along Queensland's Gold Coast with Lawrence English and heading to Brisbane airport to pick up Akio Suzuki, Lawrence said to me: "You'll have many projects left unfinished when you die." His frankness and the truth of it made me laugh. Future projects stretch before me, many unfinished, some yet to be started, more than I could accomplish even if I had the time and energy of a young person.

Increasingly I think of instruments without physical form, photographs and drawings as instruments, images as sound, sounds without sound. Their essence can be reduced to the Willing Vessel/The Radiant Surface, as I described instruments in 1975. Becoming a grandparent brings with it the feeling of seasons, respiration, transition. I practice chi kung, learning how to stand, learning how to live with myself a little better. "Love, hatred, attraction, repulsion, suspension: all are music," Trinh T. Minh-ha wrote in her essay, An Acoustic Journey. "The wider one's outlook on life, it is said, the greater one's musical hearing ability. The more displacements one has gone through, the more music one can listen to. Appeal is a question of vibration."

Silence whistles in my ears. Life is full, sometimes too full; life is empty, sometimes too empty. Never full enough; never empty enough.

David Toop      London, MMXVIII

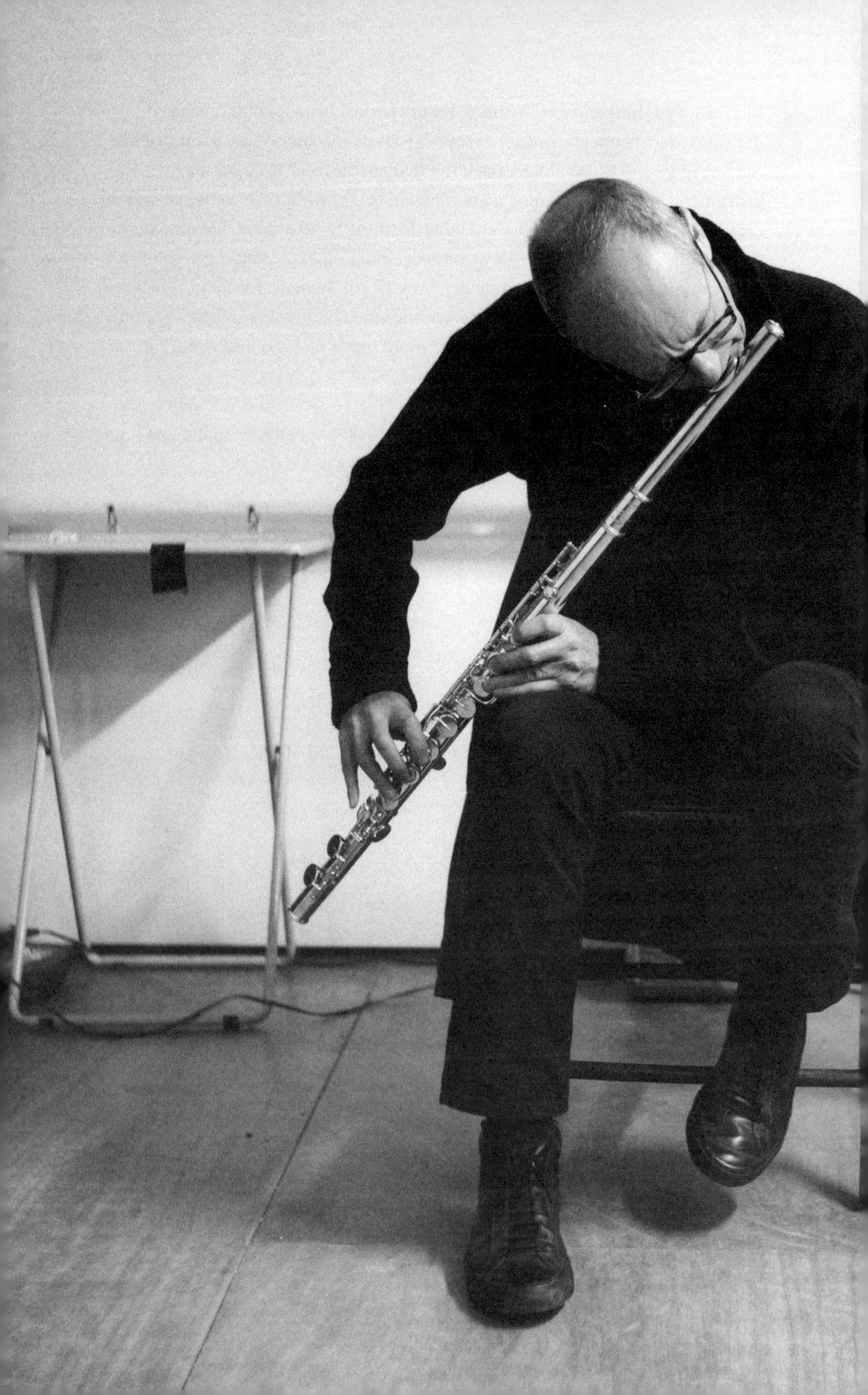

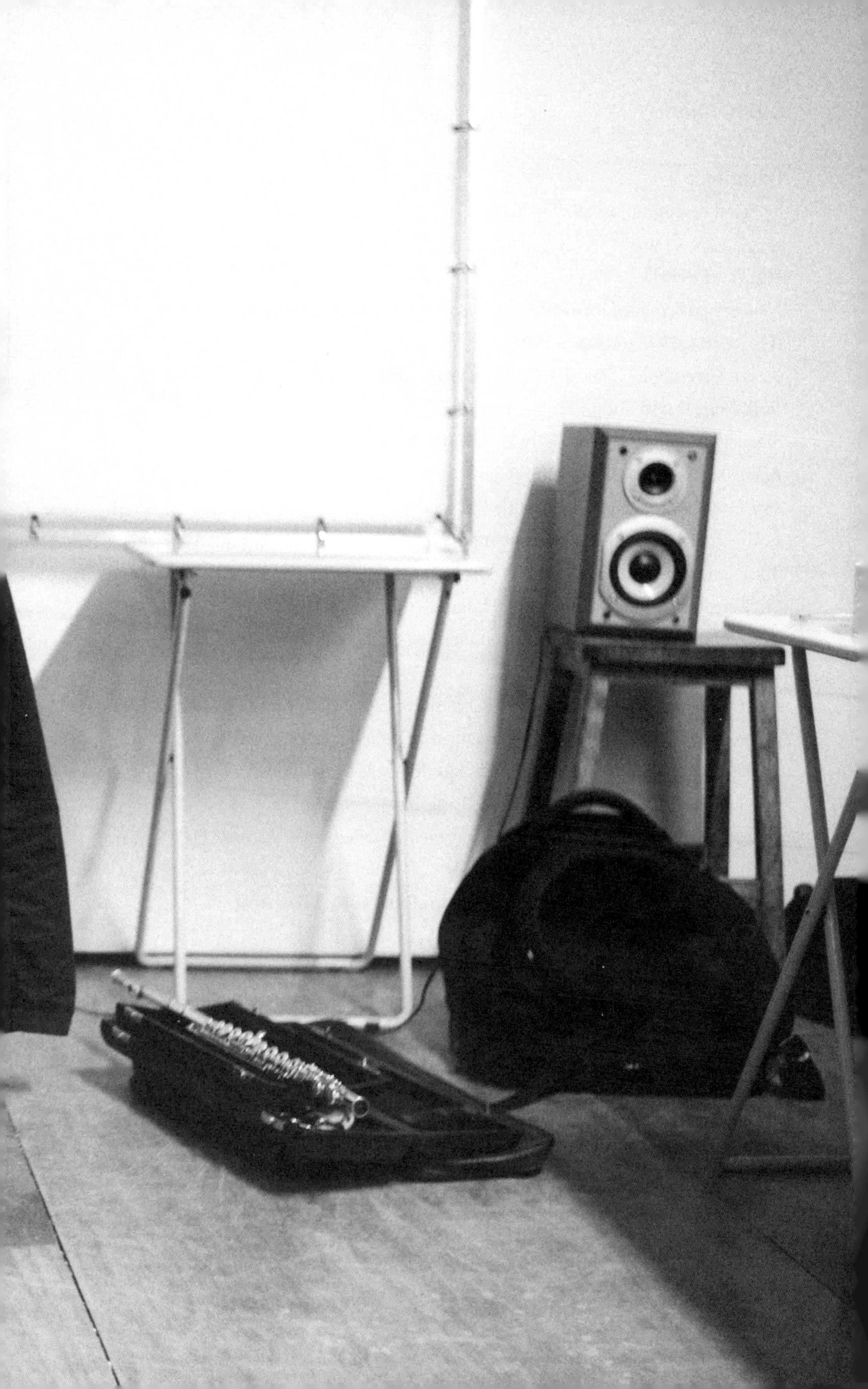

## DISCOGRAPHY

David Toop
Selected discography: 1970 – 2019

SOLO ALBUMS
*New & Rediscovered Musical Instruments*, David Toop and Max Eastley (Obscure 4, 1975, reissued 1997).
*Screen Ceremonies*, David Toop (*The Wire* Editions 9001, 1995).
*Pink Noir*, David Toop (Virgin Records AMBT 18, 1996).
*Spirit World*, David Toop (Virgin Records AMBT 22, 1997).
*Museum Of Fruit*, David Toop (Caipirinha Music, cai2022, 1998, USA).
*Hot Pants Idol*, David Toop [with Bill Laswell, Paul Schütze, Jon Hassell, Sarah Peebles, Russell Mills, Daniel Pemberton, Scanner, John Oswald, Witchman, Tom Recchion, Amelia Cuni/Werner Durand, Talvin Singh, Rhys Chatham, Slipper], (Barooni bar 020, 1999, Holland).
*37th Floor At Sunset: Music For Mondophrenetic*, David Toop (Sub Rosa SR163, 2000, Belgium).
*Black Chamber*, David Toop (Sub Rosa SR205, 2003, Belgium).
*Sound Body*, David Toop (samadhisound cd ss009, 2007, USA/UK).
*Mondo Black Chamber*, David Toop (Sub Rosa, 2014, Belgium).
*Life On the Inside*, David Toop (Sub Rosa, 2014, Belgium).
*The Myriad Creatures will be Transformed of Their own Accord*, David Toop (White Cube/The Vinyl Factory, 2015).
*Entities Inertias Faint Beings*, David Toop (ROOM40, 2016, Australia).

FIELD RECORDINGS
*Hekura: Yanamomo Shamanism from Southern Venezuela* (Quartz 004, 1980).
*Lost Shadows: In Defence of the Soul, Yanomami Shamanism, Songs, Ritual, 1978* (Sub Rosa LP/CD, 2015, Belgium).

GROUP/COLLABORATIONS ALBUMS
*Pass The Distance*, Simon Finn, Mushroom Records MR2, 1970; CD issue Durtro/Jnana 1970CD, 2004, vinyl reissue Antarctica Starts Now, 2018).
*Burwell/Toop* (Quartz/Mirliton Cassettes, QMC 1, 1976).
*Cholagogues*, David Toop, Paul Burwell, Nestor Figueras (Bead 6, 1977, reissued

by Schoolmap, CD, 2009, Italy).

*Alterations*, David Toop, Peter Cusack, Steve Beresford, Terry Day (Bead 9, 1978).

*Wounds*, David Toop, Paul Burwell (Quartz 003, 1979).

*The Flying Lizards*, The Flying Lizards (Virgin V2150, 1980).

*Circadian Rhythm*, Evan Parker, David Toop, Max Eastley, Paul Lytton, Annabel Nicolson, Paul Burwell, Hugh Davies, Paul Lovens (Incus 33, 1980).

*Whirled Music*, David Toop, Max Eastley, Steve Beresford, Paul Burwell (Quartz 005, 1980, Black Truffle vinyl reissue, 2018).

*The 49 Americans* , The 49 Americans (Choo Choo Train Records, Chug 1, 1980; CD issue Saidera SD-4018, 2002, Japan).

*Too Young To Be Ideal*, The 49 Americans (Choo Choo Train Records, Chug 2, 1982; CD issue Saidera SD-4020, 2002, Japan).

*Imitation of Life*, David Toop, Steve Beresford, Tristan Honsinger, Toshinori Kondo (Y Records, Y13, 1982).

*We Know Nonsense*, The 49 Americans (Choo Choo Train Records, Chug 4, 1982; CD issue Saidera SD-4019, 2002, Japan).

*The Promenaders*, The Promenaders (Y Records, Y31, 1982).

*Danger In Paradise*, General Strike – David Toop, Steve Beresford, produced by David Cunningham (Touch Cassettes T02, 1984; issued in CD, Piano 503, 1995, Staubgold, 2012).

*My Favourite Animals*, Alterations (Nato 280, 1985, France).

*Deadly Weapons*, David Toop, John Zorn, Steve Beresford, Tonie Marshall (Nato 950, 1986, France).

*Buried Dreams*, David Toop, Max Eastley (Beyond RBAD CD 6, 1994).

*Needle In The Groove*, David Toop, Jeff Noon (Sulphur SULCD0004, 2000).

*Alterations Live: Live Recordings 1980-83*, Alterations (Intuitive Records IRCD 1, 2000, Denmark).

*The Dreams of Inscriptions On Various Surfaces*, David Toop, Max Eastley (InterCommunication, No. 33, Summer 2000, Japan).

*Voila Enough!,* Alterations (Atavistic UMS/ALP239CD, 2001, USA).

*A Picturesque View, Ignored*, David Toop, Scanner, I/03 (Room 40, 2002, Australia).

*Doll Creature*, David Toop, Max Eastley (Bip-Hop bleep 25, 2004, France).

*Breath-taking*, David Toop, Akio Suzuki (Confront 14, 2004).
*Alterations* box set (Unpredictable series, 2016).
*Skin Tones*, Ken Ikeda, David Toop (Home Normal, 2017, Japan).
*Void Transactions*, Alterations (Unpredictable Series, 2017).
*Dirty Songs Play Dirty Songs*, Phil Minton, Evan Parker, Steve Beresford, Mark Sanders, David Toop, Dave Hunt (Audika LP & CD, 2017, USA).
*Electronic Music for Piano*, Tania Chen, Thurston Moore, Jon Leidecker, David Toop (Omnivore, 2018, USA).
*Suttle Sculpture*, David Toop & Paul Burwell (Logos/Sub Rosa, 2018, Belgium).

COMPILATION TRACKS
"Alaskan Windows Two", David Toop, Steve Beresford (*Infecund Infection*, Pinakotheka DS-0001, Japan).
"Improvised Music & Sound Works", David Toop, Hugh Davies (*Audio Arts* cassette, Vol. 4, no. 2, 1980).
"Reach For N", General Strike (*Myths 2*, Sub Rosa SUB 33002-3, 1985, Belgium).
"Stranger On the Shore", The Promenaders (*Birth Of the Y*, Y Records Y331/3, 1982).
"Shin Shin", David Toop, Kazuko Hohki (*Alternate Cake*, Nato 824, France).
"What's That", General Strike: David Toop, Steve Beresford (*Bugs On the Wire*, Foghorn 001, 1987).
"Black Dahlia", David Toop (*The Freedom Principle*, Polydor 837 925-1, 1989).
"Fe-Tshun-Ti-Fe", David Toop, Max Eastley (*A Gnomean Haignaimean*, NOY 2, Portugal).
"Normal Entrance, Abnormal Exit", David Toop, Max Eastley (*At Close Quarters*, These 7 CD, 1993).
"Burial Rites (remix)", David Toop, Max Eastley (*Isolationism*, Virgin AMBT 4, 1994).
"Mud & Quartz" (Time em:t 3394, 1994).
"Living Dust" (*Miscellaneous*, Language Word D1, 1995).
"Stones, Bones & Skin" (*Extreme Possibilities*, Lo Recordings LCD 01, 1995).
"Yanomami Shamans" (*Ancient Lights and the Blackcore*, Sub Rosa SR78, 1995).
"Bodies Of Water" (Time em:t 5595, 1995).
"Flashing Night Spirits, David Toop, Bedouin Ascent (*Collaborations*,

Lo Recordings, LCD 02, 1995).

"Unearthed", David Toop, Daniel Pemberton (*Collaborations*, Lo Recordings LCD 02, 1995).

"Iron Perm" (*Statics*, CCI Recordings, CCD25002, 1995, Japan).

"Chen Pe'I Pe'I", David Toop, John Zorn (*Ocean Of Sound*, Virgin AMBT 10, 1995).

"Bodies Of Water" (em:t explorer, Instinct ex330.2, 1996, USA).

"Reverse World" (*Eclectic Guitars*, Unknown Public 06, 1996).

"Boneless" (*The Unfinished*, Sub Rosa SR103, 1996, Belgium).

"Bodies Of Water" (*Amberdelic Space*, Dressed To Kill, DTK Box 55, 1996).

"Mr. Lullaby Should Have Rocked You" (*Future: A Journey Through the Electronic Underground*, Virgin VTDCD 118, 1997).

"House Of Traps" (*East-Westercism*, Law & Auder LA-ANGE 2CD, 1997).

"Oil Hell Murder" and "Holy Weapon", Iron Monkey (*Booming On Pluto*, Virgin AMBT20, 1997).

"Reverse World" (*Music From Nature*, Terra Nova TN9701, 1997, USA).

"I Hear Voices Too", David Toop, Neill MacColl (*Guitars On Mars*, Virgin AMBT 24, 1997).

"City On Fire" (*Roma: A Soundscape Mix*, Noteworks NW 5101 2, 1998, Germany).

"Li-Shang Yin" (*Triskel: 1990-2000 Soundworks*, Intermedia 2000, Ireland).

"Let All Mortal Flesh Keep Silence" (*hmm*, Sprawl SP-032, 2000).

"Soylent Green" (*Tin Pan* – Haruomi Hosono, Shigeru Suzuki, Tatsuo Hayashi, Daisyworld RWCL20009, 2000, Japan).

"Breath Shapes" (*Radical Fashion*, Victoria & Albert Museum, V&ACD01, 2001).

"Untitled", David Toop, John Zorn (*LMC . . . The First 25 Years*, Resonance RES8.2, 2001?).

"Untitled", David Toop, Paul Burwell (as above).

"Untitled", Alterations (as above).

"Tricyrtis Latifolia" (*Floating Foundation Vol. 2*, Sub Rosa SR191, 2002, Belgium).

"Koladé Spirit" (*Konstantin Raudive: The Voices of the Dead*, Sub Rosa SR66, 2002, Belgium).

"Buried Dreams", David Toop, Max Eastley (*The Wire: 20 Years, 1982-2002*, Mute CDStumm 220, 2002).

"Breath Shapes" (*Emit One*, QUT Creative Industries, Emit One, 2002, Australia).

"Hynogogmatist" (*Melatonin: Meditations On Sound In Sleep*, Room 40, 2004, Australia).

"Eyelash Turned Inwards", David Toop, Max Eastley (Haunted Weather, Staubgold 52, 2004, Germany).

"Mallophaga Squared" (*Secular Steel*, Gaff 67917727, 2004, USA).

"Live Excerpt, Sprawl 2004, David Toop, Scanner, Lawrence English (*Room 40*, *The Wire* Issue 266, April 2006).

"Chair Creaks, Though No One Sits There" (*On Isolation*, Room 40 EDRM410, 2006).

"Yanomamo Wayamou" (*Otherness*, Sonic Arts Network, 2007).

"David Toop & Sharon Gal" (*Art of Improvisers*, Unpredictable Series, 2017).

CURATED COMPILATIONS

*Ocean of Sound* (Virgin, 1996).

*Crooning On Venus* (Virgin, 1996).

*Sugar and Poison: Tru Life Soul Ballads for Sentients, Cynics, Sex Machines and Sybarites* (Virgin, 1996).

*Booming On Pluto: Electro for Droids* (Virgin, 1997).

*Guitars On Mars* (Virgin, 1997).

*Radical Fashion* (V&A, 2001).

*Not Necessarily "English Music"* (*Leonardo Music Journal* CD series, 2001, USA).

*Haunted Weather* (Staubgold, 2004, Germany).

CO-PRODUCTIONS (with Steve Beresford)

*We Are Frank Chickens*, Frank Chickens (KAZ, 1984).

*Get Chickenised*, Frank Chickens (Flying Lecords, 1987).

*Privilege*, Ivor Cutler and Linda Hirst (Rough Trade Records, 1983, issued on CD by Hoorgi House, 2009).

## ILLUSTRATIONS

Cover © Fabio Lugaro

pp 1,4, 8, 12, 16, 18, 27, 38-39,46, 77, 94, 102-103,108, 112, endpapers: Courtesy of David Toop

| | | |
|---|---|---|
| p 9 | David Toop performance with sounds of plastic | © Robin Parmar |
| pp 22-23, 27, 33 | Paul Burwell & David Toop Rain In the Face rehearsal Ealing College, circa 1972 | © Marie Yates |
| | Contact sheets: David Toop & Paul Burwell | © Nicholas Bechgaard |
| p 29 | The Little Theatre Club Paul Burwell & David Toop | |
| pp 42-43 | Bob Cobbing, Paul Burwell and David Toop Sound Poetry Trio Recording at the BBC Studios | Photographer unknown |
| p 44 | Almost Free Theatre | © Nicholas Bechgaard |
| p 45 | Beginner Studio, Cologne, 1979 | © Guido Conen |
| p 51 | Paul Burwell & David Toop at The Little Theatre Club | © Nicholas Bechgaard |
| p 52 | Mitsutaka Ishii, David Toop & Paul Burwell | © Nicholas Bechgaard |
| p 58 | David Toop at 'Field Working' performance at Midland Group Gallery in Nottingham, 1973 | © Odile Laperche |
| p 64 | David Toop & Paul Burwell at Logos Foundation, Gent, 1977 | © Logos Foundation |
| p 90 | White Cube Gallery, 2015 | © Fabio Lugaro |
| p 96 | Live performance, David Toop & John Butcher, 100 Years Gallery | Photographer unknown |
| p 100 | In the DJ booth with Grandmaster Flash, 1984 | © Patricia Bates |
| p 119 | David Toop compiling *Musics* | © Gérard Rouy |
| p 129 | Playing with cassette player | © David Bloor |
| p 136 | Performance at Cafe OTO (in duo with Ross Lambert) | © Fabio Lugaro |
| p 166 | Bamboo flute performance at Alterations Festival, 2017 | © Nadjib le Fleurier |
| p 172 | Unknown Devices at Tate Modern | © OCA/Marta Buso |
| p 180-181 | Camille Norment & David Toop at Venice Biennale | Photographer unknown |
| p 190 | David Toop & Tom Recchion | Photographer unknown |

David Toop is an English musician, composer, writer and sound curator. His previous books include *Ocean of Sound, Sinister Resonance* and *Into the Maelstrom*. He is currently Professor of Audio Culture and Improvisation at London College of Communication.

First published in English in MMXIX by Ecstatic Peace Library in conjunction with Omnibus Press, 14-15 Berners Street, London W1T 3LJ Great Britain

ecstaticpeacelibrary.net

All rights reserved, all wrongs reversed. All are born free and equal in rights. The past is always now, chronology and continuity broken into pieces, scattered by the pressure of living within depths of time. No part of this publication may be reproduced or reprinted, stored in a retrieval system or transmitted in any form or by any means, electronic, mechanical, photocopying, scanning, recording or otherwise without written consent and permission of the publishers.

© MMXIX David Toop
© MMXIX Thurston Moore

Flutter Echo: Living within Sound by David Toop
Publishers: Eva Prinz & Thurston Moore
Designer: Christian Corless

ISBN 978-1-78760-152-9